The Children Left Behind

The Children Left Behind

America's Struggle to Improve Its Lowest Performing Schools

Daniel L. Duke

ROWMAN & LITTLEFIELD
Lanham • Boulder • New York • London

Published by Rowman & Littlefield
A wholly owned subsidiary of The Rowman & Littlefield Publishing Group, Inc.
4501 Forbes Boulevard, Suite 200, Lanham, Maryland 20706
www.rowman.com

Unit A, Whitacre Mews, 26-34 Stannary Street, London SE11 4AB

British Library Cataloguing in Publication Information Available

Library of Congress Cataloging-in-Publication Data

Names: Duke, Daniel Linden, author.
Title: The children left behind : America's struggle to improve its lowest performing schools / Daniel L. Duke.
Description: Lanham : Rowman & Littlefield, [2016] | Includes bibliographical references and index.
Identifiers: LCCN 2015048693 (print) | LCCN 2016003136 (ebook) | ISBN 9781475823592 (hardcover : alk. paper) | ISBN 9781475823608 (pbk. : alk. paper) | ISBN 9781475823615 (electronic)
Subjects: LCSH: School improvement programs—United States. | Government aid to education—United States.
Classification: LCC LB2822.82 .D84 2016 (print) | LCC LB2822.82 (ebook) | DDC 371.2/07—dc23
LC record available at http://lccn.loc.gov/2015048693

Printed in the United States of America

To all my former and current students who have made the commitment to serve the children left behind.

Contents

Introduction

The front lines in the struggle to improve America's lowest-performing schools are the schools and classrooms. It is in these locations that educators teach, manage behavior, counsel, build relationships, handle crises, meet with parents, administer state and local tests, and undertake other daily activities intended to provide students with a fighting chance for success in life.

The struggle also goes on behind the front lines, in central offices and boardrooms, mayors' offices and state education departments, legislative bodies and the White House. The central figures include elected officials, bureaucrats, superintendents, school boards, and advisors. The question that gnaws at their conscience is a perplexing one. There are few more critical questions facing policy makers, however. Is enough being done to help students trapped in our lowest-performing schools?

This question has challenged educators, concerned citizens, and politicians for decades, but it has only been since the beginning of the 21st century that the federal government has made a concerted effort to focus policy and resources on the improvement of the nation's least-successful public schools. Soon after his election in 2000, President George W. Bush, with bipartisan support from Congress, enacted the No Child Left Behind Act in 2001. Among the provisions of No Child Left Behind (NCLB) was a graduated set of achievement benchmarks in reading and mathematics. By 2014 virtually all students in public schools were expected to achieve proficiency in these two critical subjects. Schools and school districts that failed to meet the benchmarks were subject to an escalating series of sanctions.

In 2007 the Government Accountability Office (*No Child Left Behind Act*, 2007) checked to see how improvement efforts under NCLB were coming along. The report found that 2,790 Title I schools were in some stage of corrective action, meaning that they were subject to sanctions for failing to hit prescribed benchmarks. Despite the worthy intentions of No Child Left Behind, some children clearly were being left behind.

Following the election of Barack Obama in 2008, the new administration renewed the federal commitment to helping the neediest students. Instead of guaranteeing additional funding for chronically low-performing schools, as had been standard practice previously, the prescription for special assistance called for competition. States and school districts would have to develop detailed proposals for School Improvement Grant money. Only the best proposals were to be funded. The Obama administration committed the unprecedented sum of $4.5 billion to the cause.

There can be no mistaking the commitment of the federal government. From bipartisan support for the No Child Left Behind Act to the allocation of Race to the Top funds in 2009, the objective has been clear: Improve the educational opportunities available to the neediest students and raise their academic achievement.

The federal government, however, cannot act alone to ensure that no child is left behind. Public education in the United States requires a team effort. States and local school districts do the heavy lifting when it comes to school improvement—which brings me to the purpose of this book: *The Children Left Behind* examines what states and school districts have done and are doing to respond to federal mandates and financial incentives intended to help the neediest students. If the results of these efforts so far have fallen short of the mark, one thing is certain: It has not been for want of trying.

The purpose of this book is not to determine who or what is to blame for the persistence of low-performing schools. There are no villains to be outed or conspiracies to be revealed. My primary intent is to promote understanding regarding contemporary efforts focused on the lowest-performing schools. Two sets of questions help to center the investigation. First, what have states and school districts done to respond to federal policies and financial incentives concerning these schools? Do their responses reflect convergent or divergent thinking regarding the best ways to help our neediest students?

Second, what have been the consequences thus far of state and school district responses? Have these responses, for example, affected the relationships between key players (state legislatures and local school districts, policy makers and parents, politicians and teacher unions, and so on)? Have the options available to students in low-performing schools increased or narrowed? Have federal initiatives led to the restructuring of district central offices, promoted the interests of charter schools and education management organizations, and shifted thinking about how to staff low-performing schools? Finally, is there any evidence that the prevailing policy solutions to persistent educational problems have become problems themselves?

Efforts to ensure that the children left behind receive a good education resemble in some ways a military campaign. State and local initiatives involve multiple fronts and require the mobilization of resources and political support, strategic thinking, and an array of tactical maneuvers. When it comes to making critical policy decisions, logic may give way to emotional considerations and humanitarian appeals. Shifts in control of the White House, state houses, and local districts can occasion mission adjustments, just as support for military operations ebbs and flows, depending on what happens back home as well as in the field. In one sense,

though, the analogy of a military campaign is not accurate: In the struggle to save the children left behind, there is no common mortal enemy,
only diverse opinions about how best to help.

My hope is that this book will provide policy makers, students of
education policy, educational leaders, and concerned educators and citizens with a foundation for discussing what has been gained and possibly
lost as a result of recent efforts to improve the lowest-performing schools.
Such discussions are especially important given new initiatives such as
the Common Core Standards and Smarter Balanced standardized tests
that are designed to raise the academic achievement bar even higher. If
the United States is to become more educationally competitive on the
international stage and simultaneously improve its lowest-performing
schools, current policies may need to be reconsidered. Failure to do so
could lead to even more children being left behind.

CONFLICT, CONTEXT, AND COMPLEXITY

Before addressing the specific measures taken by the federal government,
states, and school districts to improve America's lowest-performing
schools, a few words about what we know in general about policy development and implementation are in order. The "few words" are *conflict*,
context, and *complexity*; understanding how they apply is essential to any
investigation of policy making and policy execution.

If there is one aspect of policy development and implementation
about which there is general agreement, it concerns the likelihood of
resistance. This finding is hardly surprising. New policies invariably call
for change, and change invariably poses a threat to certain interests. It
might seem, for example, that nobody benefits from the continued existence of chronically low-performing schools, but past history has shown
that efforts to improve these schools often lead to pushback and protests.
Some register concern over the prescribed methods for achieving improvement. Others question how changes will impact those who are ben-
efiting from the status quo. Still others believe that resources would be
better spent on other priorities. They contend that the best approach to
persistent low performance is to close schools.

The predictability of *conflicts* illustrates the fact that policy development and implementation are inherently political processes. Malen (2006,
p. 86) makes the case in the following statement: "Political perspectives
reveal that actors at all levels of the system can influence policy implementation. They can do so by their choices regarding which policy options and designs to adopt and by their efforts to abandon or alter the
purposes and provisions of policies throughout implementation."

The potential for conflict begins well before a policy is implemented.
Stone (1997) has shown that disagreements arise early in the policy-mak-

ing process when individuals and groups offer competing causal stories concerning why a new policy is needed in the first place. Whichever causal story prevails is likely to influence the policy prescription for addressing the problem at hand.

In the case of low-performing schools, numerous causal stories have been offered to explain why they exist (Duke, Tucker, & Salmonowicz, 2014; Murphy, 2010). Some of these explanations focus on factors beyond the control of educators: poverty, poor parenting, and negative peer influence. Other causal stories emphasize the failure of government to provide the resources needed to reverse school decline. Still other causal stories attribute the problem to inadequate instruction, poor school leadership, and low expectations.

It is not difficult to understand how each causal story is likely to have defenders and opponents. Teachers, for example, are apt to become defensive if low student achievement is blamed on how they teach. Fiscal conservatives can be counted on to resist explanations of low performance that focus solely on funding of schools. These objections are unlikely to disappear once a policy for improving low-performing schools has been adopted. They can take on new life once efforts are made to implement the policy. As Malen (2006, p. 101) has noted, "policy implementation is a messy process marked by combinations of contests, contingencies, and disruptions that cannot be fully anticipated yet alone readily controlled."

When we are dealing with the implementation of federal education policy, the prospects of conflict are further heightened by the fact that implementation must take place across 50 states and the District of Columbia as well as thousands of local school districts. Implementation ultimately has to occur in individual schools. Each state, each school district, and each school constitutes a *context* with certain unique features—a history, a culture, a way of doing business, and a collection of actors. If one policy fits all of these contexts equally well, it would be a miracle. Honig (2006) points out that much contemporary research focuses on how and why interactions among policies, contexts, and actors shape implementation in idiosyncratic ways.

The focus on interactions recognizes that every policy involves particular goals or targets. At the same time, however, individual actors and groups of actors possess their own ideas about what goals or targets are and are not appropriate. These ideas, in turn, are subject to influence by contextual factors such as local and state policies, traditions, and economic conditions. The result of a policy interacting with actors and contexts can be modifications in a policy's original goals and targets.

It is easy to understand why the process of policy development is characterized by *complexity* (Honig, 2006). There are additional reasons for expecting complexity when policies actually are implemented. Sabatier (1999, p. 7) warns against assuming that there is ever a single "policy cycle focused on a major piece of legislation." The ground is always shifting beneath any particular policy. A new party comes to power. Public opinion shifts. An economic downturn occurs. Any number of unanticipated events can lead to rethinking the appropriateness of a policy and its implementation. Sometimes concern focuses on the contents of the policy or who supports it. At other times, issues arise regarding how the policy is to be implemented. In still other instances, the problem has to do with unexpected consequences of policy implementation.

Because policy development and implementation can be so complex, it is best to regard them as ongoing processes, not discrete events. Just consider how the No Child Left Behind Act evolved over time. A Democrat replaced a Republican in the White House. The U.S. economy suffered its worst economic crisis since the Great Depression. Public and professional support for important elements of NCLB began to erode. Congress failed to reauthorize NCLB, but that did not prevent executive action by the White House and the U.S. Department of Education, action that altered key portions of the bill. Sanctions were eased in some cases, waivers were permitted, new funding was found, and greater choice for states and school districts was permitted.

Yet another reason for considering policy development and implementation to be complex processes concerns the fact that they often involve a multitude of actions. In the case of a federal education initiative like Race to the Top, for example, states that hoped to compete successfully for funding first had to adopt policies that complied with Race to the Top guidelines. This meant establishing criteria for identifying "Priority Schools" and requiring teacher evaluations to be linked to student achievement on state standardized tests, among other requirements.

Once states responded to these requirements, policy implementation morphed into program implementation. Programs for turning around Priority Schools or closing them had to be implemented. New teacher evaluation procedures had to be put into practice. It was possible for states to respond successfully to federal policy objectives but falter when it came to subsequent programmatic efforts. Policy implementation without effective program implementation constitutes little more than a symbolic exercise in many instances.

Conflict. Context. Complexity. These considerations all add up to one thing: *variability*. Supovitz and Weinbaum (2008, p. 7) conclude, "Variability is not the exception to the implementation experience, but the rule." The sheer number of states and school districts in which federal policy must be implemented, not to mention the range of choices allowed these jurisdictions under Obama administration regulations, seem to all but ensure variations in policy and programmatic responses.

Nonetheless, an argument also can be made for the opposite result. The assumptions supporting the theory of institutional isomorphism suggest that, over time, organizational responses to external pressure actually can result in convergence (DiMaggio & Powell, 1983). Mimetic forces, for example, might lead states and school districts to copy the steps being taken by the states and districts experiencing the greatest success in turning around low-performing schools. Normative forces stemming from the convergence of professional opinion regarding the best ways to improve low-performing schools also could have a similar effect—the reduction of variation.

The point is this: Whether state and local responses to federal policy tend to reflect similarities or differences is an empirical question. It remains to be determined how these responses compare and the likely reasons for any similarities or differences.

STUDYING SCHOOL TURNAROUND POLICY

The purpose of this book is to investigate what states and school districts have done to respond to federal policy concerning the lowest-performing schools. In some cases, efforts to understand responses require backtracking to developments prior to the Obama administration, but most of the discussion and analysis focuses on implementation efforts prompted by Race to the Top, the School Improvement Grant program, and NCLB waivers. When appropriate, we also consider how some states and school districts went well beyond federal policy in their efforts to address the needs of the lowest-performing schools.

The preceding discussion of research on policy development and implementation provides guidance for the present investigation. An important question concerns the extent to which states and school districts vary in their responses to federal policy regarding the lowest-performing schools.

The concepts of conflict, context, and complexity can help to account for revealed variability. In what ways did different state and local conditions affect responses to federal initiatives? Was resistance to implementation efforts encountered, and if so, from what sources? How was this resistance resolved? To what extent did states and school districts opt for different courses of action in areas where federal policy permitted choices to be made?

The primary foci of this investigation are the policy and programmatic responses of states and school districts to federal initiatives during the Obama administration. The ultimate outcomes of these actions in terms of student achievement and school turnarounds lie beyond the scope of the present study, but where data is readily available on policy and program outcomes, it is included.

Various information sources have been tapped on a regular basis in order to compile chronologies of key events and descriptive profiles of policy and programmatic responses. Articles in local and national news outlets were monitored. Research reports in refereed journals and commissioned reports from nonprofit organizations were consulted. Various search engines including Google and Google Scholar were used as well as websites for state departments of education and school districts. Waiver applications and monitoring reports were accessed from the U.S. Department of Education. Online, phone, and in-person interviews were conducted with key state and local education officials.

There always are risks associated with studies such as this one that are so broad in scope. The more the aperture is opened, the greater the likelihood resolution will be lost. Still, the problem of persistently low-performing schools is not limited to particular states and localities. If coherent and effective policies are to be created for reducing the number of these schools, it is important to understand what has been tried and the reactions and responses these efforts have generated. Giving up on the children left behind, it is hoped, will never become the default position of policy makers at any level.

ORGANIZATION OF THE BOOK

The book is organized into four sections. Part I opens with an overview of the evolution of federal efforts to address the needs of low-performing schools. This account begins in 1965 with the passage of the Elementary and Secondary Education Act and works forward to the No Child Left Behind Act of 2001 and subsequent initiatives by the Obama administration to make adjustments in federal policy and practice concerning school improvement. It would be impossible to make sense of state and school district policies and programs without this grounding in actions taken by the federal government.

Chapter 2 explores one city's efforts to grapple with federal and state mandates concerning its lowest-performing schools. The case of Buffalo, New York, provides an opportunity for readers to understand the interplay of conflict, context, and complexity, and sets the stage for the remainder of the book.

Part II focuses on state-level efforts to respond to federal pressure concerning the lowest-performing schools. Rather than offering a broad survey of state actions, each chapter spotlights the efforts of several states, thereby permitting a more in-depth look at improvement initiatives. Chapter 3 examines some of the most aggressive state actions to improve failing schools, actions calling for state takeover of low-performing schools and school districts. The next chapter looks at several states that have opted to create separate districts for chronically low-performing schools. Chapter 5 examines various ways that states are ensuring that low-performing schools and districts receive the technical assistance and training needed to boost student achievement. The section's concluding chapter looks at state-based measures to expand the range of educational options available to students, increase community involvement in turning around schools, and, as a last resort, close failing schools.

Part III moves from state to local school district initiatives. Chapter 7 looks at how two urban school districts—Richmond, Virginia, and Cincinnati, Ohio—undertook to standardize the school turnaround process. Other school systems have chosen to address failing schools by relying on innovation and multiple options for students. These approaches are the focus of chapter 8. Chapter 9 reviews different ways that districts have built their capacity for assisting low-performing schools. These measures include restructuring school district operations, adjusting school financing, changing staffing practices, and rethinking how students are transported to and from school.

The final section of the book opens with a consideration of three perspectives on turning around our lowest-performing schools—the Idealist, the Pragmatist, and the Cynic. Chapter 10 goes on to review some of the accomplishments that have resulted from 15 years of intense focus on failing schools as well as what remains to be accomplished. The concluding chapter discusses lessons that have been learned since the passage of No Child Left Behind and the launching of Race to the Top. The chapter ends with some unanswered questions regarding America's efforts to leave no child behind.

Concern for the lowest-performing schools has occupied a front burner, politically speaking, for a decade and a half. Such longevity is unusual in government. It is imperative that we learn as much as possible about what is and is not working before the moment is lost.

REFERENCES

DiMaggio, P. J., & Powell, W. W. 1983. The iron cage revisited: Institutional isomorphism and collective rationality in organizational fields. *American Sociological Review, 48,* 147–160.

Duke, D. L., Tucker, P. D., & Salmonowicz, M. J. 2014. *Teacher's guide to school turnarounds* (2nd ed.). Lanham, MD: Rowman & Littlefield.

Honig, M. I. 2006. Complexity and policy implementation. In M. I. Honig (ed.), *New directions in education policy implementation.* Albany: State University of New York Press, 1–23.

Malen, B. 2006. Revisiting policy implementation as a political phenomenon. In M. I. Honig (ed.), *New directions in education policy implementation.* Albany: State University of New York Press, 83–104.

Murphy, J. 2010. *The educator's handbook for understanding and closing achievement gaps.* Thousand Oaks, CA: Corwin.

No Child Left Behind: Education should clarify guidance and address potential compliance issues for schools in corrective action and restructuring status. 2007. Washington, DC: Government Accountability Office.

Sabatier, P. A. 1999. The need for better theories. In P. A. Sabatier (ed.), *Theories of the policy process.* Boulder, CO: Westview, 3–17.

Stone, D. 1997. *Policy paradox.* New York: Norton.

Supovitz, J. A., & Weinbaum, E. H. 2008. *The implementation gap.* New York: Teachers College Press.

Part I

The Making of a Mission

America's commitment to improve its lowest-performing schools was not forged overnight. It has taken half a century to evolve, and it continues to be shaped by local, state, national, and even international developments. Our story begins in 1965 with the passage of the Elementary and Secondary Education Act, though, of course, this pivotal legislation had its antecedents. The opening chapter offers an overview of actions taken by the federal government to address the plight of America's neediest students and their schools, particularly actions taken following the reauthorization of the Elementary and Secondary Education Act (ESEA) in 2001. Although the book focuses primarily on what states and school districts have done to respond to federal policy concerning persistently low-performing schools, it is necessary to understand how such policy has unfolded in recent years.

To appreciate the conflicts, contextual issues, and complexities that arise when federal policy "trickles down" through state bureaucracy and then school district channels, chapter 2 provides a concrete example. Since the advent of the No Child Left Behind Act, the Buffalo, New York, school system has struggled to raise student achievement in its lowest-performing schools. The challenges with which Buffalo has had to deal in order to meet federal and state requirements set the stage for the remainder of the book.

ONE

The Evolving Role of the Federal Government in Helping the Lowest-Performing Schools

It is no coincidence that one of the most comprehensive and far-reaching pieces of federal legislation regarding public education became law during the term of a president who had been a school teacher. That the Elementary and Secondary Education Act (ESEA) of 1965 focused squarely on the academic needs of poor and minority children also was not a coincidence. Lyndon Baines Johnson, himself a product of impoverished parents, had made his intentions known just after assuming office when his administration launched the War on Poverty. He believed that the first line of defense against perennial poverty was a sound education. If some states, particularly states in the South, were unwilling or unable to take the necessary steps to guarantee a sound education for all children, then the federal government would have to get involved.

THE EARLY YEARS OF THE ESEA

The ESEA was signed into law on April 11, 1965, in front of President Johnson's old one-room schoolhouse in Texas. Johnson's remarks on that occasion reflected his vision for education:

> By passing this bill, we bridge the gap between helplessness and hope for more than five million educationally deprived children. We put into the hands of our youth more than thirty million new books and into many of our schools their first libraries.
> We reduce the terrible lag in bringing new teaching techniques into the nation's classrooms. We strengthen state and local agencies which bear the burden and the challenge of better education, and we rekindle

3

the revolution—the revolution of the spirit against the tyranny of ig-
norance. (Cross, 2014, p. 33)

The original version of the ESEA consisted of six sections, or "titles" as
they came to be known. Of most immediate importance for low-performing schools was Title I, which provided financial assistance to local school
districts for the education of children of low-income families. The initial
authorization called for $1 billion in funding.

It is generally accepted that the primary purpose of the ESEA was to
ensure greater educational equity for children of poverty. Clotfelter
(2004), however, offers a more nuanced view. In his account of the rise
and fall of desegregation, he argues that the primary intent of the ESEA
and Title I was to incentivize desegregation efforts in the South (p. 26).
Offering federal dollars to schools that enrolled black students served as
a carrot to balance the stick contained in the Civil Rights Act of 1964. Title
IV of the Civil Rights Act authorized the attorney general to initiate class
action lawsuits against school districts that resisted desegregation. Title
VI of the same act authorized the secretary of health, education, and
welfare to withhold funds to any school district excluding students from
school on the basis of race.

Within two years of the passage of the ESEA, the focus of assistance
was widened to encompass handicapped children (PL 89-750) and English-language learners (PL 90-247). Title IX (PL 92-318) followed in 1972,
extending special protection to female students. Then came the Education
of All Handicapped Children Act (PL 94-142) in 1975, which broadened
safeguards and services for students with disabilities. No one could claim
the federal government was unconcerned any longer about groups of
students that previously had been denied equal access to educational
benefits.

Around the same period, the federal government made another commitment that would have long-lasting implications for public education
in general and the neediest students in particular. The notion of educational accountability first surfaced in a presidential policy speech in 1970
(Lessinger, 1971). In his Education Message of March 3, 1970, President
Richard M. Nixon stated, "From these considerations we derive another
new concept: *Accountability*. School administrators and school teachers
alike are responsible for their performance, and it is in their interest as
well as in the interest of their pupils that they be held accountable" (Lessinger, 1971, pp. 62–63).

Apparently the notion of educational accountability struck a chord
with policy makers and the public because states and school systems
across the United States began to launch accountability initiatives within
a year of Nixon's address. These efforts ranged from new systems for
evaluating teachers and school administrators to performance-based
contracts with private providers. The *Washington Post* proclaimed that

American education had entered "an Age of Accountability" (Lessinger, 1971, p. 64). The focus on holding educators accountable for student achievement would intensify over the next three decades, culminating in the passage of the No Child Left Behind Act in 2001.

Despite, or perhaps because of, the new focus on accountability, the Nixon administration did not sustain the level of commitment to helping poor and minority students that had been a hallmark of the Johnson administration. James E. Allen Jr., Nixon's choice for assistant secretary and commissioner of education, tried to accelerate the process of improving failing schools, but he felt thwarted by the administration's strategy of minimal accommodation rather than active White House leadership and advocacy on behalf of the neediest students (Allen, 1970). Unable to increase federal appropriations for struggling schools or win a presidential commitment to help inner-city schools, Allen left office.

Over the ensuing years, the ESEA periodically came up for reauthorization, and these occasions provided opportunities for politicians and policy makers to revisit the challenges facing low-performing schools. Regulations were added during the 1970s to ensure that Title I funds reached the neediest students. Pulling targeted students out of their regular classes in order for them to receive special assistance seemed at first to be the best way to make certain Title I funds were used as intended, but pullout programs presented their own challenges. For one, when students were pulled out of their regular classes, they missed the instruction being received by their classmates. By 1978, concern over the negative effects of pullout programs led to an adjustment in Title I provisions. When schools enrolled 75% or more students from low-income homes, Title I funds were allowed to be spent on schoolwide improvement rather than for specific students (Part I: Title I in Perspective, n.d.). Not all eligible school systems, however, initially embraced the whole-school option.

CONCERN SHIFTS TO EDUCATIONAL EXCELLENCE

By the time Ronald Reagan was elected president in 1980, there could be no backpedaling where disadvantaged children were concerned. Schools serving poor students had come to depend on supplementary funding from Washington. Still, it is fair to maintain that the needs of America's lowest-performing schools began to be eclipsed by a new concern. America was losing business to global competitors, and much of the blame was being laid at the doorstep of public schools (Cuban, 2004). Weren't European and Asian students surpassing their American counterparts on various achievement tests? Hadn't the literacy rate in the United States dropped below that of many nations? And wasn't math achievement even worse?

It was not hard for some observers to feel that so much emphasis had been placed on raising the performance of the lowest achievers that educational excellence had been allowed to slip. By the time Ronald Reagan took office, a freestanding Department of Education was in existence (though Reagan had pledged during his campaign to close it down). Terrell Bell, Reagan's secretary of education, pressed the president to appoint a blue-ribbon commission to examine ways America could respond to the global challenges facing its economy and education system. When Reagan delayed making appointments to the National Commission on Excellence in Education, Bell himself made the appointments (Cross, 2014).

The commission's final report, provocatively titled *A Nation at Risk* (1983), left no doubt about the direction public education needed to take:

> Our nation is at risk. Our once unchallenged preeminence in commerce, industry, science and technological innovation is being overtaken by competitors throughout the world. . . . The educational foundations of our society are presently being eroded by a rising tide of mediocrity that threatens our very future as a Nation and a people. (National Commission on Excellence in Education, 1983, p. 1)

Responding to the challenges issued by the commission, state after state increased graduation requirements, required more testing and more rigorous tests, and lengthened the school year (Cuban, 2004). Mounting pressure to raise the bar for millions of American students eventually led Reagan's successor, President George H. W. Bush, to convene an unprecedented Education Summit at the University of Virginia in September of 1989. Committed to being the "education president," Bush invited to Charlottesville every state governor and most of his cabinet in order to develop a set of national education goals. General agreement was reached on six goals, though opinions varied on how best to achieve them.

The goals covered such topics as school readiness; high school graduation; science and mathematics achievement; adult literacy and lifelong learning; and safe, disciplined, and drug-free schools. Goal 3 (science and mathematics) was the most complex and captured the spirit behind the move to alter the focus of U.S. education policy:

> By the year 2000, American students will leave grades four, eight and twelve having demonstrated competency in challenging subject matter including English, mathematics, science, history, and geography; and every school in America will ensure that all students learn to use their minds well, so they may be prepared for responsible citizenship, further learning, and productive employment in our modern economy. (Executive Office of the President, 1990)

Although the goals were inclusive, referring to "all children" and "all students," they failed to include specific references to disadvantaged and struggling students or to low-performing schools. Presumably efforts to achieve the national education goals by the end of the 20th century would move ahead those youngsters furthest behind while accelerating overall student achievement and reinstating the United States at the head of the international class. Exactly how this transformation would be accomplished or who would pay for it was left to the U.S. Department of Education and state policy makers to figure out.

Not surprisingly, the push for educational excellence occasioned a counter-push by advocates for disadvantaged and struggling students. These individuals appropriated the term "at risk" from *A Nation at Risk* and used it as a general reference for the children they felt were likely to be left behind as educators increased rigor and requirements. Every new policy and program intended to advance the cause of educational excellence became an opportunity to remind people of the unmet needs of at-risk students. That the concerns of advocates for at-risk students had been heard became apparent when the ESEA was reauthorized in 1994.

RENEWED FOCUS ON THE NEEDIEST STUDENTS

Like his predecessor, Bill Clinton also considered himself to be an "education president." Soon after his election in 1992, he pressed ahead with the reauthorization of ESEA, but this time there would be significant changes to Chapter 1/Title I (Cross, 2014, pp. 112–13). States were required to develop content and performance standards for all children. Tests aligned to the standards had to be developed and administered to ensure students learned what they were expected to learn. Federal funds could not be used to teach low-level skills.

Several important provisions of the bill targeted schools serving students from low-income homes. The distribution formula for Chapter 1/Title I funds was changed so that schools with 75% or more poor students got funded before money was distributed to other schools. Schools enrolling at least 50% poor students had to screen children for health and nutritional problems. School districts with the highest poverty rates received larger percentages of federal funds, and all districts were required to allocate funds on the basis of poverty rather than student achievement, thereby removing any disincentive for raising student performance. The threshold for *schoolwide* Chapter 1/Title I programs was lowered from 75% poor students to 65% poor students, a move intended to reduce the number of pullout programs for needy students. Implementing Chapter 1/Title I interventions on a schoolwide basis—in other words, in all classrooms—promised to reduce the need to deliver student assistance outside of class.

The above provisions were contained in the Improving America's Schools Act (IASA), which was passed with bipartisan support and signed into law in October 1994. Of the bill, Christopher Cross, former assistant secretary in the U.S. Department of Education, had the following to say:

> the 1994 law placed the federal government in the position of setting the agenda for almost every school district and every state in the nation. The federal government had moved from being a passive actor, providing resources, research, and some guidance, to being a partner that provided the intellectual framework for school reform and education improvement. (Cross, 2014, p. 116)

Advocates for an expanded federal role in public education had been lucky. If the IASA had come up for congressional approval after the November 1994 elections, it might not have passed. Republicans gained control of both houses of Congress in the off-year elections and announced their intention to reduce Washington's role in state and local government.

Despite the reelection of Bill Clinton in 1996, Republicans retained control of Congress. Clinton's second term in the White House was marked by a series of bold education proposals, including a number of measures intended to improve low-performing schools. In his State of the Union address in 1997 he called for national testing in reading and mathematics, tutoring assistance for struggling students, after-school programs, and the addition of 100,000 new teachers. Republicans balked at the idea of expanding the federal role in education by initiating national tests for students (Cross, 2014). When the time came to reauthorize the ESEA toward the end of Clinton's time in office, disagreements between and within the two parties prevented passage of a new bill. The Republican-controlled Congress, however, substantially increased federal funding for education. The GOP had come to realize that being perceived as anti-education was not in its best interest. Clinton's successor would seize on this change of heart and propose the most ambitious education bill in the nation's history.

REFOCUSING ON THE NEEDIEST STUDENTS

George W. Bush wasted no time in proposing a bill to reauthorize the ESEA. Three days after his inauguration, he presented it at a press conference. The title, No Child Left Behind (NCLB), was borrowed from a slogan used by the Children's Defense Fund (Cross, 2014). NCLB entailed four main principles: (1) testing in reading and math for students in grades 3 through 8, (2) greater flexibility for state and local leaders to innovate, (3) focused assistance for failing schools, and (4) options for parents whose children attended schools that did not improve (No Child Left Behind Act of 2001).

The final version of NCLB eventually was passed with bipartisan support by both houses of Congress in December 2001. It contained nine titles and 45 separate authorizations, and ran over 1,000 pages (Cross, 2014). The authorizations extended from 2002 to 2007.

With regard to improving low-performing schools, the landmark bill's purpose was clearly stated in Section 1001 of Title I: "The purpose of this title is to ensure that all children have a fair, equal, and significant opportunity to obtain a high-quality education and reach, at a minimum, proficiency on challenging state academic achievement standards and state academic assessments" (No Child Left Behind Act, Title I, p. 1). The year 2014 was set as the date when all students would achieve proficiency. The choice of standards, tests to measure proficiency, and the test scores needed to reach proficiency were left to the states to determine.

Following the statement of purpose for the reauthorized Title I was a list of 12 ways to achieve the purpose. The first way, for example, entailed greater alignment at all levels for academic assessments, accountability systems, teacher preparation, curriculum, and instructional materials. The implication was straightforward: States needed to do a better job of ensuring that what students were taught reflected what they were tested on, which in turn must reflect state curriculum standards.

The list went on to call for a focus on low-performing subgroups, targeting of resources on students in greatest need of help, more latitude for schools to exercise authority, and extended learning time for struggling students. Other items on the list stressed the importance of scientifically based instructional strategies, professional development for teachers, close coordination between schools and other youth-serving agencies, and parent involvement in their children's schooling. Item 4 on the list of strategies contained one of the first official references to school turnaround.

> Holding schools, local educational agencies, and States accountable for improving the academic achievement of all students, and identifying and turning around low-performing schools that have failed to provide a high-quality education to their students, while providing alternatives to students in such schools to enable the students to receive a high-quality education. (No Child Left Behind Act, Title I, p. 1)

The notion of school turnaround soon would become a guiding idea for politicians, policy makers, and pundits concerned about the lowest-performing schools (Duke, 2012). For those interested in the history of public ideas, President Ronald Reagan, in a 1983 speech on education policy in Indianapolis, stressed six reforms that would "turn our schools around" (Cross, 2014). Reagan's concern was America's ability to compete against global competition. All schools, in his estimation, needed to be turned around. Two decades later in the No Child Left Behind Act, school turnaround referred specifically to schools in which large percentages of students failed to achieve proficiency in reading and mathematics. These were the students being "left behind" as America attempted to ramp up the quality of its public education.

There was something else about the notion of school turnaround that represented a departure from previous thinking. The preferred path to improving failing schools traditionally had been slow and steady change (Duke, 2012). As the idea of school turnaround gained traction, however, it came to connote quick and dramatic change. Advocates pointed to the example of turnarounds in the private sector where new leaders took over foundering businesses and initiated radical measures to save them. Nothing less, they argued, could rescue students trapped in the lowest-performing schools.

NCLB provided for a graduated set of requirements and eventual sanctions for low-performing schools that did not turn around. These steps marked a major shift in federal policy. Federal funding now came with a complex set of expectations. Instead of judging schools on the aggregated achievement of the entire student body, achievement targets had to be met by various student subgroups. Failure of any subgroup to meet a target led to consequences. Each state determined the target, referred to as adequate yearly progress, and the minimum number of students in a subgroup in order for that subgroup's test scores to be reported. Minimum subgroup numbers varied widely from state to state. Texas, for example, counted subgroup achievement if five or more students in the subgroup attended a school. Virginia set the bar at 50 students per school.

Schools that failed to hit adequate yearly progress benchmarks for one year were placed on a *watch list* and required to draft a school improvement plan (see box 1.1). After two years, the school entered *needs improvement* status and had to offer parents the option of transferring their child to a school that met adequate yearly progress. The school district had to absorb the cost of transportation for children who transferred. At least 10% of the school's Title I funds must be set aside for teacher professional development. Failure to make adequate yearly progress for a third straight year led to *corrective action*, which meant that the school had to continue offering parents the option to transfer their child as well as provide *supplemental educational services* such as after-school tutoring. The school district was required to pay for such services out of its Title I allocation.

Four consecutive years of failure to make adequate yearly progress led to *restructuring*. Besides the previous sanctions, the school had to replace its staff or make some other *fundamental* change. After five years of low performance, school *reconstitution* was mandated. This could take the form of conversion to a charter school, contracting out the management of the school to a private provider, or takeover by the state. The reconstituted school remained subject to all of the preceding provisions as well.

BOX 1.1: SANCTIONS UNDER THE
NO CHILD LEFT BEHIND ACT

Schools that fail to make adequate yearly progress for:

1 year   are placed on a "watch list" and required to develop a school improvement plan

2 years   are listed as "needs improvement" and required to offer parents the option of transferring their child to a school that has met adequate yearly progress (district pays for transportation)

3 years   are in "corrective action" status and must provide students with "supplemental educational services" (such as after-school tutoring) as well as offer parents the option of transferring their child

4 years   are in "restructuring" status and must change their staffing or make some other "fundamental change" as well as provide "supplemental educational services" and offer parents the option of transferring their child

5 years   must convert to a charter school, turn management over to a private management company, or be taken over by the state as well as the preceding provisions for schools in "restructuring" status

---

The foregoing sanctions were not the only major policy changes affecting low-performing schools. NCLB also broke new ground concerning school districts. No previous piece of federal legislation had targeted low-performing school districts for improvement. As a result of NCLB, districts with high percentages of low-performing schools also became targets for turnaround. They, too, could be identified for corrective action and required to restructure.

Early reactions to NCLB were largely favorable, though some concerns were raised. Even before Congress passed the bill, Michael Casserly, executive director of the Council of the Great City Schools, complained that NCLB failed to provide a clear definition of a failing school (Strauss, 2001). The National Education Association (2001) embraced the lofty goals of NCLB but complained about the means for achieving them. Business leaders generally applauded the aim of having all children achieve proficiency in reading and math by 2014 and supported the emphasis on greater accountability. The prospect of new funding and greater flexibility appealed to state education officials (Cross, 2014).

Like land mass forming around a coral reef, criticism of NCLB gradually began to build as educators encountered the difficulties of attaining testing benchmarks that increased with each passing year. Perhaps no individual better illustrates the shift in thinking about NCLB than veteran education scholar Diane Ravitch. In *The Death and Life of the Great American School System* (2010), she writes about her conversion from an ardent supporter of NCLB to a concerned critic:

> I can pinpoint the date exactly [November 30, 2006] because that was the day I realized that NCLB was a failure. I went to a conference at the American Enterprise Institute [AEI] in Washington, DC. . . . The various presentations that day demonstrated that state education departments were drowning in new bureaucratic requirements, procedures, and routines, and that none of the prescribed remedies was making a difference. (p. 99)

Ravitch goes on to present additional points made at the AEI conference. Experts noted that the choice provisions of NCLB were not working because only a tiny percentage of eligible students were transferring to better schools. Parents clearly were reluctant to move their children from neighborhood schools, even when those schools continued to be low performing. This was especially true for parents of English-language learners. Even the provision of free after-school tutoring for students stuck in failing schools, another requirement of NCLB, had failed to attract much interest.

Ravitch's misgivings about NCLB were confirmed in 2007 when the Government Accountability Office (GAO) issued a comprehensive report on the status of the legislation. The report indicated that 2,790 Title I schools were in some stage of corrective action or restructuring status as of the 2005–2006 school year (*No Child Left Behind*, 2007). Furthermore, the GAO predicted that the number was likely to increase as state proficiency targets approached 100% in 2014. Of the schools in corrective action or restructuring status, 42% were estimated by the GAO not to be receiving all of the required types of assistance from their school districts. An estimated 40% of these schools had failed to take any of the five required restructuring steps under NCLB. The GAO report concluded by chastising the U.S. Department of Education and calling on department officials to do a better job of addressing local compliance issues.

Nine months after the GAO report, the Department of Education's Institute of Education Sciences (IES) published a guide for educators entitled "Turning around Chronically Low-performing Schools" (Herman et al., 2008). Though the guide noted the overall weakness of research on the school turnaround process, it went on to offer four recommendations.

Educators engaged in turning around low-performing schools were exhorted to (a) "signal the need for dramatic change with strong leadership," (b) "maintain a consistent focus on improving instruction," (c) "provide visible improvements early in the turnaround process (quick wins)," and (d) "build a committed staff" (Herman et al., 2008, p. 8).

More than a guide for educators was needed, however, to ensure that low-performing schools received the assistance required to raise achievement for all students. Any new initiatives tied to school turnarounds would have to wait, though, until Americans elected a new president in 2008. It remained to be seen whether public education in general and improving low-performing schools in particular would continue to occupy the political front burner.

A NEW INITIATIVE TARGETING
THE LOWEST-PERFORMING SCHOOLS

With the election of Barack Obama in 2008 came a shift in the party in power, a new secretary of education with experience running the Chicago public schools, and the onset of a serious financial crisis. Reviving the economy took center stage. Acting quickly to stimulate the economy, the new administration got Congress to pass the American Recovery and Reinvestment Act (ARRA) on February 13, 2009. Of the $787 billion allocated to ARRA, nearly $100 billion was earmarked for education, and of that amount, $4.3 billion went to a new initiative called Race to the Top (Cross, 2014). Race to the Top represented a departure from previous federal policy in that states had to compete for funding.

Secretary of Education Arne Duncan announced that winning applications for Race to the Top grants would have to meet a number of conditions (*Race to the Top Program*, 2010). Provisions had to be included for tying teacher evaluation to student achievement. States were required to adopt new and higher standards for student learning, develop longitudinal data systems, and provide for the equitable distribution of the most highly qualified teachers across school districts.

A primary target of Race to the Top was the nation's lowest-performing schools. Duncan called for states receiving funds to identify 15% of their schools for significant interventions (Gewertz, 2009). The bottom 5% of schools were designated "Priority" Schools and required to adopt dramatic measures. The next lowest-performing 10% were designated "Focus" schools. For the first time, high schools with graduation rates below 60% qualified for funding. Instead of leaving it up to states and school districts to determine how best to turn around failing schools, the U.S. Department of Education required that one of four options had to be chosen (Race to the Top Program, 2010).

Option 1 called for closing the school and sending students to higher-performing schools. Option 2, referred to as the *restart* model, involved turning operation of the school over to a charter or education-management organization. The *transformation* model, option 3, required replacing the principal and improving the school through comprehensive curriculum reform, professional development, extended learning time, and other prescribed practices. The final option, dubbed the *turnaround* model, entailed replacing the principal, screening existing school staff and rehiring no more than half the staff members, choosing a new governance structure, and adopting reforms similar to those for the transformation model. Federal policy toward low-performing schools had crossed another threshold. As Cross (2014, p. 158) put it, "In order to get funding, states had to promise far more reform than had ever been required by the federal government."

Thirty-five states and the District of Columbia competed for the first Race to the Top awards. Tennessee and Delaware were the initial winners. Over the next two years, 17 additional states received funding. The stage was set for a concerted push at all levels—federal, state, and local—to help the children left furthest behind.

In 2012 a new competition for Race to the Top funds was announced by Secretary Duncan. This time school districts were the applicants. Awards ranging from $5 million to $40 million went to 16 districts, including three charter school organizations (Cross, 2014). Half a billion dollars in grants also was allocated for the improvement of early learning opportunities for young children (from birth to age 5).

During the Obama administration the primary vehicle for improving the lowest-performing schools was the School Improvement Grant (SIG). NCLB had authorized SIGs, but it was not until 2007 that significant funding ($125 million) was provided for this initiative. The infusion of Race to the Top money in 2009 along with an increase in the Title I allocation ($546 million) allowed the SIG program to expand greatly. Guidelines for the SIGs followed those required for Race to the Top applications. State education agencies (SEAs) were expected to administer School Improvement Grants to local school districts in order to enable the lowest-performing schools to meet accountability requirements (Perlman & Redding, 2011).

States were instructed to identify three tiers of schools (Quillin, 2011). The highest-priority schools were designated Tier I schools and represented a state's lowest-achieving 5% of Title I schools that were designated in improvement, corrective action, or restructuring, or the five lowest-performing Title I schools, whichever number was greater. Secondary schools that were eligible for, but did not receive, Title I–Part A funds and that were identified by states as "persistently lowest-achieving" were classified as Tier II schools (Perlman & Redding, 2011). Tier III included

Title I schools in improvement, corrective action, or restructuring that were not Tier I schools.

By creating the three tiers and concentrating on the lowest-performing schools, the new guidelines addressed a major concern of state education officials with NCLB. The No Child Left Behind Act led to the identification of so many schools for improvement that most states found it impossible to focus resources and closely monitor schools in greatest need of help (Hyslop, 2013). Under Race to the Top and its related SIG provisions, states were free to zero in on a smaller number of schools, the very lowest-performing schools.

When school districts applied to their SEA for SIGs, they were required to specify whether they intended to implement the restart, transformation, or turnaround model or close schools. Comparatively few school districts opted for school closure or the restart model (O'Brien & Dervarics, 2013). School Improvement Grants had to be awarded to SEAs based on the proportional share of funds they received under Title I. To assist states and school districts in interpreting the guidelines governing federal funding for school improvement, Secretary Duncan authorized the establishment of the Office of School Turnaround in 2011. The OST also was responsible for monitoring how federal funds were being used, providing technical assistance related to school turnaround efforts, and building state and school district capacity for improving student outcomes and sustaining school turnarounds.

Several years later, an office was created to help states cope with the complexities of administering and monitoring various federal grant programs (Klein, October 8, 2014). State education officials had complained about not having one point of contact when dealing with the U.S. Department of Education. The new office was responsible for coordinating Title I grants, School Improvement Grants, Race to the Top programs, and NCLB waivers, among others.

Secretary Duncan clearly expressed the administration's hopes for the Race to the Top initiative and the School Improvement Grant program in an August 26, 2009, press release ("Obama administration announces"):

> The large investment in school improvement funds made possible by the Recovery Act presents a historic opportunity to attack education's most intractable challenge—turning around or closing down chronically low-achieving schools. Our goal is to turn around the 5,000 lowest-performing schools over the next five years, as part of our overall strategy for dramatically reducing the drop-out rate, improving high school graduation rates and increasing the number of students who graduate prepared for success in college and the workplace.

MOUNTING CONCERNS AND THE ADVENT OF WAIVERS

In the years immediately following the beginning of Race to the Top and the expanded School Improvement Grant program, several efforts were made in Congress to reauthorize the ESEA, but none of them was able to overcome partisan disagreements and a lack of enthusiasm for tackling concerns about the role of the federal government in public education (Cross, 2014). In the absence of an "education Congress," the executive branch continued to take the lead in addressing pressing matters related to school improvement and accountability. In a March 2011 speech to kick off Education Month, President Obama went to Central High School in Miami to pledge his continued commitment to help the lowest-performing schools in the United States (Remarks by the president, 2011). In the fall, the administration acknowledged that states and school districts were struggling to hit the steadily rising achievement targets mandated by NCLB. Since Congress was unable to agree on how to handle the matter, Secretary Duncan announced that states could apply for waivers that provided some flexibility in how they met certain requirements under NCLB (Klein, February 1, 2012).

In the secretary's own words, "America's most sweeping education law . . . No Child Left Behind . . . is outmoded and constrains state and district efforts for innovation and reform" (States granted waivers, 2013). Continuing, he noted that "the federal government has worked with states to develop waiver agreements that unleash local leaders' energy for change and ensure equity, protect the most vulnerable students, and encourage standards that keep America competitive." Thirty-four states and the District of Columbia received waivers that ran from fall of 2012 through spring of 2014.

Some conditions, however, were tied to the waivers. A state might choose an alternative yardstick to adequate yearly progress, for example, but in return it had to agree to adopt new college- and career-ready standards. Other suggested trade-offs for waiver states included developing differentiated recognition, accountability, and support systems for schools and districts and adopting measures to support effective instruction and school leadership.

Many of the states that applied for and received waivers opted for differentiated accountability systems that combined various subgroups of students considered to be at risk by NCLB into larger super-subgroups. Virginia, for instance, chose to create three new groups (Accountability and Virginia public schools, 2013). Proficiency Gap Group 1 consisted of students with disabilities, limited-English-proficient students, and economically disadvantaged students (regardless of race and ethnicity). Proficiency Gap Group 2 included African American students, not of Hispanic origin, including those also counted in Proficiency Gap Group 1. The third group consisted of Hispanic students, including those also counted in Proficiency Gap Group 1. The target pass rates in reading and mathematics for each of these groups varied somewhat from year to year, although all three groups were expected to hit a common pass rate by the final year of the waiver (2016–2017). Interestingly, the final target pass rate in reading was 78% and in mathematics 73%, well below the 100% specified in NCLB.

Allowing more realistic pass rates was applauded by many educators, but groups advocating for disadvantaged young people saw the waivers as a form of backsliding on NCLB commitments to leave no child behind. A letter to Secretary Duncan from 13 of these groups, including the National Association for the Advancement of Colored People (NAACP) and the National Council of La Raza (NCLR), expressed the "utmost concern" that new state accountability systems (under waiver provisions) were "masking the academic performance of individual student groups, including students of color, low-income students, English-language learners, and students with disabilities" (Klein, October 24, 2014). Concern also was registered regarding differential achievement targets for different student subgroups and super-subgroups.

Negative reaction to the waivers was not the first instance when Secretary Duncan was put on the defensive. No sooner did the U.S. Department of Education roll out the four turnaround options than criticism was aired about the expanding role of the federal government in matters that were state and local business. By March 2012, however, Duncan was able to counter that a preliminary analysis of first-year test results in schools receiving SIG funds indicated that the percentage of students achieving proficiency in reading and mathematics rose in roughly 60% of the schools (Klein, March 19, 2012).

When the U.S. Department of Education conducted its second annual snapshot of the School Improvement Grant program, two thirds of the schools in their second year of funding posted gains in reading and mathematics (Klein, December 4, 2013). The other third, however, actually declined in achievement. Rural and small-town SIG schools had bigger gains than urban and suburban schools. Schools that elected to become charter schools (the restart option) generally saw bigger gains than schools choosing the turnaround or transformation option. Despite evidence that many of the lowest-performing schools had benefited from their SIG awards, congressional Republicans vowed to cut all funding for the program when the ESEA next came up for reauthorization (Klein, December 4, 2013).

By 2014 over 40 states and the District of Columbia had been granted waivers from various requirements under NCLB. Secretary Duncan's intention had been to allow states to focus more on their very lowest-performing schools. When staff members at *Education Week* reviewed Department of Education monitoring reports, however, almost half of the waiver states were found not to be following through on their plans for improving the lowest 5% of their schools (Klein, July 9, 2014). Many of the states were criticized for failing to monitor improvement efforts more closely.

Although some observers might have expected the U.S. Department of Education to tighten up on its regulations concerning waivers and the SIG program, the decision actually was made to offer states even more flexibility. Granted, this decision was prompted by congressional pressure, not the preferences of the Obama administration (Klein, September 17, 2014). Faced with what it regarded as lackluster results from federal efforts to improve the lowest-performing schools, Congress insisted on revamping the SIG program as part of the annual budget package in January 2014.

Although details were left to the Department of Education, Congress indicated that states were to be allowed to choose their own model for school turnaround in addition to those put forward by the government. When the Department of Education released the new regulations, it added an additional option of its own. Low-performing elementary schools could choose high-quality early childhood education as a turnaround strategy. This move came as no surprise, given the Obama administration's support for preschool education.

After clamoring for greater flexibility in the choice of approaches to turning around their lowest-performing schools, the states finally had gained broad discretionary authority to develop their own models. Only five states, however, took advantage of the shift in federal policy (Klein, July 2, 2015). Colorado and Texas focused on high school reform, New York stressed partnering low-performing schools with a partner having a strong turnaround track record, Minnesota made it easier for schools to retain their principals, and Rhode Island gave school districts greater control over developing turnaround plans.

At the same time that the Department of Education permitted greater flexibility for waiver states in their choice of turnaround models, it backtracked on an earlier pledge to require waiver states to provide data showing that their new models actually were improving student achievement (Klein, December 3, 2014). This shift caught many observers by surprise. Was an era in educational accountability, one anchored in yearly standardized testing, drawing to a close? Or had states already initiated a sufficient set of testing requirements to obviate the need for federal redundancy?

The revised SIG requirements did not abandon quality control entirely. Developers of whole-school reform models, for example, needed to have a track record of success in implementing their reform models in low-performing schools. In selecting interventions, school districts were required to take into consideration family and community input. Families and community members also had to be continuously engaged in the implementation of chosen interventions. When external providers were hired with SIG funds, school districts were expected to hold them accountable for outcomes.

The midterm elections in November 2014 gave Republicans control of both houses of Congress and an opportunity to reassert their influence on the nation's education agenda as well as reduce the role of the White House and the secretary of education. Knowing that momentum finally was building to push through a reauthorization of the ESEA, Secretary Duncan laid out the administration's expectations for a new bill. A billion dollars in additional assistance for the lowest-performing schools and new funding for preschool education topped his list (Layton, January 13, 2015). Duncan also called for a continued commitment to testing all students in reading and mathematics, an acknowledgment on his part of the mounting campaign by various groups to curtail standardized testing.

Congress debated reauthorization through the late summer and early fall of 2015, but stalled when differences developed between the House bill and the Senate bill (Camera, 2015). Interestingly, both bills called for eliminating the School Improvement Grant program for the lowest-performing schools. The House bill required states to set aside 7% of their Title I funds for school improvement and to intervene in Title I schools that were not performing well. States would not be told how to intervene, however. The Senate bill left decisions about how to fix schools to school districts with help from states. The bill expressly prohibited the federal government from telling states and districts how to improve failing schools.

Perhaps sensing that the Republican-controlled Congress was committed to undoing many of the measures that he had championed, Secretary of Education Duncan announced that he planned to resign in December 2015. His successor was John B. King Jr., former commissioner of education for New York State. Duncan's legacy would be based, in part, on his willingness to bypass a gridlocked Congress in order to adopt landmark changes in how the federal government and the states addressed the needs of the children left behind.

THE EVOLUTION OF FEDERAL POLICY

The half century of federal education policy from 1965 to 2015 can be analyzed in various ways. Those who expect to find consistency and continuity may come away from such analysis disappointed. As former assistant secretary of education Christopher Cross put it:

> It should be clear . . . that we, as a nation, do not have a national education policy, though most people assume that we do. Instead we have a hodgepodge of federal laws, executive branch policy decisions, regulations, and incentives that have accumulated like so many geolog-

ical layers since the passage of the National Defense Education Act in
1958. (Cross, 2014, p. 167)

If Cross's assessment is correct, it may be due to the fact that the locus of
influence over education policy at the federal level has shifted back and
forth from the White House to Congress. With the advent of a stand-
alone Department of Education in 1980, secretaries of education, depending on the individual, also have become important players in developing
education policy.

Since the passage of the Elementary and Secondary Education Act in
1965, the federal government has made a sustained commitment to helping schools that serve students from low-income homes. The essence of
this commitment has varied, however, depending on the party in power
and the nature of competing priorities. From time to time, for example,
concern about educational excellence and the need for higher academic
standards has displaced the improvement of low-performing schools as
the top priority. Since the passage of the No Child Left Behind Act, however, the federal government has focused both policy and funding
squarely on turning around the nation's lowest-performing schools together with greater educational accountability at the state and local levels.

The strategies and programs for helping struggling schools and their
students have evolved over the years. What began in the early days of
Title I as supplementary funding has grown into a combination of guaranteed funding, competitive school improvement grants, and sanctions
for schools that fail to improve. The buzzwords used to characterize the
improvement strategy du jour have shifted from effective schools to
school restructuring to comprehensive school reform to school turnaround. Over the years, the expected timetable for school improvement
has shortened substantially. Instead of gradual gains over extended periods, schools receiving SIGs now have three years to effect dramatic improvements in student achievement. Targeting low-performing schools
has been expanded to include low-performing school districts as well.
The search for solutions has widened beyond the confines of traditional
public education to include charter schools and educational management
organizations.

A disturbing milestone in American public education was noted at the
beginning of 2015. For the first time in at least a half century, more than
50% of the public school students in the United States lived in poverty
(Layton, January 17, 2015). Whether this fact will mean that the "policy
window," to use Kingdon's (1995) terminology, will remain open for
efforts to address the problem of low-performing schools remains to be
seen. One thing, however, is certain: As long as there are children born
and forced to live in poverty, the likelihood of children being left behind
remains great.

REFERENCES

Accountability and Virginia public schools. 2013. Richmond: Virginia Department of Education.

Allen, J. E. 1970. An interview with James Allen. *Harvard Education Review, 40*(4), 533–46.

Camera, L. 2015, August 5. Collision alert: House, Senate ESEA rewrites. *Education Week,* 1, 20–21.

Clotfelter, C. T. 2004. *After Brown: The rise and retreat of school desegregation.* Princeton, NJ: Princeton University Press.

Cross, C. T. 2014. *Political education: Setting the course for state and federal policy* (2nd ed.). New York: Teachers College Press.

Cuban, L. 2004. *The Blackboard and the bottom line.* Cambridge, MA: Harvard University Press.

Duke, D. L. 2012. Tinkering and turnarounds: Understanding the contemporary campaign to improve low-performing schools. *Journal of Education for Students Place at Risk, 17*(1– 2), 9–24.

Executive Office of the President. 1990. *National goals for education.* Washington, DC. ED 319 143.

Gewertz, C. 2009, July 21. Duncan's call for school turnarounds sparks debate. *Education Week.* Retrieved from http://www.edweek.org/ew/articles/2009/07/21/37turnaround.h28.html?tkn.

Herman, R., Dawson, P., Dee, T., Greene, J., Maynard, R., & Redding, S. 2008. *Turning around chronically low-performing schools.* Washington, DC: Institute for Education Sciences, U.S. Department of Education.

Hyslop, A. 2013. *It's all relative: How NCLB waivers did—and did not—transform school accountability.* Washington, DC: New America Education Policy Program.

Kingdon, J. W. 1995. *Agendas, alternatives, and public policies* (2nd ed.). New York: Longman.

Klein, A. 2012, March 19. Early SIG data looks promising, Duncan says. *Education Week.* Retrieved from http://blogs.edweek.org/edweek/campaign-k-12/2012/03/early_sig_data_looks_promising.html.

———. 2012, February 1. Eyebrows raised over initial NCLB waiver requests. *Education Week,* 17.

———. 2014, October 8. Federal monitoring set to take team approach. *Education Week,* 17.

———. 2015, July 2. How many states decided to develop their own turnaround strategies? Not many! *Education Week.* Retrieved from http://blogs.edweek.org/edweek/campaign-k-12/2015/07/how_many_states_decided_to_dev.html.

———. 2013, December 4. Latest SIG school snapshot paints mixed improvement picture. *Education Week,* 23.

———. 2014, December 3. New guidance offers states roadmap to NCLB waiver renewal. *Education Week,* 16, 19.

———. 2014, September 17. New turnaround options detailed in draft SIG program guidance. *Education Week,* 18.

———. 2014, October 24. Poor and minority kids must count in NCLB waivers, civil rights groups say. *Education Week.* Retrieved from http://blogs.edweek.org/edweek/campaign-k-12/2014/10/civil_rights_groups_to_arne_du.html.

———. 2014, July 9. School turnarounds proving heavy lift for waiver states. *Education Week,* 24, 32.

Layton, L. 2015, January 13. Education secretary: Keep annual tests, add preschool funding. *Washington Post,* A-5.

———. 2015, January 17. Most public school students now living in poverty. *Washington Post,* A-1, A-10.

Lessinger, L. M. 1971. The powerful notion of accountability in education. In L. H. Browder (ed.), *Emerging patterns of administrative accountability.* Berkeley, CA: McCutchan, 62–73.

National Commission on Excellence in Education. 1983. *A nation at risk.* Washington, D.C.: U.S. Department of Education.

National Education Association. 2001, December 11. *Education bill: Right goals, wrong means* [press release].

No Child Left Behind Act of 2001, Pub.L.No.107-110. Retrieved from www.ed.gov/legislation/esea02/.

No Child Left Behind: Education should clarify guidance and address potential compliance issues for schools in corrective action and restructuring status. 2007. Washington, DC: Government Accountability Office.

Obama administration announces historic opportunity to turn around nation's lowest-achieving public schools. 2009, August 26. *U.S. Department of Education.* Retrieved from http://www2.ed.gov/print/news/pressreleases/2009/08/08262009.html.

O'Brien, E. M., & Dervarics, C. J. 2013. *Which way up?* Washington, DC: Center for Public Education, National School Boards Association.

Perlman, C. L., & Redding, S. (Eds.). 2011. *Handbook on effective implementation of School Improvement Grants.* Lincoln, IL: Center on Innovation & Improvement.

Quillin, J. 2011. *Snapshot of SIG: A Look at Four States' Approaches to School Turnaround.* Washington, DC: Center for American Progress.

Race to the Top Program: Guidance and Frequently Asked Questions. 2010. Washington, DC: U.S. Department of Education.

Ravitch, D. 2010. *The Death and Life of the Great American School System.* New York: Basic Books.

Remarks by the President at Miami Central High School in Miami, Florida. 2011, March 4. Retrieved from http://www.whitehouse.gov/the-press-office/2011/03/04/remarks-president-miami-central.

States granted waivers from No Child Left Behind allowed to reapply for renewal for 2014 and 2015 school years. *U.S. Department of Education.* 2013, August 29. Retrieved from http://www.ed.gov/news/press-releases/states-granted-waivers-no-child-left-behind-allowed.

Strauss, V. 2001, August 28. Lawmakers struggle to define failing schools. *Washington Post,* A-8.

TWO

"If You Can Turn Around Buffalo, You Can Turn Around Anything"

It's one thing to consider conflict, context, and complexity in the abstract, and quite another to see these concepts played out in an actual school district struggling to meet federal and state mandates. The statement that serves as this chapter's title was voiced by New York governor Andrew Cuomo in his State of the State address in January 2015 (Newberg, January 22, 2015). Cuomo's frustration was evident as he noted that state aid for each Buffalo student was double that of the state average, yet this investment had failed to produce desired results. Just as frustrating as the wasted dollars, however, were the abandoned plans, the battles between the school board and the Buffalo Teachers Federation, turnover in district leadership, and the bitter disappointment of parents.

The chapter opens with a profile of Buffalo and the circumstances that placed the city and its school system in difficult straits. The heart of the chapter is a chronological account of the events following Buffalo's receipt of Race to the Top funds. The chapter concludes with the lessons to be learned from Buffalo's efforts to respond to federal and state requirements concerning the school district's lowest-performing schools.

A CITY LOOKING FOR ANSWERS

There was a time in the not too distant past when Buffalo boasted a vibrant economy and a population of more than half a million. Like many Rust Belt cities, Buffalo's industrial base began to decline in the 1960s as global competition intensified. The opening of the St. Lawrence Seaway in 1957, however, had an even more devastating effect on the local economy. Buffalo had grown rich on the trade that came as a result of its

23

location at the junction of the Great Lakes and the Erie Canal. The seaway allowed vessels to bypass Buffalo.

Between 1960 and 2000, Buffalo's population declined by 240,000. The worsening economic crisis eventually resulted in the creation in 2003 of the Buffalo Fiscal Stability Authority to oversee the city's finances. The Fiscal Stability Authority was established by New York State. As will become evident when we examine Buffalo's school system, it would not be the only instance of state intervention in the city's affairs.

Buffalo's economy began to improve as the new century progressed. Residents became hopeful that their city would experience a Rust Belt Renaissance, but local leaders understood that such a turnaround could not occur without significant improvements in local schools. When the No Child Left Behind (NCLB) Act was passed in 2001, Buffalo Public Schools consisted of 76 schools with a total enrollment of 44,849 students (Sunderman & Kim, 2004). Almost three out of four students were classified as minority students, and 82% came from low-income homes.

In the 2002–2003 school year, the first year when NCLB regulations took effect, 31 of Buffalo's 76 schools made the watch list as schools in need of improvement (Sunderman & Kim, 2004). Only 3% of third graders scored proficient in reading, while half of third graders scored proficient in mathematics. These percentages were 16 points and 17 points below third graders in New York City (Sunderman & Kim, 2004). If higher student achievement was a key to economic revival, Buffalo educators clearly had a lot of work to do.

Under NCLB guidelines, students from schools identified as in need of improvement could transfer to any school in the district that had not been so identified. Education leaders in Buffalo decided to exclude public schools with admission requirements from the list of possible transfer schools. Once these magnet and special schools were ruled out, there were few nonimprovement schools available for transfers (Kim & Sunderman, 2003). As if the short list of possibilities were not problem enough, a survey of Buffalo parents revealed that 75% of them did not even realize their child attended a school designated in need of improvement (Kim & Sunderman, 2003). Communication issues between Buffalo Public Schools and the community would become a persistent source of concern over the ensuing years.

The enrollment and number of schools in Buffalo continued to shrink in the early years of the 21st century. By 2014, 57 schools enrolled 32,762 students. Of this number, 3,879 students were English-language learners and 8,384 were students with Individual Education Plans (District Directory Information, 2013–2014). Under New York State accountability guidelines, 27 of these schools were Priority Schools, indicating that they were among the lowest-achieving schools in the state. Another 16 were Focus Schools, just a notch above Priority status. Only 14 schools were listed as being in Good Standing. As a result, Buffalo Public Schools was classified as a Focus District.

THE PROMISE OF RACE TO THE TOP

When the Obama administration announced the Race to the Top competition and New York State decided to submit an application, educational leaders throughout the Empire State hoped that significant funding would become available for school improvement. Ninety-one percent of New York's public school districts, including Buffalo, submitted a Memorandum of Understanding (MOU) confirming their support of the state's application. The application committed New York to adopting internationally benchmarked standards and assessments, recruiting and rewarding effective teachers and principals, building instructional data systems, and turning around the lowest-performing schools. School districts that had schools identified as "persistently lowest-achieving" were expected to adopt one of four turnaround models: turnaround, restart, transformation, or closure.

After failing to win a Race to the Top grant in the first round of competition, New York State was notified on August 24, 2010, that its second application had succeeded. The award was $696,646,000, one of the two largest awards given under the program. Florida obtained a similarly impressive award. Half of the amount was earmarked to be sent directly to New York school districts and charter schools that signed the MOU.

In order to be a Race to the Top winner, New York State needed to enact several pieces of legislation. One statute (S.7991/A.11171) established the requirements for new, more rigorous evaluations of classroom teachers and building principals (Legislation in support, 2010). Other laws raised the cap on the number of charter schools permitted to operate in New York and provided funding to implement a state longitudinal data system (Legislation in support, 2010).

Within two months of the announcement that New York had won a Race to the Top grant, the New York State Department of Education notified Buffalo Public Schools that it would receive $7.9 million in School Improvement Grant (SIG) funds for the 2010–2011 school year. The money was intended to help turn around four persistently low-performing Buffalo schools: Bennett High School, M. L. King Multicultural Institute, International School, and South Park High School. The school district chose the transformation option for all four schools. Considered the "least disruptive" school turnaround model, transformation was the most popular of the four options across the United States (Maxwell, 2010).

An outside observer might have expected the citizens of Buffalo to be pleased that additional funds had been obtained for their schools. After all, Buffalo Public Schools was reported to be the third most underfunded school district in the United States (Press release, July 15, 2011). The problem was that Buffalo had requested a much larger allocation from Albany and been turned down. Blame for the rejection was directed at Superintendent James A. Williams.

The transformation model required replacing the school principal, among other measures. In July 2010, Williams refused to replace principals in three of Buffalo's seven lowest-performing schools, thereby depriving the strapped school system of badly needed improvement funds. The *Buffalo News* (Pasciak, July 25, 2010) reported that Williams said, "You can sit in Albany and just say, 'Remove that principal, they've been there longer than two years.' But who am I going to replace them with? There's a shortage of leaders in this country." Apparently the Buffalo School Board disagreed with Williams about the shortage of leaders along with other aspects of Williams's stewardship.

Albany had other concerns regarding Buffalo's request for SIG and Race to the Top funds. Williams, for example, was criticized for failing to include the Buffalo Teachers Federation (BTF) in the turnaround planning process or secure its support for the final plans (Telephone polls, 2011). Buffalo did receive almost $8 million to turn around the aforementioned quartet of struggling schools, but its application had sought $42 million! Critics reasoned that if Williams had played by the rules, the school system would have received the full amount.

Alarmed at the prospect that Williams and the school board would miss a second opportunity to secure federal SIG funds for all seven priority schools, the District Parent Coordinating Council and parent representatives from the Priority Schools met in July 2011 to develop a plan of action. They blamed the Buffalo Teachers Federation for publicly declaring that it would not support any district turnaround plan that called for moving even one teacher (Press release, July 13, 2011). The parent group decided to appeal for help to Buffalo's representative on the New York State Board of Regents as well as its congressional representative.

Parent activism paid off to some extent. On August 9, 2011, the New York State Education Department awarded $9.2 million to Buffalo to fund turnaround efforts at six schools. Funding for three other schools, however, was rejected because their plans did not meet state and federal guidelines. On the same day, the school board voted to dismiss Williams. The head of the BTF, who up to this point had supported Williams because he had not pressed for teacher transfers from Priority Schools, also came to the conclusion that the time had come for a new superintendent.

On September 7, 2011, Amber Dixon was named interim superintendent. An insider, she formerly held the position of executive director of evaluation, accountability, and project initiatives for Buffalo Public Schools.

Soon after her appointment, Dixon received a letter from New York commissioner of education John B. King informing her that Buffalo's School Improvement Grant had been suspended (Letter dated January 3,

2012). The school system had failed to comply with various federal requirements associated with the transformation model chosen in its application for funding. The commissioner noted that Buffalo's collective bargaining agreement with teachers and principals unions needed to be modified in order to provide for evaluations that were based, in part, on student growth in academic achievement. Evidence of a rigorous evaluation process for teachers, including observations and assessment tools, was judged insufficient. Dixon was instructed to cease obligating SIG funds. She also was warned that Buffalo's Race to the Top funding could be jeopardized because of noncompliance.

A DISTRICT ADRIFT

As Buffalo began to search for a new superintendent, state education officials continued to monitor the district's efforts to comply with federal regulations for schools choosing the transformation model. Dixon requested a hearing by the New York State Education Department (NYSED) to address the suspension of 2011–2012 funding for six transformation schools.

Knowing that Buffalo's teacher evaluation system was a major sticking point with NYSED, Dixon tried to restart negotiations with the teachers union. Negotiations had broken down in December 2011 over the issue of student absenteeism. At the time, the union argued that the achievement of students who were chronically absent should not be counted for the 20% of each teacher's Annual Professional Performance Review (APPR) that NYSED said had to be based on student achievement. In March 2012, the union and the school district agreed to submit a new evaluation proposal to Albany, one that involved scaling back teacher performance goals in schools with higher-than-average student absenteeism. That proposal was rejected by the NYSED (Cramer, 2012).

In a letter dated May 3, 2012, Commissioner King also warned Dixon that failure to resolve issues concerning the evaluation of teachers and principals could jeopardize their SIG funding for 2012–2013 (Pasciak, May 4, 2012). In addition, he pointed out that lack of agreement between BPS and the BTF on evaluation plans could lead to the loss of $57 million in state aid and federal funds.

The commissioner's letter also referenced BPS's applications for new SIG funds for seven additional Priority Schools. None of the new applications involved the transformation model, however. Buffalo Elementary School of Technology, Waterfront Elementary, Lafayette High School, and East High School chose the restart model, while Bilingual Center, Futures Academy, and Dr. Charles R. Drew Science Magnet opted for the turnaround model. Pending district response to various issues identified by the commissioner, six of the seven applications seemed destined for approval. Submission of a satisfactory evaluation plan (APPR) for the restart schools and specification of locally adopted competencies to be used to screen staff for the turnaround schools were two of the requirements noted by King in his letter. He also indicated that a "distinguished educator" might be appointed by his office to assist the school district with improvement plans for its lowest-performing schools.

Buffalo was not the only school system in New York to be faced with the loss of federal funds over the issue of teacher evaluation. A total of 10 districts were threatened with sanctions. In June 2012, Dixon received the news that Commissioner King had accepted Buffalo's revisions and restored its federal funding. Of the 10 out-of-compliance districts, only New York City remained under sanction.

Unfortunately for Dixon, this good news was followed by the school board's announcement that it had passed over the locally popular interim superintendent in favor of an outsider. Dixon supporters claimed that race had played a part in the selection: The new superintendent was African American; Dixon was white.

CHANGING OF THE GUARD

The beginning of the 2012–2013 school year in Buffalo found two new figures in key roles in the school district. Dr. Pamela Brown, Buffalo's new superintendent, was a graduate of Harvard's prestigious urban superintendents program and a former central office administrator in Richmond, Virginia, and Philadelphia. When interviewed concerning her strategy for improving Buffalo Public Schools, she responded, "My number one priority now is to engage all the stakeholders and to bring together a broad representation of the community, including teachers, teacher assistants, principals, bus drivers, food service workers, parents, foundations, unions—because everybody in this community has a stake in the future of our children" (Scrivani, n.d.).

The second new figure also was new to Buffalo. Dr. Judy Elliott became the first distinguished educator ever appointed by the New York State commissioner to assist a low-performing school district (Pasciak, October 8, 2012). Elliott previously had served as a high-ranking administrator in the Los Angeles Unified School District before having her contract bought out. Though many regarded Elliott as an outsider, she actually had spent three decades in western New York before going west.

Confusion regarding Elliott's role characterized her early days in Buffalo. Some observers considered her to be Commissioner King's resident spy (Pasciak, October 8, 2012). They reasoned that King and New York State regent Bob Bennett actually were planning a state takeover of Buffalo Public Schools once pending takeover legislation was passed. This law required, however, that a distinguished educator first had to be appointed and take a shot at improving conditions before a state takeover could proceed.

Elliott pointed out that her role was neither to pave the way for a takeover nor to fix individual struggling schools (Pasciak, October 8, 2012). Her charge, she insisted, was to facilitate a turnaround of the entire Buffalo school system. The responsibility for fixing struggling schools, she went on to note, belonged to Superintendent Brown.

One thing was certain. The challenges facing Brown and Elliott were staggering. As local news reporter Mary Pasciak (October 8, 2012) put it:

> Truancy is rampant—one-third of high school students missed more than seven weeks of school in a recent year, nearly half of kindergartners missed nearly a month. The district suspends students at four times the statewide rate. Less than a third of elementary and middle school students can read or do math at grade level. Only about half of all students graduate from high schools—and only one out of four black males graduate.

Elliott spent the late summer and early fall compiling data and meeting with people, including the principals of Buffalo's 28 Priority Schools. On October 5, 2012, she presented the results of her efforts in the form of an action plan to guide Brown's efforts to turn around Buffalo Public Schools. Elliott's recommendations were preceded by an analysis of problems with the existing organization of the school district. Buffalo was faulted, for example, for being too highly centralized, providing too little support for low-performing schools, privileging a group of special schools with admission requirements, failing to use data to drive instructional decision making, and failing to offer a districtwide continuum of services for students with disabilities (Elliott, October 5, 2012).

The action plan addressed nine different aspects of district operations. The goals for these nine areas are listed in box 2.1 (Elliott, October 5, 2012).

BOX 2.1

Deliverable Area 1: Governance
   Goal: Move from a totally centralized system to one that is more school based, with oversight, and that allows for gradual release of centrally held decision making to Priority School principals.

Deliverable Area 2: Organizational
   Goal: Align Central Office departments and functions so that they are responsive, proactive, and coherent in supporting Priority Schools.

Deliverable Area 3: Articulation and Coordination

Goal: Establish and maintain monthly professional development and meeting structures for Priority School principals to further develop and enhance their instructional leadership.

Deliverable Area 4: Leadership

Goal: Establish a coherent, talented leadership team and organization at Central Office that is accountable, data driven, and able to provide immediate, responsive service and support to Priority Schools.

Deliverable Area 5: Use of Data

Goal: Establish a culture of data-based decision making, align data systems and tools, and create a unified data platform for teachers and principals that is responsive and easily accessible in real time.

Deliverable Area 6: Curriculum

Goal: Evaluate and ensure that the outlined curriculum, across grade levels and content areas, is being consistently implemented and monitored with fidelity, that there are instructional materials and textbook in classes, and that progress is monitored regularly.

Deliverable Area 7: Instruction

Goal: Align all efforts in Central Office to be focused on instruction, including the transition to the Common Core Standards and pedagogy, for all students, including English learners; create a continuum of services for students with disabilities; and set performance targets for the Priority Schools.

Deliverable Area 8: Assessment

Goal: Develop a written plan for implementing a comprehensive assessment system and using data for instructional decisions.

Deliverable Area 9: Operations and Management

Goal: Establish, in writing: (1) procedures, timelines for dissemination, and expectations of Central Office processes (e.g., textbook ordering, closure of under enrolled classes, student placement decisions, hiring/staffing) that directly impact Priority Schools; (2) a plan to expand student support services to directly address chronic absenteeism that includes multiagency efforts and city/countywide collaboration.

In the details accompanying each goal area were lots of suggestions for improving services to Buffalo's 28 Priority Schools. Elliott recommended that Priority Schools be accorded discretionary authority regarding their budgets and other site-based matters that previously were handled by the central office. Priority School personnel were called on to report on the extent to which they were receiving support and assistance from "community superintendents" and their staffs. Superintendent Brown was called upon to visit Priority Schools and have conversations with their principals on at least a monthly basis. Special efforts were recommended regarding alternative education for suspended students and credit recovery for students at risk of not graduating.

Elliott planned to spend between five and ten days a month in the district. Her time was covered by BPS, not the NYSED, a provision that did not sit well with many Buffalo residents, especially since her hourly rate exceeded the superintendent's pay rate (Pasciak, October 8, 2012). Much of her time was reserved for reviewing the improvement plans for the Priority and Focus Schools. She had the option to accept a school's plan or recommend modifications to the school board and commissioner.

Things were looking up early in the new year when Pamela Brown received notice from Commissioner King that Buffalo's proposed Annual Professional Performance Review plan had been approved (Letter dated January 17, 2013). The commissioner's letter did contain the following warning, however: "Please be advised that . . . the Department will be analyzing data . . . and may order a corrective action plan if there are unacceptably low correlation results between the student growth sub-component and any other measures of teacher and principal effectiveness and/or if the teacher or principal scores or ratings show little differentiation across educators."

Two months later, Brown received a letter from Dr. Julia Rafal-Baer, executive director of the Office of Teacher and Leader Effectiveness, Policy and Programs at the NYSED (Letter dated March 25, 2013). The Education Department had monitored the Buffalo Teacher Federation's website and noticed that it contained information that contradicted what the school district had agreed to regarding the approved APPR. The website reported, for example, that "No teacher will be negatively affected by the results of their evaluation rating for the 2011–2012 and 2012–2013 school years." Clearly this statement violated the approved APPR, New York Education Law 3012-c(1), and the federal requirements for low-performing schools choosing the transformation model. Brown was warned that Buffalo could lose its SIG money if the website was not brought into alignment with the approved APPR.

The NYSED went ahead, despite the warning, and allocated $22.5 million in SIG funds to Buffalo. This sum amounted to over one quarter of all SIG funds awarded to New York school districts. In the roller coaster world of Buffalo Public Schools, however, good news invariably is followed by bad news. In April 2013, Commissioner King went on record as saying that the federal money that had been spent at four failing Buffalo schools had yielded disappointing results (Pasciak, April 10, 2013). Drawing on site visits by NYSED monitors and a progress report filed by

Judy Elliott, King told the Buffalo news media that promises made in Buffalo's School Improvement Grant applications were not being fulfilled.

King's concerns about Buffalo's efforts to turn around the initial four failing schools were registered in the spring of 2013, the third and final year of federal SIG funding for those schools. By this time Buffalo school district officials were projecting a $51 million deficit for the 2013–2014 school year. The end of SIG funding for the four schools contributed to the dire financial circumstances (Pasciak, April 10, 2013). Commissioner King reminded Buffalo educational leaders that the SIG funds were intended to build local capacity for improvement, not to become permanent supplements to the local budget. He went on to warn that the state had the authority to revoke a school's registration, thereby effectively shutting down the school.

NO END TO BAD NEWS FROM ALBANY

As if the spring of 2013 was not trying enough for Buffalo Public Schools, Superintendent Brown received a letter on May 29 from Ira Schwartz, the assistant commissioner in charge of New York's Office of Accountability (Letter dated May 29, 2013). Schwartz indicated that his office had received a complaint from Samuel Radford III, president of the Buffalo School District Parent Coordinating Council. Radford accused the school district of failing to comply with the provisions of Section 1116 of the No Child Left Behind Act. The provisions required that students in Priority and Focus Schools be given an opportunity to choose another public school.

After an investigation, Schwartz's office found that 95 Buffalo students who were eligible for the choice option in 2012–2013 had been denied a transfer. Schwartz pointed out that the school district's claim that it lacked the capacity to accommodate a change of schools for the 95 students was an unacceptable reason for denial. Brown was told that a Corrective Action Plan (CAP) addressing the problem had to be submitted. The CAP eventually was approved in November 2013, but the NYSED informed Brown that a midyear inventory to identify all available seats in Good Standing Schools had to be conducted "so as to offer as many parents as possible choice for second semester placement" (Letter dated November 6, 2013).

Buffalo received another unwelcome directive from Albany over the summer when Commissioner King informed district officials that they would have to involve their regional Board of Cooperative Educational Services (BOCES) in plans to address low graduation rates at East and Lafayette High Schools. State officials blamed the district for failing to come up with viable turnaround plans for the two Priority Schools (Newberg, July 23, 2013).

Buffalo Public Schools at the time had been conducting promising discussions with Johns Hopkins University regarding its involvement as a lead partner in turning around East and Lafayette. Superintendent Brown clearly preferred an alliance with the prestigious university to an imposed partnership with BOCES, one that would permit students to take courses at the regional center at the school district's expense. Commissioner King, having found Buffalo's turnaround plans for East and Lafayette unacceptable, also denied the school district millions of dollars in badly needed federal funds, funds that would have been used in part to hire Johns Hopkins as a lead partner. If Buffalo Public Schools wished to retain the services of Johns Hopkins, it would have to find the needed $3.6 million from other sources.

A month after mandating that Buffalo engage the Erie County BOCES in its turnaround efforts, Commissioner King took the unprecedented step of summoning Superintendent Brown and her leadership team to Albany (Williams, August 23, 2013). Convinced that Buffalo lacked the expertise to develop viable turnaround plans for four of its Priority Schools, King ordered state officials to provide direct, face-to-face assistance. After a full day of consultation, "properly completed" turnaround plans were created for both East and Lafayette High Schools as well as Buffalo Elementary School of Technology and Highgate Heights Elementary School. In an unexpected switch, the plans called for Johns Hopkins University to serve as the "operator"—or superintendent—of the four schools. The Buffalo Board of Education was expected to monitor Johns Hopkins's work.

The mood at the central office of Buffalo Public Schools following the trip to Albany was understandably upbeat. Not only had acceptable turnaround plans been developed, plans that allowed the district to work with its desired partner, but badly needed federal funds were reinstated. It did not take long, however, for the mood to turn sour once again.

In the fall of 2013, a team from the NYSED visited three of Buffalo's Priority Schools as part of a routine review (Tan, November 11, 2013). So concerned were team members by what they saw that they conducted an unprecedented immediate return visit to offer technical assistance. Among the identified issues were school leadership problems, inadequate instruction for English-language learners, and a lack of central office support for turnaround efforts in the schools. As a consequence of the team's report, Pamela Brown asked for the resignation of Buffalo's administrator in charge of school turnaround planning.

If Brown believed that this action would deflect attention from her own precarious status, she was mistaken. She already had narrowly escaped dismissal in September when the school board voted 5 to 4 to retain her (Lankes, December 30, 2013). Carl Paladino, a board member, announced his intention in December to introduce another resolution calling for Brown's ouster along with a companion resolution requiring the entire school board to resign and asking the state to appoint a special master to take control of Buffalo Public Schools. At the same time, it came to light that a group of local business leaders had offered Brown half a million dollars to buy out her contract (Lankes, December 30, 2013).

When interviewed by the press, Brown indicated that she had no intention of accepting the buyout offer (Lankes, December 30, 2013). She went on to defend her leadership, pointing out that short-term suspensions and student absenteeism had decreased during her watch. What's more, student enrollment and the graduation rate had inched up.

Brown's encouraging assessment of progress did not prevent a parent active on the District Parent Coordinating Council from filing a complaint with the U.S. Department of Education's New York Office for Civil Rights. The complaint alleged that Buffalo Public Schools discriminated against nonwhite students (Pasciak, March 13, 2014). Evidence offered to support the claim included the racial breakdown for students at City Honors High School. While Buffalo Public Schools enrolled 22% white students, City Honors enrolled 66% white students. Only 21% of City Honors students were black. In March 2014, federal authorities agreed to investigate the disparity.

Spring brought Buffalo yet another controversy, this one involving the district's efforts to secure a consulting firm to handle turnaround training for staff members at nine low-performing schools. The Arizona firm Evans Newton Inc., which had submitted the lowest bid, did not receive the highest rating when school board members reviewed the applications. Furthermore, board members registered concern that Evans Newton once had retained the services of several district administrators who were fired because they lacked the appropriate credentials (Williams, April 3, 2014). Brown again found herself in the spotlight because she had hired these former Evans Newton consultants and because the Evans Newton firm had not been disclosed on the applications for SIG funds that the school board approved. In the face of mounting criticism, Evans Newton elected to withdraw its bid, leaving the school district to continue its search for a turnaround partner.

Facing a divided school board and mounting criticism of stalled turnaround initiatives, Pamela Brown negotiated a very favorable resignation in June (Tan, June 16, 2014). Will Keresztes, a high-ranking administrator with the school district, was appointed interim superintendent until July when newly elected board members would be installed and the new school board could take up the matter of replacing Brown.

FAMILIAR PROBLEMS FOR A NEW LEADER

The French idiom claims that the more things change, the more they remain the same. Yogi Berra put it more simply, "It's déjà vu all over again." Regardless of the expression, a disconcerting sense of history repeating itself followed closely on the heels of Donald Ogilvie's appointment as interim superintendent on July 9, 2014.

Members of the new school board sidestepped Keresztes and chose the former superintendent of the Erie County BOCES without conducting a formal search and interview process (Lankes, July 7, 2014). Ogilvie's charge was to implement the plan for school reform that the board majority drafted the previous week. The plan called for increasing the number of open spots for students in high-performing schools, encouraging more charter schools to open, and lobbying the state to take over the district. Having authored a critical report on the state of public education in Buffalo in 2010, Ogilvie understood the challenges that had to be overcome in order to turn around the district and its lowest-performing schools.

No sooner had Ogilvie assumed office than Johns Hopkins University announced its intention to cancel the contract to serve as the de facto superintendent for East High School and Lafayette High School (Tan, August 13, 2014). Johns Hopkins built its school turnaround track record on consulting with struggling schools on matters such as curriculum alignment, data analysis, assessment, and instructional improvement, not on handling such matters as governance, hiring personnel, and evaluating principals and teachers. Representatives of Johns Hopkins complained that so much time was required to address these latter concerns that they were unable to focus on the former. With schools set to open within a few weeks, the timing of the announcement could not have been worse. Besides leaving the two Priority Schools in the lurch, Johns Hopkins's withdrawal placed their federal SIG funds in jeopardy.

But this was not the only looming financial disaster. Of greater consequence was the state's withholding $36 million in federal aid because the school district had failed in the past to involve parents and the District Parent Coordinating Council in drafting various proposals and plans, including school turnaround plans (Williams, August 15, 2014). Parent representatives offered assurances, however, that the plans currently before the school board had benefitted from their participation. While Will Keresztes was interim superintendent, he had engaged the American Institutes for Research (AIR) to solicit parent input in order to redesign turnaround plans. The District Parent Coordinating Council urged the school board to approve the revised plans and forward them to Albany in the hope that the commissioner would release the badly needed funds.

Stung by Johns Hopkins's decision to cancel its contract with Buffalo Public Schools, the school board began to question why so much district money was being allocated for consulting services (Tan, August 24, 2014).

Board members complained that there was no consistent or deliberative process for evaluating the work of consulting companies and determining whether these companies deserved repeat business. One board member questioned why the school district couldn't assemble its own in-house group of school turnaround experts.

Despite their concerns, the school board went ahead and approved plans in late August to solicit proposals from external providers to turn around Bennett High School (Williams, August 27, 2014). After three years of efforts supported by a School Improvement Grant, Bennett remained a failing high school. District officials had hoped to convert Bennett to a science and technology specialty school, but Albany rejected the proposal and forbid the high school from accepting any freshman for the coming school year. If improvements could not be made quickly, Bennett would have to close. A similar fate awaited East High School, Lafayette High School, and Martin Luther King Elementary School. The state agreed, however, to give the district one more year to develop acceptable turnaround plans for the four schools.

No sooner had the state agreed to extensions for the failing schools than Commissioner King took Buffalo Public Schools to task for not making better use of its federal SIG money. King told the press that district administrators had failed to deliver on the promises they made in past turnaround plans (Tan, September 18, 2014). As an example, he indicated that prescribed teacher training never took place because district and teacher union officials could not agree on how to provide it.

In October the New York State Education Department took the unprecedented step of inviting a new round of charter school proposals solely for Buffalo (Tan, October 12, 2014). It seemed that Buffalo was earning the dubious distinction of prompting the state to take unprecedented actions to help students stuck in low-performing Buffalo schools. Predictably, the move drew harsh criticism from the Buffalo Teachers Federation and the minority bloc on the school board that opposed charter schools.

In fall meetings, the school board approved the phase-out of East High School, Lafayette High School, Bennett High School, and Martin Luther King Multicultural Institute in their existing form and development of plans for new schools at the four locations (Tan, October 12, 2014). With Commissioner King's announcement regarding charter schools, independent charter operators also were invited to tender proposals to operate each of the four persistently failing schools. By the fall of 2014, Buffalo already had 16 charter schools serving more than 7,000 students (compared to 34,000 students in public schools). Partnerships with outside operators were an additional option for the four schools, but officials at the NYSED indicated that they had learned a lesson from the Johns Hopkins pullout. No partnership would be considered unless "work rule flexibility" was agreed to by the teachers union (Tan, October 12, 2014).

The school board announced that plans for reinventing or taking over the four failing schools needed to be submitted by December 12, 2014. The plans then would be reviewed by the school board. A board-approved plan had to be sent to Albany by January 30, 2015. The NYSED insisted that the school district provide each of the four schools with a full-time facilitator to assist with preparing turnaround plans.

In November amidst public demonstrations opposing an expansion of charter schools and increasing rancor between factions on the school board, representatives from Lafayette High School proposed that the school become a "newcomer academy" catering to immigrants and refugees needing intensive assistance with English literacy. Modeled after a Rochester school, the Lafayette International Newcomer Academy (LINA) would be a two-year rapid immersion school for new English-language learners. Each student would receive an individualized learning plan. With over 70% of Lafayette's students already being immigrants and refugees, the proposal made sense to many supporters of "community" (as opposed to charter) schools, but the school board postponed its review of the proposal. The majority bloc on the board may have hoped that a charter school proposal for Lafayette would be submitted before the December 12 deadline.

Meanwhile Bennett High School alumni and administrators put forth their own proposal. Hoping to recapture the glory of Bennett's past, former students pressed for a school turnaround based on honors courses and career programs. Instead of drawing students from across the city, Bennett would function as a neighborhood school catering to residents of University Heights, North Buffalo, and the Buffalo Promise Neighborhood Zone (Tan, November 30, 2014). At the same time the turnaround plan for Bennett was being drafted, a charter school organization also expressed interest in the school. A local newspaper editorial speculated that it was the prospect of competition from Tapestry Charter School that prompted Bennett alumni to develop their own turnaround plan (Opinion, December 2, 2014).

Claiming that the district had been slow to hire planning facilitators and that a November snowstorm had resulted in the loss of planning time, representatives from East High and Martin Luther King Multicultural Institute asked the school board for an extension on the December 12 deadline. The request was denied on the grounds that the school board needed the time between December 12 and January 30 to thoroughly review the proposals for all four failing schools. East High made the deadline with a proposal to convert the school to a community school with extended hours, vocational training, and a high school equivalency program. That left Martin Luther King as the only one of the four without a district-sponsored turnaround plan. A charter organization and a local group interested in teaching by the Socratic method, however, did submit plans for converting the elementary school.

Buffalo educators and residents who felt that Albany had been too heavy-handed in dealing with their failing schools got an early Christmas present when Commissioner John King announced his resignation at the beginning of December. King had been asked to become a senior advisor to U.S. secretary of education Arne Duncan. King's departure left Buffalo wondering about the fate of plans for the four failing schools as well as their share of federal school improvement funds.

THE GOVERNOR GETS INVOLVED

Commissioner King might have departed for the nation's capital, but that did not mean that fair winds began to blow from Albany to Buffalo. With the new year came harsh words for Buffalo from Governor Andrew Cuomo. In his State of the State address, he noted that Buffalo had been a failing district for many years despite receiving twice the state average in per pupil aid (Newberg, January 22, 2015). Cuomo went on to propose an agenda for statewide education reform that included bonuses for top-performing teachers and a takeover plan for persistently failing schools. Such schools would be turned over to a nonprofit organization, another school district, or a turnaround expert.

Several weeks after his State of the State address, Cuomo expressed an interest in turning over control of failing schools to independent "czars" (Tan, February 13, 2015). A similar "receivership" model already was in place in neighboring Massachusetts, and the governor asked the NYSED to find out how it was working. A receiver would have broad authority to hire and fire, override union contracts, and shut down schools.

While Cuomo explored his options, the Buffalo School Board decided on a new tack of its own. The five-person majority bloc agreed to refuse to act on turnaround plans submitted by the four failing schools until a new contract could be negotiated with the Buffalo Teachers Federation (Lankes, February 9, 2015). If the strategy failed to gain concessions from the union, the four failing schools would continue to be phased out of existence. Union president Philip Rumore predicted that such an outcome would lead to the opening of more charter schools.

As the 2014–2015 school year wound down, turmoil and uncertainty remained the hallmarks of public education in Buffalo. One member of the school board majority, Carl Paladino, called for the immediate resignation of interim superintendent Donald Ogilvie. Paladino accused Ogilvie of conspiring against the majority that hired him (Lankes, March 28, 2015). While other board members refused to support Paladino's move, they agreed that Ogilvie should depart at the end of the school year. Once again Buffalo would be searching for someone to lead the school system.

School board president James Sampson admitted, "Whoever comes in is going to have to be incredibly adept at balancing competing and intense interests" (Lankes, March 28, 2015).

As the school board geared up for the superintendent search, a host of issues remained unresolved. The possibility of a federal discrimination lawsuit still loomed. The fate of the four failing schools was yet to be determined. No new contract with the Buffalo Teachers Federation had been negotiated. The threat of Governor Cuomo assigning a receiver to take charge of part or all of Buffalo Public Schools continued to be discussed. And the deep division among board members persisted. Finding a capable leader willing to face these challenges would be difficult. Meanwhile, more and more children in Buffalo's schools found themselves being left behind.

WHAT CAN BE LEARNED FROM THE BUFFALO CASE?

In thinking about the recent history of Buffalo Public Schools, several questions come to mind. What factors contributed to the sorry state of public education in so many Buffalo schools, and why hadn't the school district, the city, and the state been able to address the problem effectively?

Deborah Stone (1997) suggested that serious social problems typically inspire competing causal stories—narratives constructed to account for unfortunate developments. In Buffalo's case, there is no shortage of plausible causal stories to explain the persistence of failing schools.

Competing priorities. The importance of a laserlike focus on a particular challenge is a popular theme in many manuals for organizational leaders. Focus can be especially important in a struggling organization where confidence is likely to be lacking and the numbers of problems are overwhelming. Trying to tackle all the problems at the same time is likely to exceed the organization's capacity for improvement and maximize the likelihood of failure, thereby reinforcing an already existing sense of futility and despair.

There is evidence in the preceding case that Buffalo Public Schools grappled with competing priorities. On one hand, district officials faced demands to turn around a large number of low-performing schools. At the same time, they understood the pressure to preserve their selective high-performing schools. The unspoken fear was that moving students from low-performing to selective schools could dilute the quality of the latter, causing even more parents to abandon the public schools for private, parochial, and charter schools.

One causal story, therefore, could be that Buffalo Public Schools, in its efforts to maintain the exclusivity of its top schools while simultaneously addressing issues in its Priority and Focus Schools, lost the focus required to address effectively the needs of its lowest-performing schools.

Dysfunctional district organization. It also could be argued, of course, that a well-organized school district with competent leadership should have been able to manage both academic excellence and educational equity. The case study reveals, however, that Buffalo Public Schools suffered from serious organizational problems. Perhaps the most glaring problem was the high turnover in district leadership. Buffalo earned a reputation for being an unwelcoming place for superintendents.

Despite the creation of a special office to handle school turnaround planning and monitoring, Buffalo repeatedly failed to prepare turnaround plans that met state requirements. When plans finally passed muster with the NYSED, district administrators then failed to monitor the implementation of the plans sufficiently to ensure that promised changes actually were made. It did not help that the district continually found itself in serious financial straits, partly due to the mismanagement of federal funds. The disorganized state of Buffalo's district administration was responsible, at least in part, for Johns Hopkins's decision to cancel its contract to work with failing schools.

Board politics. A third causal story to account for Buffalo's struggles involves school board politics. The case can be made that the deeply divided board contributed to the high turnover of superintendents and to the district's seeming inability to address competing priorities effectively. The majority bloc's commitment to expand charter schools and engage the state in directly overseeing district operations did little to inspire district employees or promote their loyalty. These positions also alienated many parents and community members who opposed the creation of more charter schools. The school board's reluctance to open access to Buffalo's selective schools upset parents of students stuck in failing schools. Generating positive momentum is difficult when a majority of the school board lacks confidence in its professional educators and when a significant number of citizens lack confidence in the school board.

Teacher union recalcitrance. Some might argue that the reason why many of Buffalo's turnaround plans were rejected by the NYSED concerned the refusal of the Buffalo Teachers Federation to be flexible on such matters as school hours and professional development. The BTF also opposed wholesale reconstitution of faculties at failing schools and any staffing arrangement that overrode seniority. Examples of successful school turnarounds in the absence of significant personnel changes and alterations in working conditions are relatively rare.

The BTF also voiced serious reservations concerning changes to teacher evaluation required by the federal government in return for Race to the Top funds and School Improvement Grants. New regulations required that part of each teacher's annual evaluation had to be based on student achievement. The BTF pointed out that many Buffalo students were absent from school a significant number of days each year. It was unreasonable, union representatives argued, to hold teachers accountable for the achievement of students who were frequently absent. In an ironic twist, it is worth noting that Buffalo teachers had the highest rate of teacher absenteeism for 40 metropolitan school districts (Chronically absent teachers, June 11, 2014). Nearly 40% of Buffalo teachers missed 18 or more days of school a year! This high rate of teacher absenteeism, in and of itself, might constitute a legitimate causal story for failing schools in Buffalo.

No shortage of possible causes. District dysfunctionality, school board politics, and teacher union recalcitrance are but three possible explanations for Buffalo's inadequate efforts to serve its lowest-performing schools. Other possibilities abound. Teacher competence, for instance, could be an issue. It is well known that urban school systems struggle to attract and retain talented teachers. The problem is most acute for teachers in the lowest-performing schools. Capable teachers often try to transfer to higher-performing schools at the first opportunity.

The creation of charter schools in Buffalo also might be blameworthy. An argument could be made that these schools syphoned off more motivated and successful students and more involved parents, thereby leaving public schools with higher concentrations of struggling students and disengaged parents. Such a process can be a recipe for teacher discouragement and student alienation. To make matters worse, charter schools also drain away badly needed funds. Buffalo's perennial financial problems cannot have helped the district's efforts to improve its lowest-performing schools.

The variety of possible causal stories that can be offered for Buffalo's struggles illustrates the challenges that must be overcome to save the children left behind, not just in Buffalo but across the nation. The Buffalo case examined some of the steps that New York State took in order to address these challenges. They included rejecting unacceptable school and district improvement plans, providing technical assistance on how to develop good plans, allocating federal SIG funds along with state money, appointing a distinguished educator to guide turnaround initiatives, requiring Buffalo Public Schools to work with the Erie County BOCES, instructing the school system to engage the services of outside providers, threatening to appoint a receiver to take control of improvement operations, and allowing Buffalo to have more charter schools.

In the following chapters, we investigate similar measures as well as different approaches being taken by other states and school districts to turn around their lowest-performing schools. Perhaps some of the steps being taken elsewhere offer hope for Buffalo.

REFERENCES

"Chronically absent" teachers. 2014, June 11. *Education Week,* p. 5.

Cramer, P. 2012, March 30. From Buffalo, a warning for local consensus on absent students. *Chalkbeat.* Retrieved from http://ny.chalkbeat.org/2012/03/30/from-buffalo-a-warning-for-local-consensus-on-absent-students/.

District directory information, 2013–2014. n.d. *National Center for Education Statistics.* Retrieved from http://nces.ed.gov/ccd/districtsearch/district_detail.asp?ID2=3605850.

Elliott, J. 2012, October 5. Distinguished educator action plan. *Buffalo Public Schools.* Retrieved from http://www.buffaloschools.org/district.cfm?subpage=90207.

Kim, J., & Sunderman, G. L. 2003. Findings from the first phase of school choice implementation in three districts: Buffalo, New York, Richmond, Virginia, DeKalb County, Georgia. Paper presented at the annual meeting of the American Educational Research Association, Chicago, Illinois, April 21–25, 2003.

Lankes, T. 2013, December 30. Buffalo school chief "never contemplated" taking offer to leave. *Buffalo News.* Retrieved from http://www.buffalonews.com/city-region/buffalo-public-schools/buffalo-school-chief-8216never-contemplated8217-taking-offer-to-leave-20131230.

———. 2014, July 7. New board looks to Ogilvie to reset district's course. *Buffalo News.* Retrieved from http://www.buffalonews.com/city-region/buffalo-public-schools/new-board-looks-to-ogilvie-to-reset-districts-course-20140707.

———. 2015, February 9. School board majority links reform plans to BTF contract. *Buffalo News.* Retrieved from http://www.buffalonews.com/city-region/buffalo-public-schools/school-board-majority-links-reform-plans-to-btf-contract-20150209.

———. 2015, March 28. New Buffalo superintendent will face a demanding board with shifting alliances. *Buffalo News.* Retrieved from http://www.buffalonews.com/city-region/buffalo-public-schools/new-buffalo-superintendent-will-face-a-demanding-board-with-shifting-alliances-20150328.

Legislation in support of Race to the Top application. 2010. Retrieved from http://usny.nysed.gov/rttt/application/legislation.html.

Letter dated January 3, 2012, from John B. King to Amber Dixon. *New York State Education Department.* Retrieved from New York State Education Department website. http://usny.nysed.gov/docs/sig-letters/buffalo.pdf.

Letter dated January 17, 2013, from John B. King to Dr. Pamela Brown. *New York State Education Department.* Retrieved from New York State Education Department website. http://www.nctq.org/docs/buffalo-appr-plan.pdf.

Letter dated March 25, 2013, from Dr. Julia Rafal-Baer to Dr. Pamela Brown. *New York State Education Department.* Retrieved from New York State Education Department website. http://blogs.edweek.org/edweek/state_edwatch/BuffaloPublicSchools25Mar2013.pdf.

Letter dated May 29, 2013, from Ira Schwartz to Dr. Pamela Brown. *New York State Education Department.* Retrieved from New York State Education Department website. http://www.p12.nysed.gov/accountability/T1/titleia/docs/buffalo-cap-noncompliance-letter.pdf.

Letter dated November 6, 2013, from Ken Slentz to Dr. Pamela Brown. *New York State Education Department.* Retrieved from New York State Education Department website. http://www.p12.nysed.gov/accountability/T1/titleia/docs/buffalo-psc-cap-approval-letter.pdf.

Maxwell, L. A. 2010, August 11. Least-disruptive school turnaround model proving to be most popular. *Education Week,* p. 30.

Newberg, R. 2013, July 23. BPS has failed 2 high schools for yrs. *WIVB.* Retrieved from http://www.wivb.com/dpp/news/buffalo/bps-have-failed-2-high-schools-for-yrs.

———. 2015, January 22. Education criticized in Buffalo. *WIVB.* Retrieved from http://wivb.com/2015/01/22/education-criticized-in-buffalo/.

Opinion. 2014, December 2. *Buffalo News*. Retrieved from http://www.buffalonews.com/opinion/20141202.

Pasciak, M. 2010, July 25. Williams will keep principals at three failing schools. *Education Resource Strategies*. Retrieved from http://www.erstrategies.org/news/williams_will_keep_principals_at_schools.

———. 2012, May 4. Read King's letter approving 2012-13 plans, tying money to teacher evals. *Buffalo News*. Retrieved from http://schoolzone.buffalonews.com/2012/05/04/read-kings-letter-approving-2012-13-plans.

———. 2012, October 8. Distinguished educator: Buffalo schools' hired "help." *Buffalo News*. Retrieved from http://www.buffalonews.com/apps/pbcs.dll/article?aid=20121007/cityandregion/121009573/1020.

———. 2013, April 10. Funds for 4 failing Buffalo schools reaping little. *Buffalo News*. Retrieved from http://www.buffalonews.com/20130410/funds_for_4_failing_buffalo_schools_reaping_little.html.

———. 2014, March 13. U.S. Department of Education to probe racial bias in Buffalo Public Schools admissions. *Buffalo News*. Retrieved from http://www.buffalonews.com/city-region/buffalo-public-schools/us-department-of-education-to-probe-racial-bias-in-buffalo-public-schools-admissions-20140313.

Press release. 2011, July 13. Parents at failing schools meet to discuss district's failure to submit turnaround plans. Provided by Sam Radford, District Parent Coordinating Council of Buffalo.

———. 2011, July 15. *U.S. House of Representatives*. Retrieved from http://www.house.gov/index.php?option=com_content&task=view&id=2520&Itemid=100065.

Scrivani, M. n.d. Q&A: Pamela Brown. *Buffalo Spree*. Retrieved from http://www.buffalospree.com/Buffalo-Spree/September-2012/Q-A-Pamela-Brown/.

Stone, D. 1997. *Policy paradox*. Norton: New York.

Sunderman, G. L., & Kim, J. 2004. *Increasing bureaucracy or increasing opportunities? School district experience with supplemental educational services*. Cambridge, MA: Civil Rights Project, Harvard University.

Tan, S. 2013, November 11. Sykes forced to resign key post with Buffalo schools after state blasts turnaround plans. *Buffalo News*. Retrieved from http://www.buffalonews.com/city-region/buffalo-public-schools/sykes-forced-to-resign-key-post-with-buffalo-schools-after-state-blasts-turnaround-plans-20131111.

———. 2014, August 24. Buffalo School Board questions millions spent on education consultants. *Buffalo News*. Retrieved from http://www.buffalonews.com/city-region/buffalo-public-schools/buffalo-school-board-questions-millions-spent-on-education-consultants-20140824.

———. 2014, June 16. Pamela Brown gets big payout for leaving; Keresztes named interim chief. *Buffalo News*. Retrieved from http://www.buffalonews.com/city-region/buffalo-public-schools/pamela-brown-gets-big-payout-for-leaving-keresztes-named-interim-chief-20140616.

———. 2014, September 18. Education commissioner says district didn't keep promises on spending of school turnaround money. *Buffalo News*. Retrieved from http://www.buffalonews.com/city-region/buffalo-public-schools/education-commissioner-says-district-didnt-keep-promises-on-spending-of-school-turnaround-money-20140918.

———. 2015, February 13. Governor wants study of school district takeover model. *Buffalo News*. Retrieved from http://www.buffalonews.com/city-region/buffalo-public-schools/governor-wants-study-of-school-district-takeover-model-20150213.

———. 2014, August 13. Johns Hopkins wants to cancel pact on school turnarounds. *Buffalo News*. Retrieved from http://www.buffalonews.com/city-region/buffalo-public-schools/johns-hopkins-wants-to-cancel.

———. 2014, October 12. State allows more charter school proposals. *Buffalo News*. Retrieved from http://www.buffalonews.com/city-region/buffalo-public-schools/state-allows-more-charter-school-proposals-x2013-just-for-buffalo-20141012.

————. 2014, November 30. Bennett alumni push honors, career programs to save school. *Buffalo News*. Retrieved from http://www.buffalonews.com/city-region/buffalo-public-schools/bennett-alumni-push-honors-career-programs-to-save-school-20141130.

Telephone polls and turnaround plans: The full story on both. 2011, May 1. *Buffalo News*. Retrieved from http://schoolzone.buffalonews.com/2011/05/01/telephone-polls-and-turnaround-plans-the-full-story-on-both/.

Williams, D. 2013, August 23. Turnaround plans for troubled Buffalo schools now "properly completed." *Buffalo News*. Retrieved from http://www.buffalonews.com/city-region/turnaround-plans-for-troubled-buffalo-schools-now-properly-completed-20130823.

————. 2014, April 3. Consultant process by schools questioned. *Buffalo News*. Retrieved from http://www.buffalonews.com/city-region/buffalo-public-schools/consultant-process-by-schools-questioned-20140403.

————. 2014, August 15. $36 million rides on plan to improve Buffalo schools. *Buffalo News*. Retrieved from http://www.buffalonews.com/city-region/36-million-rides-on-plan-to-improve-buffalo-schools-20140815.

————. 2014, August 27. District gets more time for Bennett turnaround plan. *Buffalo News*. Retrieved from http://www.buffalonews.com/city-region/buffalo-public-schools/district-gets-more-time-for-bennett-turnaround-plan-20140827.

Part II

The States' Growing Impact on the Lowest-Performing Schools

Ask most state legislators if public education in the United States is still primarily a matter of local control, and they probably will agree, either for political reasons or because they actually believe it. In reality, however, the state's role in local schools has been significant for over a century. Recently that role has expanded with regard to persistently low-performing schools and districts. A report from the Institute on Education Law and Policy at Rutgers University found, for example, that 24 states have laws that allow them to take over a school district, while 15 states are empowered to take over individual schools (*50-state report*, n.d.). In 1989, New Jersey became the first state to take over a district (Newark), followed in the same year by Kentucky (Oluwole & Green, 2009). Not all district takeovers are due to low performance, of course. Fiscal mismanagement, inadequate administration, and corrupt governance all can lead to such action. In recent years, though, the primary reason for state takeover has been persistent failure to meet state academic standards.

Just because a state takes over control of a school district or school does not necessarily mean that the state is equipped to handle the challenge of raising academic performance. A brief from the U.S. Institute of Education Sciences (*State capacity*, 2015) found, in fact, that 38 states (76%) reported significant gaps in expertise for supporting school turnaround. Many states were compelled to rely on intermediaries to provide the know-how to improve the lowest-performing schools.

This section examines a variety of ways in which states are addressing failing schools and districts. The section opens with several cases involving some of the most serious state actions—school and district takeover. Subsequent chapters discuss other types of state intervention, including special state districts, school closure, reconstitution, charter schools, and technical assistance.

REFERENCES

50-state report on accountability, state intervention and takeover. N.d. New Brunswick, NJ: Institute on Education Law and Policy, Rutgers University.

Oluwole, J. O., & Green, P. C. 2009. State takeovers of school districts: Race and the Equal Protection Clause. *Indiana Law Review, 42,* 343–409.

State capacity to support school turnaround. 2015. Washington, DC: Institute of Education Sciences, U.S. Department of Education.

THREE

State Takeovers and the Complexities of Policy Making for the Lowest-Performing School Districts and Schools

The most drastic action that a state can take with regard to persistently failing schools is to take them over or close them. In the preceding case of Buffalo, the New York State Education Department gave serious consideration to a takeover of the troubled school district. A majority of the newly elected school board, in fact, took the unusual step of pressing the state to do so.

The No Child Left Behind Act provided a legal basis for state takeover of failing school districts. NCLB required a state to take at least one corrective action to address districts that consistently failed to meet Adequate Yearly Progress. Three of the specified corrective actions provided a basis for state takeovers:

1. Replacement of district personnel
2. Appointment of a trustee or receiver through the state department of education to manage the district's affairs
3. Restructure or dissolution of the school district (Oluwole & Green, 2009)

Even before the passage of NCLB, however, many states had laws on the books permitting state takeovers. When Rudo (2001) examined state laws in 2001, she reported that 27 states possessed takeover provisions. She did not distinguish, however, between state takeovers of school districts and state takeovers of individual schools. That distinction was made in an undated report by the Institute on Education Law and Policy at Rutgers University (*50-state report*, n.d.). The report indicated that 24 states

47

have laws allowing the state to take over school districts, while 15 states permit state takeover of individual schools.

Having a legal basis for state takeover is extremely important, as Virginia's governor Robert F. McDonnell (Republican) learned when he tried to implement a state-run K–12 district for low-performing schools. The so-called Opportunity Educational Institution (OEI) constituted a new executive-branch agency reporting directly to the governor, not to the state superintendent of schools. The Virginia School Boards Association (VSBA) in conjunction with the Norfolk City School Division brought a lawsuit against the OEI, claiming that no provision for state takeover of schools existed in the Virginia Constitution. The VSBA prevailed.

The present chapter focuses on the efforts of one state, Indiana, to come to grips with the issue of state takeover. The Indiana case illustrates the fact that policy making around the issue of the state's role in improving its lowest-performing schools is clearly a process, not an event. In its efforts to determine how best to champion the welfare of the students left behind in failing schools, Indiana policy makers, to use a popular expression, have been building the bridge while crossing it. Just as it appears a definitive course of action has been determined, some shift in local sentiment, state politics, or federal regulations occurs to disrupt progress and divert policy makers. Such complexities, it should be added, are often overlooked in general reports on corrective actions associated with school turnaround (Rudo, 2001).

INDIANA ADOPTS PUBLIC LAW 221

In 1999, two years before the No Child Left Behind Act, the Indiana General Assembly passed Public Law 221. The bill gave the Indiana Board of Education (IBOE) the authority to choose from a set of five options when a school reached six consecutive years rated in the state's lowest performance category (Elliott, 2013). The options included:

- Revising the school's improvement plan
- Merging the school with a higher-scoring school
- Following the Indiana Department of Education's recommendation, such as assigning a lead partner to assist the school
- Following recommendations made at a public meeting, including closing the school
- State takeover of the school

Public Law 221, however, did not include authorization for a state takeover of an entire school district.

Over a decade would pass before the state actually exercised the options provided in the law. The reason for the delayed action concerned the rating system for schools. Not until 2005 did Indiana begin counting a school's consecutive years in the lowest rating category (Elliott, 2013). Since a school had to occupy the lowest rating for six consecutive years, the state would have to wait until at least 2011 before choosing one of the five options.

In the meantime, other measures were taken by the state to address the needs of low-performing schools. In the summer of 2010, for example, the Indiana Department of Education (IDOE) awarded a $500,000 grant to Marian University to develop a leadership academy for turnaround principals. The selection of relatively unknown Marian over such major institutions as Indiana University surprised many observers. Some maintained that the award had been an inside job, since Marian president Daniel Elsener served on the state education board and the wife of state superintendent Tony Bennett worked part-time at Marian (Radical school turnaround, 2010). The leadership academy planned to prepare 500 new principals in five years, using a combination of in-class study and on-the-job mentorship.

The state superintendent also created an Office of School Turnaround and appointed a director of school turnaround to oversee the identification and improvement of low-performing schools. Among the responsibilities of the role were the review of progress of schools designated for takeover and the vetting of possible outside operators that could take charge of school turnarounds.

As 2011 neared and the prospect of state takeover for persistently low-performing schools loomed, public concerns began to be expressed. The prospect of turning over control of a school to a private, for-profit entity troubled Indianapolis superintendent Eugene White (Fosmoe, 2010). Others voiced concern about circumventing collective bargaining agreements if a school takeover occurred. Despite the misgivings of many, the state proceeded to warn failing schools that they were in danger of takeover and began to identify possible outside operators with the capacity to assume control of these schools. By January 2011, the IDOE had narrowed the list of approved private operators from 11 to five.

The provisions for Turnaround School Operators (TSO), as they were dubbed, were articulated by Lee Ann Kwiatkowski, Indiana's director of school turnaround:

> If the board decides to go with a TSO for a school, that's when we will enter into a long-term contract (five years) with the TSO. It will be renewable annually. The TSO will have the same accountability requirements as traditional public schools. I would even argue that there will be additional accountability. We will choose any number of TSOs or all five of them. We'll try to make the best match for the school. (McCollum, January 23, 2011)

Five schools—four in Indianapolis and one in Gary—received notification in 2011 that they would become the first schools taken over by the state under Public Law 221. Regulations called for a "transition" year in 2011–2012, followed by assignment of each school to an approved TSO. The four Indianapolis schools were assigned to charter school operators, while the Gary school was assigned to EdisonLearning, an education management organization (EMO). Two other Indianapolis schools were assigned to lead partners, a lesser form of state intervention (Elliott, 2013). Lead partners provided technical assistance, such as teacher training and data analysis, but they did not constitute independent operators.

Soon after these initial state takeovers, Tony Bennett, Indiana's state superintendent of schools, was being credited with implementing a novel and promising approach to improving low-performing schools (Hess, 2011). Bennett's assistant superintendent for innovation and improvement, Dale Chu, noted that he and his boss had been impressed by Louisiana's Recovery School District, but they worried that it constituted another state bureaucracy. Chu went on to observe that Indiana did not want to be in the business of directly operating low-performing schools (Hess, 2011).

Neither the state takeover nor Tony Bennett fared very well. After failing to win reelection in 2012, Bennett moved to Florida as education commissioner but resigned in August 2013 after less than eight months on the job when he was accused of rigging the grade given to a charter school while he was Indiana's state superintendent. The charter school had been backed by influential Republican donors. Bennett eventually was exonerated of the charges by a state ethics commission. He admitted, however, that he had improperly used state-owned computers during his reelection campaign (Ujifusa, 2014). As for the schools taken over during his tenure in Indiana, most remained among the state's lowest-performing schools, and only one rose above an F grade (Elliott, 2013).

Bennett's successor for the position of Indiana state superintendent of schools campaigned against state takeover and vowed not to resort to the intervention. Glenda Ritz closed down Bennett's Office of School Turnaround. The Indiana Board of Education, which Ritz chaired, then negotiated an arrangement with Mayor Greg Ballard of Indianapolis. Ballard's charter school office would assume day-to-day oversight of the four Indianapolis schools previously taken over by the state. Ballard agreed to use the same evaluation process for the four schools as was used with Indianapolis charter schools.

In March 2014, Indiana lawmakers passed Public Law 1321, which enabled the Indianapolis Public Schools (IPS) to enter into agreements with outside management organizations to create Innovation Network Schools (Superville, June 11, 2014). The new law was hailed in the *Wall Street Journal* for granting schools autonomy from the central district bureaucracy and allowing schools to circumvent collective bargaining agreements (Hubbard, 2014). IPS proceeded to solicit proposals for unique schools that could provide opportunities previously unavailable to many Indianapolis students. The solicitation produced proposals for single-gender schools, boarding schools, year-round schools, STEM-focused schools, and other novel designs.

Public Law 1321 also contained other provisions, including one that allowed IPS to close schools that received a state grade of D or F for three consecutive years. The closed schools then would be available to winners of the Innovation Network competition. Charter school operators were permitted to occupy closed schools as well. Schools in the network were required to admit any student living in their designated attendance area.

CONFLICT OVER CONTROL OF EDUCATION POLICY

No sooner had Glenda Ritz replaced Tony Bennett as state superintendent than she struggled to find common ground with Governor Mike Pence and members of the Indiana Board of Education. The first indication of trouble occurred when the 10 board members who were appointed by the governor signed a letter asking legislative leaders "to intervene in the calculation of A–F letter grades" assigned to Indiana schools (CECI: Governor Pence, n.d.). Ritz sued the board over this action on the grounds that they had violated Indiana's Open Door Law.

Then in August of 2013, Governor Pence announced the creation of a new state agency, the Center for Education and Career Innovation (CECI). Glenda Ritz only learned about the new agency just before Pence made the announcement. Charged with aligning the state's workforce development efforts, CECI also housed the Indiana Board of Education staff. A spokesperson for the governor stated that the Department of Education, which Ritz headed, should not be the fiscal agent for the IBOE because "their responsibilities came from a different place in Indiana code" (CECI: Governor Pence, n.d.). The creation of CECI marked the beginning of a bitter political battle over who controlled education policy in Indiana—the elected state superintendent (a Democrat) or the governor (a Republican).

While educational politics grew ever more contentious in the capital, the Evansville–Vanderburgh School Corporation chose a path toward improving its low-performing schools that eventually would have a major impact on state policy. With state takeovers of low-performing schools out-of-favor, Evansville school officials elected to contract with an out-of-state group—Boston-based Mass Insight Education—to help establish an in-district entity in charge of turning around the district's low-performing schools (Stokes, 2013). The entity, called the "transformation zone," in effect became an in-district lead partner. Evansville told the state that it preferred to oversee its own turnaround initiatives rather than have the IDOE or IBOE appoint a lead partner.

Evansville superintendent David Smith decided not to wait to intervene until a school had six consecutive years of F ratings. When a school began to register academic problems, a collection of district employees focused solely on turnaround efforts was assigned to the school. Teachers at the school were given the opportunity to transfer elsewhere if they were not willing to rise to the turnaround challenge. Teachers who elected to stay were assigned mentor teachers to help support their efforts. Partnerships were developed with local organizations interested in providing volunteers and other resources.

A year after Evansville rolled out its new turnaround plan, the IBOE held its regular December meeting and heard an outside consultant's recommendations and the board's own School Turnaround Committee's recommendations for options regarding Indiana's nine failing schools (Morello, December 3, 2014). At the top of the list was the transformation zone model from Evansville. By accepting this recommendation, the IBOE would be endorsing a turnaround strategy that placed the onus of change on local school systems instead of the IDOE or IBOE.

Another recommendation eliminated the lead partner model. No doubt this suggestion was prompted by the fact that all lead partners that previously had been appointed to assist with school turnarounds in Indiana had withdrawn from their assigned schools.

The third recommendation concerned the timing of state intervention. Instead of waiting until a school had received six consecutive F's, the state would offer assistance after four F's. Improvement strategies also could be suggested for D as well as F schools under the proposed revisions.

The final recommendations seemed to contradict the reasoning behind the first recommendation. A specific turnaround unit to manage state intervention activities under the auspices of the IBOE was proposed. Furthermore, the Indiana Board of Education would be granted the authority to take over management of failing school districts as a last resort.

No mention was made of a role for the Department of Education in these recommendations. State superintendent Ritz, who chaired the IBOE, voted against the recommendations, one of only two negative votes. Her argument that the Department of Education was the proper agency for handling school turnarounds because it received federal school improvement dollars failed to convince the majority of board members.

The day after the IBOE voted to accept the aforementioned recommendations, Governor Pence captured the headlines with two announcements. The first was clearly a reaction to Glenda Ritz's opposition to the previous day's recommendations. Pence stated his intention to advise the Indiana General Assembly to pass legislation allowing the IBOE to elect its own chair (Morello, December 4, 2014). If approved, the bill would mean that the state superintendent no longer would assume automatically that position.

Regarding Pence's threat, House minority leader Scott Pelath was quoted as saying, "They [IBOE] have this pesky lone Democrat that was elected. They didn't expect it and now they have to do something about it and they're grossly overreacting and they're showing themselves, I think, to be extraordinarily paranoid and insecure" (Morello, December 4, 2014).

Pence's second announcement seemed even more curious than the first. He signed an executive order dissolving the Center for Education and Career Innovation, the agency that he had created the previous year. The explanation for this action must have struck many as odd, given the fact that he also was making moves to circumvent the authority of the Indiana Department of Education by creating a new turnaround unit under the auspices of the IBOE. Pence was quoted as saying, "Frankly there are too many entities with overlapping responsibilities in education at the highest levels in Indiana. For education to work in our state, it has to work at the highest levels, and somebody's got to take the first step to restore harmony and trust among those that are charged with overseeing education in our state" (Morello, December 4, 2014).

Just as odd as Pence's proposal, however, was the decision by the IBOE to entertain a proposal from the Gary Community School Corporation to have EdisonLearning serve as its external lead partner (McCollum, December 4, 2014). Three years earlier the IBOE had removed a Gary school from school district control and appointed EdisonLearning to operate the school. The relationship between the district and Edison-Learning had not gone well, and the takeover school continued to earn an F grade. Subsequently, however, relations between Gary and Edison-Learning improved, and the district actually requested that the Tennessee-based company become the lead partner for the entire school system. When the IBOE endorsed Gary's interest in working with EdisonLearning, it seemed to contradict one of the recommendations that the IBOE had just approved—the recommendation that the transformation zone model calling for in-house coordination of school turnarounds replace the external lead partner option.

One possible interpretation of the state board's seemingly contradictory action was that it represented yet another effort to diminish the Department of Education's role in school turnarounds. Because Gary had a "high risk" designation as a school district and was the only Indiana district with an F rating, Glenda Ritz had appointed an individual to serve as director of district improvement in Gary. This individual oversaw federal programs and classroom instruction in Gary and led the state intervention team. Approving a relationship with EdisonLearning therefore could be regarded as a vote of no confidence in the IDOE's and Glenda Ritz's efforts to assist Gary.

Early in 2015, the proposals approved by the IBOE were put forward with the governor's blessing in House Bill 1638. The bill went through several months of tweaking before it finally passed in May. The provision that would have allowed the state to take over a failing school district was removed when Senator Earline Rogers, Democrat representing Gary, won support for an amendment to HB 1638 (Weddle, 2015). Gary likely would have been the first school district to be taken over had the provision remained.

The version of HB 1638 that eventually was signed into law replaced the requirement for the IBOE to hire an external provider to help run or fully operate a failing school with the transformation zone option originally developed by Evansville. This change essentially returned control of turnaround initiatives to local school districts. The bill's author, Representative Robert Behning, Republican from Indianapolis, commented on the purpose of HB 1638: "The goal is not to be in the takeover business—that is really what the purpose of this bill is. To get out of the takeover business and let's give schools the ability to transform themselves" (Weddle, 2015).

Despite Behning's seeming preference for local control, his bill moved up the timeline for state intervention in failing schools from six years to four years. HB 1638 also contained a provision that allowed members of the Indiana Board of Education to select a chairman. No longer would the state superintendent automatically chair the board.

Residents of Gary also must have wondered about the validity of Rep. Behning's claim that local school systems should have the authority to transform themselves. Just weeks before the passage of HB 1638, after all, the IBOE had voted to close Gary's Dunbar-Pulaski Academic and Career Academy.

REFLECTING ON INDIANA AND STATE TAKEOVERS

Indiana's efforts to improve its lowest-performing schools, like Buffalo's experience, illustrate the themes of conflict, context, and complexity. In both instances, for example, political infighting served to distract from, rather than shine a spotlight on, the plight of children stuck in persistently low-performing schools. Instead of helping to pinpoint important issues regarding school decline and improvement, contentious debate often centered on who was in charge of turnaround efforts, who got to set policy, what sanctions should be employed, and what special interests to protect. Too frequently the result of all the volleying back and forth was to characterize educators as the causes of low performance rather than caring public servants committed to helping young people. Only in rare cases did policy makers seem interested in finding common ground concerning how best to serve the children left behind.

Although New York and Indiana share some similarities, they also are sufficiently different to make context an important key to understanding policy. Democrats played a more influential political role in New York than in Indiana, where Republicans controlled the statehouse and the legislature. Tension between the governor and the state board of education, on one hand, and the state superintendent and department of education, on the other, was a key factor in Indiana, but not in New York. Buffalo's political infighting took place instead at the school board level.

Regardless of context, complexity constituted a challenge in each case. Endless tinkering characterized policy makers' efforts to deal with the lowest-performing schools. Some favored state takeover of individual schools. Others considered takeover of failing school districts to be the key. Still others argued that states should not be in the business of taking over schools or districts. Improvement, they contended, had to come from local initiatives. These disputes resulted in an array of trial policies involving lead partners, external school operators, local change agents, and charter schools.

Among the complex issues associated with state takeovers are the timing of a takeover, the form of a takeover, the duration of a takeover, and the consequences of a failed takeover. Let us briefly examine each of these issues.

Timing of Takeovers

For how long should a school be allowed to fail? That is the fundamental question state policy makers must ponder when addressing the issue of takeover timing. With the passage of HB 1638, Indiana legislators decided that six consecutive years of school failure was too long. They opted to move the timing of state intervention up to four years. Indianapolis Public Schools earlier had been allowed to act after only three years.

Related to the timing issue is the matter of prerequisite action by the state, the local district, or both. What measures by the state or district, in other words, should have to be taken before resorting to the drastic step of state takeover? Appointing a distinguished educator to oversee turnaround plans in Buffalo is one such measure. Others might involve technical assistance from state department of education specialists, pairing a low-performing school with a high-performing school, and requiring a school to work with a lead partner.

A consideration of prerequisite measures leads to another issue. What evidence should be considered in determining whether or not the prerequisite measures succeeded? Is it sufficient that some progress was made, even if state or federal targets were not hit? Such considerations have generated much debate in recent years. Opinions vary greatly about the length of time it takes to turn around a persistently low-performing school. Ultimately the time that should be allowed for prerequisite measures to take effect boils down to a judgment call. Is more harm to children likely to result from extending the time for pre-takeover measures to work or from interrupting the implementation of these measures as a result of state takeover?

Form of Takeovers

The Indiana case illustrates several different forms that a state takeover can take. Early on, the preferred form was assigning responsibility for turning around a school to an external operator such as a charter school organization or for-profit provider like EdisonLearning.

Who chooses the external operator also is a concern. Buffalo resented having the state require the Erie County BOCES take control of school turnaround. Eventually Buffalo elected to work with Johns Hopkins, but this arrangement disintegrated over scope-of-work and governance issues.

When external providers in Indiana pulled out of the schools to which they had been assigned, the IBOE grew disenchanted with this option and moved to approve in-house providers—the so-called transformation zone model piloted in Evansville. Later in this chapter, another option is examined. Massachusetts chose to assign a new leader to oversee schools taken over by the state.

Some states even have opted to place takeover schools in a separate, state-managed school system. The next chapter reviews such efforts in Louisiana, Tennessee, and Michigan. As indicated earlier, the option to take over an entire school district also exists in some states. This option was recommended for HB 1638 by Governor Pence but eventually removed from the final version of the bill.

When a state takes over an entire school system, it can replace key individuals such as the superintendent and school board members. Another possibility is to retain these individuals as an advisory group reporting to state officials. Some states even have turned over control to city mayors. Indiana explored this option for failing schools in Indianapolis. In Boston, Chicago, Cleveland, and Detroit, control of the entire school district, not just low-performing schools, was shifted to the mayor's office.

Duration of Takeover

How long should a takeover school or district be given to achieve an acceptable turnaround? Research-based guidelines on this matter are scarce. Schools that receive federal School Improvement Grants have three years in which to effect a turnaround. When the Council of the

Great City Schools (*School Improvement Grants*, 2015) examined the impact of SIG funding on student achievement in urban schools, it found that three years was sufficient to reduce the percentage of students in the lowest-proficiency categories and narrow the gap in student achievement between SIG-funded and SIG-eligible (but not funded) schools. The gap also was reduced between SIG-funded schools and schools that were not eligible for SIG funding.

New Jersey has taken over several school districts for various reasons, including mismanagement and endemic academic problems. The districts include Newark, Jersey City, Paterson, and Camden. Camden was returned to local control after a year, while Newark and Paterson remained under state control for over two decades (Oluwole & Green, 2009; Superville, September 9, 2015).

Logically speaking, a takeover should end when the school or district has met the targets required for all schools, but such precise language does not always appear in state policy. Determining exit criteria for schools can be just as complex a matter as deciding on the timing and form of takeovers. Is it sufficient, for example, for a takeover school to hit its target once, or should it be required to sustain gains for several years before exiting its takeover status? How much credit should a low-performing school or district get for improving, even if targets are not reached?

New Jersey's provisions for state takeover are relatively clear and straightforward: A failing district is placed under state control for at least five years (*50-state report*, n.d.). The state can replace the superintendent and board of education with new appointees. Within six months of takeover, the district must present a corrective action plan. If after five years the state commission finds that the corrective action plan has not been sufficiently implemented, the state can retain control of the district. Otherwise, the district returns to local control. What is uncertain about the exit process in New Jersey, however, are the criteria by which administrators determine implementation sufficiency.

Failed Takeovers

What if a state takeover fails? Indiana faced this situation when external providers approved by the state withdrew after their assigned schools continued to receive an F grade. School closure would seem to be a logical next step, but as we shall see in chapter 5, such a decision is likely to encounter considerable local resistance. Indiana legislators determined that the state should not be in the business of taking over the lowest-performing schools. Instead they shifted responsibility back to local school districts by endorsing the in-house transformation zone model.

When the focus of state takeover is an entire school district, the challenge becomes much greater. It is no simple matter to shut down an entire school district, although such action has been taken on rare occasions.[1] Previously it was noted that New Jersey continues to operate failing school districts when they do not turn around in the prescribed five-year period. In the case of the Orleans Parish school system, the state placed most of its schools in the Recovery School District, leaving only a handful of relatively high-performing schools in the system. The intent of the state was to convert the transferred public schools to charter schools.

Of all the states that have experimented with taking over low-performing schools and school districts, Massachusetts is arguably one of the most successful. The concluding section examines the nature of takeovers in the Bay State.

EMPOWERING THE STATE TO ACT

Massachusetts legislators passed An Act Relative to the Achievement Gap in 2010, thereby providing the Office of District and School Turnaround in the state's Department of Elementary and Secondary Education with the authority to take over both schools and districts. The act gives the commissioner of education the authority to assign "Level 4" status to schools that are among the lowest-performing 20% of schools in Massachusetts. When a school is given the Level 4 designation, the district superintendent must design and implement a turnaround plan.

Should the turnaround plan fail, the school or district moves to Level 5 status, meaning it is "chronically underperforming." The commissioner of education assumes responsibility for designing the turnaround plan and may allow the district to implement it or may choose a third party "receiver" to operate the school or district and implement the plan.

What distinguishes Massachusetts's approach to its lowest-performing schools from Indiana's is the former's willingness to entertain a variety of options. While Indiana legislators rejected district takeover as a possibility, Massachusetts accepted it. As of 2015, the district takeover option had been exercised in Lawrence and Holyoke. Indiana originally focused on assigning an external operator to take the lead when it took over persistently low-performing schools. Later the Indiana Board of Education decided that it preferred districts to develop an in-house unit to guide school turnarounds. Massachusetts has maintained both options, leaving the ultimate decision to the commissioner of education.

Commissioner Mitchell Chester has used both options, depending on his assessment of local needs and capacity. In Boston, for instance, takeover schools were assigned to a pair of education nonprofits, Unlocking Potential and Blueprint Schools Network. In New Bedford, however, Chester elected to assign turnaround responsibility for an elementary school and a high school to the incumbent superintendent, Pat Durkin. Durkin reported directly to Chester on each school's progress.

One other distinction between the takeover experience in Indiana and Massachusetts should be noted. Massachusetts never experienced the prolonged infighting and jockeying for power that Indiana did. To say it is a challenge to make headway against persistently low-performing schools when the governor and his appointed state board of education cannot get along with the elected state superintendent and her department of education risks serious understatement.

Plans for school turnarounds in Massachusetts must receive local input from an advisory group of parents and community members, but they are drafted by the appointed receiver and the state commissioner. No two plans are identical, but they all allow the receiver to circumvent the collective bargaining process and require that professional staff reapply for their jobs. Needless to say, teacher unions have not been pleased with these arrangements. Demonstrations opposing state takeover have been organized across the state.

It is hard to find fault with the state-approved plans for Level 5 schools. In the case of New Bedford's Parker Elementary School, for example, the state commissioner mandated four areas of focus: (1) increased rigor in classroom instruction, (2) school systems and structures that ensure instruction is delivered by effective teachers, (3) data-driven differentiated instruction and intervention, and (4) a school climate focused on learning and family engagement (DeCosta, 2014). Parker's turnaround plan included provisions for an extended school day for students and staff and extensive professional development. Mitchell Chester also insisted that implementation of the plan be accompanied by a new performance-based teacher evaluation system. Funds to help implement the plan were provided by the federal government and the state.

The Massachusetts Department of Elementary and Secondary Education retained the services of the Institute for Strategic Leadership and Learning (ISLL) to assess how well efforts to improve Level 4 schools were working (Lane, Unger & Rhim, 2013). These are schools that may be subject to state takeover if student achievement does not rise. Of the original 34 schools designated as Level 4 in 2009, 14 schools were reported to be on target to meet their three-year goals, and 11 schools were "partially on target to meet their goals" (p. i).

The ISLL report went on to identify differences between the improving schools and schools where little progress could be detected. Of the Level 4 schools that replaced over half of their teachers in the first year of the turnaround process, 89% made significant progress. All nine of the schools that made little progress had teacher replacement rates of 35% or less in their first year.

Another difference noted in the ISLL report concerned the allocation of resources. Schools that were on target to meet their three-year goals tended to allocate higher percentages of funds to student instruction and teacher professional development. Nonimproving schools spent a higher percentage of funding to address student social-emotional and behavioral issues. It is unclear, however, whether these schools had students with higher levels of social-emotional and behavioral issues to begin with.

ISLL researchers also found that actions by school districts were closely related to progress (or lack of it) in Level 4 schools. Constructive actions included (1) district focus and/or reorganization to support turnaround initiatives, (2) district willingness to grant schools autonomy and flexibility, (3) investment in a coherent curriculum aligned with state standards, (4) district support for assessments and data analysis to inform decisions, and (5) support for the effective integration of external partners.

In 2014 ISLL completed another report on the Level 4 schools (Lane, Unger & Souvanna, 2014). After three years of state support and oversight coupled with district action, 14 of the original 34 schools exited Level 4 status, 15 schools continued as Level 4 schools, four schools dropped to Level 5 and therefore faced state takeover, and one school closed. Despite the mixed track record, the report's authors concluded that "there is clear evidence that districts and local school committees have used state law and federal policy to change and vastly improve the conditions needed for successful turnaround" (p. 17). Comments like this attracted the attention of other states, including New York (see chapter 2) and Pennsylvania (Real accountability, 2015).

The ISLL report focused on Level 4 schools. Although a comparable examination of state takeover schools (Level 5) and districts has not been conducted, there are promising indications that placing the Lawrence, Massachusetts, school system under receivership has begun to make a difference. After five years of direct state control, math achievement in the 14,000-student district climbed from 28% to 41% proficient (Superville, May 6, 2015). English/language arts inched up from 41% to 44% proficient. The graduation rate rose from 52% to 67%. The number of Level 1 schools (schools that met all state performance requirements) grew from two in 2011 to six in 2014.

One key to the encouraging developments in Lawrence has been the emergence of constructive relations between the state-appointed receiver, Jeffrey Riley, and the local teachers union. Early concerns expressed by the union faded after a year with the implementation of career ladders that offered teachers opportunities to earn more money based on performance and leadership. It also helped that Riley insisted that all Lawrence teachers join the teachers union.

Other measures that have helped to turn around Lawrence schools included greater autonomy for school principals, longer school days, and training for teachers and principals in data analysis. Riley also garnered praise for reducing the size of the district central office by 30% and redirecting the resulting savings to the schools. Several schools have been turned over to charter-management organizations, and in a unique move, the Lawrence teachers union agreed to operate an elementary school in partnership with the district.

The willingness to remain flexible, entertain multiple options, and work in concert with teacher unions are distinguishing characteristics of Massachusetts's approach to state takeovers. The next chapter examines an alternative form of state takeover, one in which the state creates a special school district for some of its lowest-performing schools.

REFERENCES

CECI: Governor Pence's new, controversial state education agency. n.d. *Indiana Public Media.* Retrieved from http://indianapublicmedia.org/stateimpact/tag/center-for-ed-ucation-and-career-innovation.

DeCosta, S. 2014, March 8. Parker school turnaround plan changes teachers' pay. *South Coast Today.* Retrieved from http://www.southcoasttoday.com/article/20140308/NEWS/403080330/0/.

Elliott, S. 2013, November 21. The basics of state takeover in Indiana: Getting tough with failing schools. *Chalkbeat.* Retrieved from http://in.chalkbeat.org/2013/11/21/the-basics-of-state-takeover-in-indiana-getting-tough-with-failing-schools/.

50-state report on accountability, state intervention and takeover. n.d. New Brunswick, NJ: Institute on Education Law and Policy, Rutgers University.

Fosmoe, M. 2010, October 29. Public speaks out about school takeover proposal. *South Bend Tribune.* Retrieved from http://articles.southbendtribune.com/2010-10-29/news/29168202_1_teacher-contracts-school-takeover-proposal-administrators.

Hess, R. 2011, September 22. Indiana's phased turnaround model. *Education Next.* Retrieved from http://educationnext.org/indianas-phased-turnaround-model/.

Hubbard, A. 2014, September 13–14. Liberating Indianapolis schools from district control. *Wall Street Journal,* p. A-11.

Lane, B., Unger, C., & Rhim, L. M. 2013. Emerging and sustaining practices for school turnaround. Institute for Strategic Leadership and Learning. *Executive Office of Education* (Massachusetts). Retrieved from http://www.mass.gov/edu/government/de-partments-and-boards/ese/programs/accountability/.

Lane, B., Unger, C., & Souvanna, P. 2014. Turnaround practices in action. Institute for Strategic Leadership and Learning. *Executive Office of Education* (Massachusetts). Retrieved from http://www.mass.gov/edu/government/departments-and-boards/ese/programs/accountability/support-for-level-3-4-and-5-districts-and-schools/school-and-district-turnaround/.

McCollum, C. 2011, January 23. IDOE continues to move forward with state interven-tion. *Times of Northwest Indiana.* Retrieved from http://www.nwitimes.com/news/local/lake/hammond/idoe-continues-to-move-forward-with-state-intervention/arti-cle_0625ebaf-2483-5f5c-952e-54e3ef6be9a7.html.

———. 2014, December 4. Gary schools to tap EdisonLearning as partner. *Times of Northwest Indiana.* Retrieved from http://www.nwitimes.com/news/local/lake/gary/gary-schools-to-tap-edisonlearning-as-partner/article_2dff433f-b827-5db9-b94b-13e9aa570e96.html.

Morello, R. 2014, December 3. Turnaround efforts take center stage at state board meeting. *Indiana Public Media.* Retrieved from http://indianapublicmedia.org/sta-teimpact/2014/12/03/turnaround-efforts-takes-center-stage-state-board-meeting/.

———. 2014, December 4. Pence signs executive order dissolving CECI. *Indiana Public Media.* Retrieved from http://indianapublicmedia.org/stateimpact/2014/12/04/pence-sign-executive-order-dissolving-ceci/.

Oluwole, J. O., and Green, P. C. 2009. State takeovers of school districts: Race and the equal protection clause. *Indiana Law Review, 42,* pp. 343–409.

Radical school turnaround. 2010, July 21. *Indianapolis Star*. Retrieved from http://www.indystar.com/article/20100721/OPINION04/7210313/1038.

Real accountability, real results. 2015. *PennCAN: The Pennsylvania Campaign for Achievement Now*. Retrieved from http://www.info@penncan.org.

Rudo, Z. H. 2001. *Corrective action in low-performing schools and school districts*. Southwest Austin, TX: Southwest Educational Development Laboratory.

School Improvement Grants: Progress report from America's great city schools. 2015. Washington, DC: Council of the Great City Schools.

Stokes, K. 2013, December 5. Why Evansville school leaders say they don't need state help to turn around a troubled school. *Indiana Public Media*. Retrieved from http://indianapublicmedia.org/stateimpact/2013/12/05/evansville-school-leaders-turn-troubled-school/.

Superville, D. R. 2014, June 11. Indianapolis district hosts contest for innovative schools. *Education Week*, p. 12.

———. 2015, May 6. State takeover gives Mass. District a fresh start. *Education Week*, pp. 1, 18–21.

———. 2015, September 9. Newark schools' journey to local control begins. *Education Week*, 1, 15.

Ujifusa, A. 2014, August 6. Indiana's A-F issues linger, despite Bennett exoneration. *Education Week*, 1, 15.

Weddle, E. 2015, March 30. School intervention overhaul faces increased scrutiny. *WBAA Public Radio*. Retrieved from http://wbaa.org/post/school-intervention-over-haul-faces-increased-scrutiny.

NOTE

1. An example of shutting down a school district is Michigan's decision to close the Inkster School District outside of Detroit in 2013. Students from the struggling district were transferred to neighboring Romulus schools.

FOUR

An Alternative Form of State Takeover

The Special State District for Low-Performing Schools

For some states, assigning an educational management organization or receiver to operate a low-performing school or district is not sufficient. To protect the interests of the children left behind, Louisiana, Tennessee, and Michigan have created independent, state-authorized and resourced districts. Other states, including Arkansas, Georgia, Nevada, and Pennsylvania, are exploring this option (Tatter, July 7, 2015).

The chapter opens with the evolution of the oldest of these special state districts: Louisiana's Recovery School District. Subsequent segments examine Tennessee's Achievement School District and Michigan's Education Achievement Authority. Several alternative types of special state systems for low-performing schools are described in the following segment. The chapter concludes with a discussion of several challenges involved in running a special state district.

THE RECOVERY SCHOOL DISTRICT

At the beginning of the 21st century, few places in the United States had a higher percentage of children left behind than New Orleans. The Recovery School District (RSD) began in 2003 as a small-scale pilot program that granted charters to four persistently low-performing schools from the Orleans Parish school system. Then, in August 2005, Hurricane Katrina made landfall and devastated New Orleans. Students and teachers evacuated the city. Most school buildings were damaged or destroyed.

With local sources of revenue all but nonexistent, the parish school system was effectively bankrupt.

Faced with such dire circumstances, elected officials determined that the hurricane had created an opportunity "for a radical overhaul of a system they had long been seen as plagued by academic failure and corruption" (Harris, 2013, pp. 1–2). Within six months of Katrina and with federal and foundation support, almost all of the public schools in New Orleans were moved from the Orleans Parish School Board to the Recovery School District. Paul Vallas, former CEO of the Chicago Public Schools and superintendent of Philadelphia Public Schools, was hired to run the RSD. Most of the RSD schools soon became charter schools managed by charter management organizations. Students could choose to attend any RSD school as long as space was available. Young and often inexperienced teachers were recruited from across the United States to teach in the RSD. None of them worked under a union contract.

Of the 32,000 students in 107 RSD schools when Vallas arrived, 85% were at least a year and a half to two years behind grade level (Nossiter, April 30, 2008). A third of the RSD students were four years below grade level (Vallas, Duke, & Smalley, 2011). Vallas and his colleagues had to address the enormous needs of these young people while simultaneously erecting an organization that was capable of rebuilding educational facilities, nurturing newly formed charter organizations, recruiting qualified educators, and holding schools accountable.

By the fall of 2010, the RSD had closed some schools and launched 46 charter schools. Vallas planned to convert the remaining 22 schools in the RSD to charters as soon as possible. The mission of the RSD was totally consistent with Vallas's misgivings about bureaucracy. "I view myself as a liberator of bureaucracies," he told the author (Vallas et al., 2011, p. 12). "I am here to liberate people by giving the organization a purpose, a mission, goals, deliverables, and then . . . finding the talent . . . and putting them in the most appropriate leadership positions."

Practically speaking, Vallas followed a five-step theory of action that he had tested and refined in Chicago and Philadelphia (Vallas et al., 2011). The five steps consisted of "critical functions," beginning with the identification of best practices related to curriculum, instruction, and assessment. These best practices, overseen by his Office of Curriculum and Instruction, became the drivers of change for the RSD.

The collection, analysis, and dissemination of data on student achievement, program effectiveness, and school safety constituted the second critical function. Vallas believed that all decisions, including personnel decisions, should be data driven.

The third critical function involved the acquisition and development of "human capital." Vallas blamed many of public education's problems on misguided notions about recruitment, selection, placement, and development of educators. He was determined to make the RSD a laboratory for examining new ways to staff schools.

Sound financial management was the fourth critical function in Vallas's theory of action. New Orleans, he understood, had a history of corruption and fiscal mismanagement. When Vallas replaced Robin Jarvis as superintendent of the RSD 20 months after Hurricane Katrina, barely a tenth of the $241 million allocated by the federal government to rebuild New Orleans schools had been expended (Nossiter, May 5, 2007). Besides developing a massive capital improvement initiative, he needed to create an effective funding mechanism for dozens of new charter schools and handle substantial grants from private foundations.

The final and, to Vallas, the most important component of his theory of action concerned school management. He was quoted as saying, "Turnaround is not just taking over a failing school and then not having a clue of how to fix it. A lot of turnaround schools, they'll just take a successful principal and stick him in a school thinking by osmosis that school is going to get better. You've got to have a turnaround plan" (Vallas et al., 2011, p. 14).

Vallas and his staff made certain that every school's plan reflected research-based best practice. Take instructional time, for example. The children left behind could never catch up with their peers, especially after the dislocations of Katrina, without greater time for learning. All RSD schools operated on the basis of an 11-month school year. The school day, as well, was lengthened, running 8 hours and 15 minutes from 7:30 a.m. to 3:45 p.m. for high schools and 8:00 a.m. until 4:15 p.m. for elementary schools from Monday through Thursday. Vallas boasted that RSD students received an additional 22,000 minutes of instruction as a result (Vallas et al., 2011, p. 15).

Believing that his ambitious plans were contingent on attracting talented young teachers who were willing to try new approaches, Vallas launched an innovative system for identifying prospective candidates. The RSD paid student teachers from various colleges a subsidy to complete their student teaching in New Orleans. Room and board also were provided. If they performed well as student teachers, individuals were offered contracts to be teacher aides. Then the most capable teacher aides were given opportunities to teach summer school. Those who were effective in their summer school assignments were recruited to become full-time RSD teachers.

By the beginning of the 2009–2010 school year, there was ample evidence that Vallas's human resources strategy was paying dividends. The RSD had an average of 24 applicants vying for every opening in its teacher recruiting and training program, Teach NOLA. Vallas made no apologies about his preference for energetic young teachers over seasoned veterans (Vallas et al., 2011).

Principals for RSD schools were handpicked for their initiative and entrepreneurial skills. These qualities were regarded by Vallas as essential because principals were accorded a great deal of autonomy in such matters as hiring, budgeting, and program development. The RSD held principals accountable, however, for their school's performance.

From the beginning of his tenure with the RSD, Vallas's intention was to convert virtually every RSD school to a charter school. As more schools underwent the conversion process, Vallas was able to downsize his central office staff. By the beginning of the 2009–2010 school year, he reported cutting about one third of the full-time office staff.

Fast forward six years to 2015. Vallas had departed for other educational and political challenges, leaving an RSD that became 100% charter. The last five schools run directly by the RSD were closed in May 2014 (Smith, 2015).

By 2015, the profile of the teaching force in New Orleans had changed dramatically from what it had been prior to Katrina (Significant changes, 2015). The percentage of African American teachers had shrunk from 71% in 2005 to 49%. The percentage of teachers with five or fewer years of experience increased from 33% to 54%, while the percentage of teachers who were certified fell from 79% to 56%. The RSD central staff had shrunk to 92, down from a high of 568, and the budget was down to $19.6 million. In 2012–2013, the budget was $306.9 million. Besides overseeing its New Orleans charter schools, the RSD also added charter schools in Baton Rouge and Shreveport to its collection.

Questions predictably have been raised about the need to continue operating the RSD. In an opinion piece entitled "What's the point of the Recovery School District now?" (Dreilinger, September 26, 2014), various critics voiced their belief that the RSD had outlived its usefulness. Among the most vocal critics were representatives of the Orleans Parish School Board (OBSP) who were anxious to have schools return to the city school system. Charter school operators did not share this desire, however. Of 36 charters that were eligible to rejoin the Orleans Parish School Board, only two have elected to do so (Smith, 2015).

It appears that local residents tend to side with the charter school operators. When Tulane University's Cowen Institute polled voters in New Orleans, only 29% favored returning schools to the OPSB, while 41% indicated that they were fine with charter schools making their own decisions on whether to return (Dreilinger, September 26, 2014). Sixteen percent wanted the charter schools to remain in the RSD.

The Orleans Parish School Board apparently has gotten the message that charter schools represent the future of education in New Orleans. In May 2015, the OPSB unanimously approved two new charter school applications, bringing its total to nine charter schools since 2011. The comments by OPSB superintendent Henderson Lewis on the occasion of the approval of the new charters sounded a lot like Paul Vallas. "We are extremely excited to increase the number of high-quality school options for the families of New Orleans," Lewis proclaimed. "As a nationally recognized charter authorizer, it is important that we consider schools that utilize innovation, best educational practices, and most of all, serve the needs of the community" (Press release, May 22, 2015, pp. 1–2).

When Patrick Dobard, RSD superintendent, addresses the special district's future, he sees an expanding role. In an interview in September 2014, he articulated a broad vision for the RSD: "We exist to ensure that all students have access to an excellent public education" (Dreilinger, September 26, 2014, p. 2). As proof of Dobard's intentions, the RSD has begun to share certain citywide educational services with the OPSB.

One example of shared services involves OneApp, a centralized enrollment system for all RSD schools and most schools in the OPSB. OneApp spares parents the need to submit separate applications to schools of their choosing. The RSD also has opened a truancy center for all students in New Orleans and a Student Hearing Office to handle cases involving pending school expulsions. Since the Student Hearing Office was created, expulsions citywide have dropped by 25% (Smith, 2015).

One area where work remains to be done is special education. In 2010 the Southern Poverty Law Center sued the Louisiana Education Department and the Orleans Parish School Board on the grounds that children with disabilities were not receiving an adequate education "in the fragmented network of charter and district schools that [has] sprung up in New Orleans after Hurricane Katrina" (Dreilinger, December 19, 2014).

A settlement finally was reached in December 2014. Its terms included oversight of special education programs by an independent monitor and a state-developed plan for identifying and evaluating all children suspected of having a disability. The RSD was required to do a better job of tracking young people with disabilities and finding appropriate placements for them. The settlement also required that charter schools be held accountable for serving students with disabilities.

Louisiana legislators followed the settlement with a new law, Act 833, that gave school-based teams "the power to develop course-completion and graduation standards for certain students with disabilities" (Samuels, 2015, p. 17). Aspects of Act 833 were immediately challenged, however, by federal officials who claimed that the new law could be implemented in a way that violated the No Child Left Behind Act and the Individuals with Disabilities Education Act. One concern involved Act 833's provision that teachers can create their own assignments to gauge the learning of special education students who repeatedly fail state standardized tests.

As the most extensive experiment in school choice in the United States, the RSD has attracted attention from other states. Policy makers wonder whether the young people of New Orleans are better off as a result of the conversion of low-performing public schools to charter schools. There are a variety of ways, of course, to evaluate the impact of the RSD.

If the results of state standardized testing are used as indicators, students in RSD schools clearly have benefited. RSD New Orleans schools led Louisiana in performance growth on the 2013 tests (RSD schools, n.d.). Patrick Dobard, the RSD superintendent, reported that 57% of RSD students scored proficient on state tests in 2013–2014 (Smith, 2015, p. 10). By contrast, only 23% of Orleans Parish students had scored proficient when the RSD took over most OPSB schools after Katrina.

Despite having 94% of its students eligible for free or reduced-price lunch, the RSD has outpaced the annual state average for academic improvement from 32 percentage points in 2008 to 12 percentage points in 2014 (Recovery School District, 2015). Black student performance in New Orleans is higher than the overall average for black students in Louisiana. ACT scores are rising along with test scores for students with disabilities (Recovery School District, 2015). Superintendent Dobard (2015) boasted that the percentage of students in New Orleans attending failing schools had plummeted from 63% in 2005 to 7% in 2015. The high school graduation rate over the same period rose from 54% to 73%.

Although these results are very encouraging, RSD students still have a great distance to travel in order to meet the more rigorous standards associated with "college and career readiness." Just 12% of RSD students performed at the mastery level on the 2014 state tests compared to 42% in the OPSB schools (Smith, 2015, p. 13). It should be noted, however, that six of the OPSB schools have academically based admissions requirements.

Beyond test scores, there is the matter of school choice. Some observers believe that providing poor families with the opportunity to choose where their children attend school is of significant value, regardless of how well the children perform. It is noteworthy, in this regard, that the Brookings Institution ranked the RSD first among more than 100 large school districts on its Choice and Competition Index, a measure of access to school choices and the quality of support structures (Smith, 2015, p. 9).

TENNESSEE'S ACHIEVEMENT SCHOOL DISTRICT

Modeled after Louisiana's RSD, the Achievement School District (ASD) resulted from Tennessee's successful application for a Race to the Top grant in April 2010. Prior to Tennessee receiving one of the first two grants, Democratic governor Phil Bredesen had backed new legislation that empowered the state commissioner of education to create a special state school district for persistently low-performing schools. The legislation passed, setting the stage for the ASD. Twenty-two million dollars from Tennessee's $500 million Race to the Top grant was set aside to launch the new district.

In May 2011, Chris Barbic, founder of Houston's highly touted YES Prep program, was chosen to be the ASD's first superintendent. Barbic brought with him a keen understanding of charter schools and how to orchestrate educational innovation. His theory of action, like Vallas's, consisted of five elements:

1. Recruit and invest in top talent
2. Build and manage a portfolio for high quality
3. Find strong school operators
4. Give schools autonomy in key areas
5. Shift power from stagnant bureaucracies to school leaders and parents (Smith, 2013)

The ASD was granted authority to remove persistently low-performing schools from their home districts for a period of at least five years. The schools would either be managed directly by the ASD or operated by a charter organization chosen by the ASD superintendent. Teachers in ASD schools relinquished their prior contract rights and were required to reapply for their jobs if they desired to remain at their school. No teacher was guaranteed reinstatement, however.

In three of the initial schools assigned to the ASD, only 30% of the teachers chose to reapply for their jobs (Editorial, December 31, 2012). Eventually the ASD established a salary scale for its direct-run schools that exceeded what teachers could earn in the local school system.

Guidelines for the ASD called for partnerships with organizations specializing in recruiting and training principals and teachers (Smith, 2013). An estimated 600 teachers would be needed during the initial phase of recruiting. Tennessee's Race to the Top application also called for the establishment of an investment fund to support the development of several Tennessee-based charter networks with the capacity to create new charter schools.

Before Barbic arrived in Nashville to assume his duties as ASD superintendent, five low-performing schools in Chattanooga and Memphis were designated to be comanaged by the ASD and their local districts. This awkward arrangement was quickly abandoned, however. The following year, Barbic announced that the ASD would launch with six Memphis schools, three managed by the ASD and three managed by charter operators. He expressed his belief that taking in a large number of schools at first, as the RSD had done after Hurricane Katrina, would be a mistake (Smith, 2013).

The summer of 2012 was a busy one, with 80 teachers beginning the ASD teacher induction process and principals attending turnaround leader training at the University of Virginia. Barbic also formed an

Achievement Advisory Council to assist in the process of matching charter operators with school sites.

Barbic held no illusions about the challenges that lay ahead, but even he reported being stunned when early testing results for the six ASD schools were released in October 2012 (Roberts, October 22, 2012). Students were performing at the 16th percentile in the nation in reading and math. The ASD's goal of moving these schools from the lowest 5% to the top 25% in five years seemed close to impossible, especially since new schools would be added to the ASD each year. Plans called for 35 schools by 2014–2015.

The ASD may have been modeled after the RSD, but there are important differences in how the two special state districts function. Unlike the RSD, which was assigned schools by the state after Katrina, school selection for the ASD involved judgment calls by Barbic. Schools with a strong principal in their first or second year were given a chance to improve on their own, as were low-performing schools showing some early signs of progress (Smith, 2013). Community input was solicited through the Achievement Advisory Council before a charter operator was matched to a school. Such matches in New Orleans were made by the RSD administration.

Another important difference concerned access to schools. RSD students, at least in theory, could choose to attend any school in the district. Schools in the ASD were required to draw students from preassigned attendance areas. Charter-operated schools were expected to serve every child zoned to the school (Roberts, November 8, 2012). Parents who did not want their children in an ASD school had the right to transfer to another school, however.

Several changes in ASD regulations that resulted from legislation signed by Governor William Haslam in May 2012 also distinguished the ASD from the RSD. One provision stated that an ASD school would not return to its home district if that district was itself "in need of improvement" (Smith, 2013). The school also was allowed to remain in the ASD if 60% of parents petitioned to do so. Regarding charters, the legislation specified that they would remain in the ASD until the end of their 10-year charter term.

The 2012 legislation included one other provision that helped school districts initiate their own turnaround process if they desired to avoid losing low-performing schools to the ASD (Smith, 2013). Tennessee districts were permitted to create "Innovation Zones," similar in design to Indiana's transformation zones. Innovation Zones were granted authority over financial, programmatic, staffing, and time allocation decisions. Federal School Improvement Grants provided funding for these initiatives. The Innovation Zones not only enabled in-house turnarounds, but they also provided a home for ASD schools when and if they returned to their district. Shelby County Public Schools, which merged with Memphis Public Schools in 2013, became the first district in Tennessee to establish an Innovation Zone.

By the 2014–2015 school year, the ASD managed five schools directly. Eighteen other schools were charter schools, with an additional six charters set to be added the following year (Smith, 2015). While chartering schools had clearly emerged as Barbic's preference for the ASD, charters also presented some of his greatest challenges. Three highly respected national charter organizations announced their intention to scale back plans to take over failing schools in Memphis (Prothero, April 21, 2015). The organizations included YES Prep, Chris Barbic's former home base, the Knowledge Is Power Program (KIPP), and Green Dot Public Schools.

One of the reasons these organizations questioned working with the ASD concerned the requirement that charter operators take on students already in the schools' attendance zones. Charter schools typically prefer to open a school with families that choose to be there rather than being assigned to the school, according to Barbic (Prothero, 2015, p. 2). Charter organizations also like to begin with one grade level and grow the school. The ASD required them to take over an existing school with all of its grade levels.

The ASD's experience with national charter organizations, as with Indiana's, raises questions about their level of interest in tackling the challenge of turning around the lowest-performing schools. Barbic was quoted as saying, "The bottom line is that there are not a lot of great charter operators to begin with, and there are even fewer who understand how to do turnaround" (Tatter, July 7, 2015, p. 3).

In an effort to placate charter operators, Governor Haslam signed a bill in 2015 that allows charter schools in the ASD to enroll students who are not residentially zoned to the schools. This provision only applies, however, to charter schools that meet student growth expectations (Tatter, April 23, 2015).

As of 2015, the track record for the ASD was mixed. According to one report (Smith, 2015), the ASD schools averaged gains of 2.92% in math and 0.72% in English/language arts over a two-year period. Another report (Achievement School District, 2015) boasted that six ASD schools no longer were in the bottom-performing 10% of Tennessee schools, and 86% of parents graded their child's ASD school an A or a B. One of the most interesting analyses of performance data compared the ASD's early academic results with those of the Shelby County Innovation Zone schools (Howard, 2014). The Innovation Zone schools were reported to have made greater gains than the ASD schools.

In a comprehensive review of ASD progress, Smith (2015) argued that the special state district had produced an unexpected outcome. "Recent statewide data suggests that the existence of the ASD may be producing one desired result," he wrote, "lighting a fire under all districts that house Priority schools in the bottom 5 percent" (p. 15). He went on to note that improvement for Priority Schools on the state's accountability scale far exceeded that of non–Priority Schools statewide.

The year 2015 brought several significant changes to the ASD. Founding superintendent Chris Barbic decided to leave the ASD, claiming a new leader was needed to stabilize early gains. In parting, he also offered a sobering warning regarding overreliance on charter schools. "As a charter school founder, I did my fair share of chest pounding over great results," he wrote in an e-mail. "I've learned that getting these same results in a zoned neighborhood school environment is much harder" (Burnette, 2015, p. 2).

The second change involved a greater voice in local ASD decisions for Priority School communities. Initially matches between Priority Schools and approved operators were made by the ASD superintendent. In order to engage the community more in the turnaround process, neighborhood advisory councils have been established for Priority Schools under consideration for the ASD (Skinner, 2015). Council members are charged with reviewing applications to run Priority Schools from outside operators and tendering their recommendations. The final decision regarding operators, however, remains with the ASD administration.

The most recent change authorized two charter organizations, KIPP and Knowledge Academies, to open ASD schools in Nashville. Allowing charters to develop new schools instead of taking over existing neighborhood schools represents a significant departure from previous ASD practice and an acknowledgment of the ASD's need to attract more charter operators (Tatter, August 7, 2015).

MICHIGAN'S EDUCATION ACHIEVEMENT AUTHORITY

Both the RSD and the ASD faced their share of conflict and complexity in their efforts to gain traction, but their trials seemed relatively small in comparison to the first years of Michigan's Education Achievement Authority (EAA). From a precipitous drop in first-year student enrollment to political infighting over expansion plans, the EAA's very survival might be regarded as something of a surprise.

The EAA was intended to be a special district for low-performing schools across Michigan, but five years after the idea for the EAA was conceived, only schools from Detroit were involved. Some of the EAA's subsequent problems can be traced to the conditions under which it was established (Smith, 2014). While the RSD and the ASD operate as state agencies codified in state law, the EAA started as an interlocal agreement between Detroit Public Schools and Eastern Michigan University. Add to this unusual arrangement the fact that the EAA initially relied on donations rather than stable state funding and it is easy to understand why the EAA's early going was rough.

Shortly after Rick Snyder (Republican) was elected governor of Michigan in 2010, he tackled the issue of the state's failing schools by promoting the EAA. According to Guyette (2014, p. 1), "The legal loophole through which the EAA slipped into being is a little-used state law that allows two units of government, acting in cooperation, to create a third public entity." Governance of the EAA rests with an 11-person board, with seven members appointed by the governor, two members by the Eastern Michigan University Board of Regents, and two members by Detroit Public Schools' emergency manager.

To lead the EAA, the board hired John Covington, who resigned his position as superintendent of the Kansas City, Missouri, school system to accept the post. A proponent of "student-centered" learning and innovative uses of technology, Covington's arrival signaled a new approach to turning around failing schools. Neither the RSD nor the ASD had made a point of emphasizing innovative models of learning.

The EAA's website (http://www.michigan.gov/eaa) provides vivid details about what students can expect if their school becomes part of the special district. The school year runs for 210 days, 30 days longer than most Michigan schools, and the school day has been lengthened to seven and a half hours, an hour longer than the average school day. The website boasts that these increases place the EAA schools "on par" with schools in Japan, China, and Singapore.

The next section of the website page addresses student-centered learning:

> Individual attention is provided for each student. The traditional education model involves a "one size fits all" approach in which students advance through school based on their age or the amount of time they have spent sitting in a classroom. EAA schools organize students by instructional level based on the content of the courses they have completed, rather than grade levels. Students advance as rapidly as they can master course content.

In order for students to advance based on content mastery instead of arbitrary semester beginnings and endings, EAA schools implement a sophisticated digital learning system, one that Covington had learned about during his time in Kansas City. Every student is allocated a computer. Students are divided into small learning groups based on their level of achievement. Each student's growth, the website proclaims, will be assessed four times a year, reducing the likelihood that any student falls too far behind. The notion of course failure is eliminated under the new instructional model because students are allowed to keep working on course content at their own pace until they have mastered it.

Despite these innovative features, many parents balked at sending their children to the initial group of 15 EAA schools from the Detroit system. In their first year of operation, EAA schools lost almost one quar-

ter of their students (Cwiek, 2013). Critics of the EAA seized on the enrollment decline to call for scrapping the new venture.

There were additional developments that made the future prospects
of the fledgling district look dim. On the eve of launching the EAA,
administrators learned that a large portion of $24 million of Title I funds
that Detroit Public Schools was supposed to forward to the special district was being held back (Smith, 2014). Had it not been for a successful
eleventh-hour appeal to private philanthropic organizations, the EAA
might never have launched.

Problems locating charter operators also confronted the EAA. Govern-
or Snyder's intention was for the EAA to follow the RSD model and
convert low-performing Detroit schools to charter schools. EAA administrators met with 23 potential charter operators in March 2012. Of these,
only three made the deadline for applying to run a school. Ultimately the
EAA found itself with only one charter operator willing to take on the
challenge. The newly formed Michigan Educational Choice Center
(MECC) contracted to serve as a single charter district overseeing three
EAA schools (Smith, 2014). The MECC secured the services of Performance Academies to handle operations at the three schools.

A serious threat to the EAA's existence followed a referendum vote in
November 2012 to overturn Public Act 4, which enabled the state to appoint emergency managers. Detroit Public Schools had been put under
state-directed emergency management in 2009 (Smith, 2014). When Public Act 4 was struck down, the Detroit School Board voted to sever its
contract with Eastern Michigan University and withdraw its schools from
the EAA. Unwilling to see his signature education initiative fail, Govern-
or Snyder signed a new bill, Public Act 436, that restored emergency
manager powers to the state. It would not be the last time Snyder went on
the offensive. The new act nullified the school board's vote and preserved
the EAA, at least for the time being.

A new threat to the EAA's existence surfaced in the fall of 2013 when
professors at Eastern Michigan University pressed their institution to end
its relationship with the special district. Faculty members claimed they
had no input concerning how the EAA was run and they opposed how it
was being operated (Strauss, 2013). Among their dislikes was the EAA's
reliance on young and inexperienced teachers, many of whom were
drawn from Teach for America, and the fact that many teachers lacked
appropriate credentials.

Since the interlocal agreement that created the EAA carried with it a
15-year obligation, there was not much the faculty could do. The Michigan legislature, however, was another matter. Legislators on both sides of
the aisle opposed any effort to expand the EAA beyond Detroit, despite
pressure from the state superintendent (Eggert, 2014). It was no coincidence that legislative opposition to EAA growth surfaced after test re-

sults for EAA schools were published (Smith, 2014). The pace of academic progress in EAA schools disappointed many legislators.

Immediately following the release of the test data, Mike Flanagan, state superintendent, announced that the Michigan Department of Education intended to withdraw from its contract with the EAA in 2015. This action would enable the state to use other agencies for turning around low-performing schools, an apparent effort by the administration in Lansing to circumvent the legislature and its unwillingness to expand the EAA beyond Detroit.

June 2014 brought the bad news that the EAA's FY 2015 budget reflected a $26 million drop in revenue. The same day the news became public, John Covington resigned. Veronica Conforme, former chief operating officer of New York City Public Schools, took over as interim chancellor. Later in the year she was offered the position of chancellor when the only other candidate withdrew.

Conforme brought a level of transparency to the position that had not characterized her predecessor's regime. She let it be known that she was displeased with the slow rate of progress in the EAA schools (Smith, 2015). In February 2015, she announced new policies giving all EAA schools greater autonomy over programs, resources, and professional development. Instead of a single innovative model, which had been Covington's preference, Conforme invited principals to explore their own approaches.

Several months before Conforme's invitation to principals to think creatively, an investigative reporter unearthed e-mails that raised serious questions about Covington's commitment to one particular model of instruction (Guyette, 2014). The reporter pointed to conflict of interest, poor judgment, and efforts to conceal flaws in the highly touted digital learning system that Covington had championed for the EAA after trying it in Kansas City. Teachers who were interviewed by the reporter indicated that students who failed to perform well on the system's tests were allowed to retake the tests in order to improve results and make the learning system look better.

Instead of initially pilot-testing the learning system, Covington insisted that all schools adopt it. The investigative reporter offered the following scathing indictment: "one question needs to be answered: How do the leaders involved in creating the EAA, the board charged with overseeing it, and the educators responsible for running it justify allowing a terribly flawed program to be used for two years on 10,000 children in schools that were already deemed to be failing?" (Guyette, 2014, p. 8).

While Conforme worked to correct the missteps of her predecessor and boost student achievement in the 15 EAA schools in Detroit, Governor Snyder launched a new initiative reminiscent of Governor Mike Pence's establishment of CECI in Indiana. Having apparently given up on a legislature that opposed expanding the EAA and a state superintendent he regarded as resistant to his vision for education in Michigan, Snyder issued an executive order in March 2015 that transferred the school turnaround functions of the Education Department to the Department of Technology, Management, and Budget, an agency over which he had direct control (Murray, 2015).

The Michigan Board of Education challenged Snyder's action, claiming it violated the state's constitution by stripping the state superintendent's authority to execute the board's policies. Snyder declared that he was dissatisfied with the slow pace of change in Michigan's lowest-performing schools (Murray, March 17, 2015). The transfer of turnaround authority to the Department of Technology, Management, and Budget allowed him to circumvent constraints on the EAA and address failing schools across the state. It is noteworthy that the first action ordered for the new turnaround operation was a performance review of the EAA.

While Governor Snyder was wresting control of the EAA from the Education Department, an ongoing federal corruption probe focused on former and current top EAA officials as well as several principals (Wisely & Zaniewski, 2015). Records were subpoenaed from various companies that supposedly provided services to EAA schools.

ALTERNATIVE SPECIAL STATE DISTRICTS

While several states have sought to create special state districts that closely resemble the RSD or the ASD, other states have explored unique alternatives.

Hawaii

Public schools in Hawaii make up a single, statewide school district. As part of its Race to the Top grant, the Hawaii Department of Education proposed the creation of two Zones of School Innovation (ZSI), each to function like a separate school district. One ZSI represents the Big Island's sprawling Kau-Keaau-Pahoa complex area; the other covers the Nanakuli-Waianae complex area on Oahu. Both areas consist of high percentages of disadvantaged families, many of whom are of native Hawaiian descent.

Each ZSI consists not only of persistently low-performing schools on Hawaii's list of Priority Schools but also of feeder schools and local charter schools. The two complexes are located in remote rural areas where schools have been hard to staff. Six of Hawaii's seven Priority Schools are located in one of the two special state districts.

The ZSIs have enabled the state to provide a comprehensive range of services and additional resources to these clusters of very needy schools. Instructional time has been increased, including summer programs and extended school days. Financial incentives have been made available to attract highly qualified teachers. A common curriculum has been put in place across the ZSIs, and the latest technology has been implemented to increase teacher and student access to new learning opportunities. ZSI principals enjoy greater autonomy than their colleagues in other schools. Finally, support services—including medical care, mental health counseling, and nutrition education—are provided to students and their families.

Early indications are that the ZSIs have had a positive impact. By 2014, eight of the 18 ZSI schools were meeting performance targets. In more than half of the schools, student growth outpaced state averages in both reading and mathematics (Hawaii Zones, 2014). Problems remain, however, with regard to the recruitment of capable teachers and securing the resources to sustain reforms beyond the end of Race to the Top funding.

Colorado

Unlike the previous special state districts, Colorado's Turnaround Network is a purely voluntary operation. The website (www.cde.state.co.us/accountability/turnaroundnetwork) describes the Turnaround Network (TN) as "a highly collaborative and accountable endeavor between local schools, their districts, and the Colorado Department of Education." The TN welcomed its first nine schools in the summer of 2014.

By working closely with the Colorado Department of Education (CDE), member schools have access to a variety of services, including diagnostic review and planning support, performance management, personalized professional learning opportunities, supplemental grant funding, and a cohort of peer schools. Network schools are required to engage a "district partner" as well. This individual, preferably a senior-level district staff member, serves as an advocate for the school at the district level. The district partner works in tandem with the principal and his or her leadership team to ensure that the conditions for school improvement are in place.

The CDE does not require participating schools to conform to a particular reform model (Garcia, 2014). Schools can decide on the changes that are most likely to address student needs. The laissez-faire approach of the TN does not mean that schools avoid the state's accountability timetable, however. Persistently low-performing schools in the TN still face state sanctions if they fail to improve in five years.

Connecticut

Established by the Connecticut General Assembly in 2012, the Commissioner's Network (CN) is a hybrid, operating primarily as an opt-in special state system, but with the option of having low-performing schools assigned to it. The CN's website (www.sde.ct.gov/sde/cwp/view.asp?a) bills the system as "a commitment between local stakeholders and the Connecticut State Department of Education (CSDE) to dramatically improve student achievement in up to 25 schools." Participating schools remain in the CN for three to five years, but they also continue to be part of their local school districts.

The schools in the CN are chosen by the state commissioner, with preference given to schools that volunteer to participate and to schools located in a district where the existing collective bargaining agreement with certified employees expires for the school year in which a turnaround plan will be implemented. The second provision makes it possible to require all faculty members to reapply for their positions, thereby giving the principal an opportunity to reconstitute the staff.

When a school is selected for the CN, the local school board must establish a district turnaround committee and permit the CSDE to conduct an operations and instructional audit of the school. Once a turnaround plan has been drafted, it must be approved by the Connecticut State Board of Education. The plan has to specify student achievement goals and strategies for accomplishing them. Turnaround plans may involve an external partner or educational management organization, and they may include provisions for altering the hours and schedules of teachers and administrators. If deemed appropriate, the commissioner is empowered to appoint a "special master" to oversee implementation of the turnaround plan.

CN schools enjoy access to technical assistance and operational support from the CSDE. The commissioner also provides supplemental funding, possibly including additional financial support for teachers and administrators.

By 2015 the CN was serving more than 9,000 students in 16 schools across nine districts. Not everyone, however, was pleased with how the CN was progressing. Conncan, a public advocacy group, issued a detailed report (Addressing Connecticut's education, 2015) calling for an overhaul of the CN's policies and operational conditions. The report also criticized the fact that less than half of the CN's 16 schools met the criteria for lowest-performing schools.

In the report, Louisiana's RSE and Tennessee's ASD as well as Massachusetts's receiver system were held up as models of what Connecticut should be doing. The report implied that giving preference to schools that volunteered to participate in the CN might not be the best way to ensure that the needs of the children left behind were being served. It also recommended that turnaround plans conform to specified guidelines rather than being completely discretionary.

IRONING OUT THE KINKS

With the possible exception of the Recovery School District, the special state districts are works in progress. Even the RSD, however, has to determine a new mission now that all of its schools have been converted to charter schools. The ASD and EAA have made an effort to include charters as an option, but both have experienced difficulty recruiting suitable charter operators. The ASD discovered, for example, that charter operators prefer to start a school from scratch rather than take over an existing public school and all of its students.

Charter schools, of course, have become a hotly contested political issue. Advocates for public education and teacher union representatives are unlikely to embrace special state districts intended to convert the lowest-performing schools to charters. They are more likely to accept special districts that directly run these schools and return them to local control when they have been turned around.

The question that has yet to be answered convincingly is this: Are special state districts capable of directly running low-performing schools until they improve significantly? Many state departments of education scaled back operations during the recession of 2008–2010. They received a financial boost from Race to the Top funds, but this money runs out in 2014–2016, depending on the state. The track record of direct-run schools has been mixed at best.

In a report on the RSD, ASD, and EAA, Nelson Smith (2015, p. 8), former president of the National Alliance for Public Charter Schools, makes the following point: "One can't help but notice that opposition to such endeavors [special state districts] has mostly been driven not by voices demanding other kinds of rigorous change, but by those defending the status quo: local control, local prerogatives, untouchable teacher contracts, and the preservation of adult jobs." Smith goes on to observe: "And there is the problem—a state trying to confront broad swaths of dysfunction is far less likely to succeed if its dysfunctional schools are stuck with the same staff, leader, school board, and comatose or corrupt central office."

It is worth noting, in light of Smith's critique, that special state districts tend to be championed by Republican governors. Traditionally, Republicans have favored local control and nongovernmental solutions to problems, and they often have campaigned for reductions in state agencies. Why special state districts seem to be an exception to these positions is worth considering. The most obvious answer is that Republicans see these districts as a means to increase charter schools and school choice (Ujifusa, 2015).

One other point regarding special state districts needs to be made. The schools in the RSD, ASD, and EAA are predominantly African American, well over 90% in most cases. By clustering together these schools, states can be accused of reifying de facto segregation. The RSD at least has created a charter-based market where parents have choices. Such choices are very limited in the ASD and EAA, and, in any event, parents likely are choosing between one all-black school and another all-black school.

REFERENCES

Achievement School District: Year two results. 2015, January 30. *Achievement School District*. Retrieved from http://achievementschooldistrict.org/wp-content/uploads/2015/01/ASD-Second-Year-Results.pdf.

Addressing Connecticut's education: Improving turnaround measures for our lowest performing school. 2015. *Conncan*. Retrieved from http://www.conncan.org.

Burnette, D. 2015, July 17. Chris Barbic, founding superintendent of state-run Achievement School District, to exit. *Chalkbeat*. Retrieved from http://tn.chalkbeat.org/2015/07/17/chris-barbic-founding-superintendent-of-achievement-school-district-to-exit/#.Vm2lgEorLIU.

Cwiek, S. 2013, November 22. Enrollment plummets in state-run Education Achievement Authority schools. *Michigan Radio*. Retrieved from http://michiganradio.org/post/enrollment-plummets-state-run-education-achievement-authority-schools#stream/0.

Dobard, P. 2015, August 26. New Orleans' Recovery District chief: "A steady focus on what's best for children." *Education Week, 24*, 18.

Dreilinger, D. 2014, September 26. What's the point of the Recovery School District now? *Times-Picayune*. Retrieved from http://www.nola.com/education/index.ssf/2014/09/whats_the_point_of_the_recover.html.

———. 2014, December 19. Landmark New Orleans special education case is settled, parties say. *Times-Picayune*. Retrieved from http://www.nola.com/education/index.ssf/2014/12/parties_ask_federal_judge_to_a.html.

Editorial. 2012, December 31. *Memphis Daily News*. Retrieved from http://www.memphisdailynews.com/editorial/Article.aspx?id=73622.

Eggert, D. 2014, February 15. Expansion of Michigan school turnaround initiative stalled. Retrieved from http://www.freep.com/article/20140215/NEWS06/302150049/Expansion-of-Michigan-school-turnaround-initiative-stalled.

Garcia, N. 2014, July 10. 8 struggling schools opt in to Colorado's new turnaround network. *Chalkbeat*. Retrieved from http://co.chalkbeat.org/2014/07/10/8-struggling-schools-opt-in-to-colorados-new-turnaround-network/.

Guyette, C. 2014, September 24. The EAA exposed: An investigative report. *Detroit Metro Times*. Retrieved from http://www.metrotimes.com/detroit/the-eaa-exposed-an-investigative-report/Content?oid=2249513.

Harris, D. N. 2013. *The post-Katrina New Orleans school reforms: Implications for national school reform and the role of government*. New Orleans, LA: Education Research Alliance for New Orleans.

Hawaii Zones of School Innovation committed to improvement. 2014. Retrieved from http://sites.ed.gov/progress/2014/06/hawaii-zones-of-school-innovation-committed-to-improvement/.

Howard, E. 2014, September 9. Just the facts: ASD vs. iZone performance Part I, Bluff City Education (blog). Retrieved from http://www.bluffcityed.com/2014/09/just-facts-asd-vs-izone-performance/.

Murray, D. D. 2015, March 17. State school board says Snyder violated Constitution by reorganizing school reform board. *Daily Tribune* [Metro Detroit]. Retrieved from http://www.dailytribune.com/general-news/20150317/state-school-board-says-snyder-violated-constitution-by-reorganizing-school-reform-board.

Nossiter, A. 2007, May 5. Prominent education reformer to lead New Orleans schools. *New York Times*, p. 1.

————. 2008, April 30. Against odds New Orleans schools fight back. *New York Times*, p. 1.

Press release. 2015, May 22. Orleans Parish School Board unanimously approves two Type 1 charter school applications. *Orleans Parish School Board*. Retrieved from http://opsb.us/2015/05/orleans-parish-school-board-unanimously-approves-two-type-1-charter-school-applications/.

Prothero, A. 2015, April 21. Charter operators pull back from Memphis turnaround effort. *Education Week*. Retrieved from http://www.edweek.org/ew/articles/2015/04/22/charter-operators-pull-back-from-memphis-turnaround.html.

Recovery School District 2014 Annual Report. 2015. Retrieved from http://lrsd.entest.org/2014%20RSD%20annual%20Report.pdf.

Roberts, J. 2012, October 22. Achievement School District gets jolt: Low test scores. *Commercial Appeal* [Memphis]. Retrieved from http://www.commercialappeal.com/news/achievement-school-district-gets-jolt-low-test-scores-ep-514665213-329200391.html.

————. 2012, November 8. Tennessee achievement district to take over 10 more Memphis city schools. *Huffington Post*. Retrieved from http://www.huffingtonpost.com/2012/11/08/10-more-memphis-schools-t_n_2091860.html.

RSD schools in New Orleans show highest growth in 2013 state tests. n.d. *Recovery School District*. Retrieved from http://www.rsdla.net/apps/news/show_news.jsp?REC_ID=273983.

Samuels, C. A. 2015, January 21. La. Struggles in rolling out new authority for IEP teams. *Education Week*, pp. 17, 20.

Significant changes in the New Orleans teacher workforce. 2015, September 9. *Education Week*, 5.

Skinner, K. 2015, September 22. Seven questions parents are asking about the ASD and its school takeover and turnaround process. *Chalkbeat*. Retrieved from http://tn.chalkbeat.org/2015/09/22/seven-questions-parents-are-asking-about-the-asd-and-its-school-takeover-and-turnaround-process/.

Smith, N. 2013. Redefining the school district in Tennessee. Washington, DC: Thomas B. Fordham Institute.

————. 2014. Redefining the school district in Michigan. Washington, DC: Thomas B. Fordham Institute.

————. 2015. Redefining the school district in America. Washington, DC: Thomas B. Fordham Institute.

Strauss, V. 2013, October 25. Faculty fight university's link to controversial school turnaround district. *Washington Post*. Retrieved from http://www.washingtonpost.com/blogs/answer-sheet/wp/2013/10/25/faculty-fight-universitys-link-to-controversial-school-turnaround-district/.

Tatter, G. 2015, July 7. More states look to Tennessee's Achievement School District as a school turnaround model. *Chalkbeat*. Retrieved from http://tn.chalkbeat.org/2015/07/07/more-states-look-to-tennessees-achievement-school-district-as-a-school-turnaround-model/#.Vmya6korLIU.

————. 2015, August 7. Achievement School District announces KIPP, Knowledge Academies to open Nashville schools. *Chalkbeat*. Retrieved from http://tn.chalkbeat.org/2015/08/07/achievement-school-district-announces-kipp-knowledge-academies-to-open-nashville-schools/#.Vri70VJUVS0.

————. 2015, August 23. As Tennessee lawmakers end session, did legislature "get education right." *Chalkbeat*. Retrieved from http://tn.chalkbeat.org/2015/04/23/as-tennessee-lawmakers-end-session-did-legislature-get-education-right/#.VmyazUorLIU.

Ujifusa, A. 2015, July 8. Budgets, testing issues took legislative state. *Education Week*, p. 13.

Vallas, P. G., Duke, D. L., & Smalley, E. F. 2011. Building the plane while flying it. In D. L. Duke and E. F. Smalley (Eds.), *Essentials for Education Executives*. Charlottesville,

VA: Darden/Curry Partnership for Leaders in Education, University of Virginia, pp. 11–19.

Wisely, J., & Zaniewski, A. 2015, October 21. Top officials, bank records focus of school probe. *Detroit Free Press*. Retrieved from http://www.freep.com/story/news/local/michigan/detroit/2015/10/20/federal-probe-eaa/74297446/.

FIVE

Technical Assistance and Training

Among the narratives that are given to explain why some schools fail while others succeed is one rooted in a pervasive lack of educational expertise. As the story goes, persistently low-performing schools struggle to attract and retain highly qualified principals and teachers. The educational professionals who staff these schools are characterized as well meaning and caring for the most part but deficient in the technical skills of effective instruction, classroom management, student assessment, data analysis, and instructional intervention.

Sometimes school districts possess the expertise to help school-based personnel develop competence in these areas so that they can turn around their schools. Unfortunately, as we have seen in cases like Buffalo, district expertise also can be lacking. In these instances, states have several options. They can contract directly with commercial and nonprofit providers or require schools and districts to contract with such organizations, including lead partners and educational management organizations. Some state departments of education also have developed the in-house capacity to deliver technical assistance and training to failing schools. This chapter describes some of these state-based efforts.

In a policy brief for the Education Commission of the States, Christie (2007, p. 1) discussed the challenge of technical assistance for state agencies:

> The goal of state intervention in a school or district designated as low-performing is not to punish. It is to help figure out how to improve student learning. The challenge, particularly for a chief state school officer or state board of education, is how best to leverage assistance to schools that have varying degrees of need. . . . How to proceed with limited funding and staffing is the truly difficult questions.

83

The chapter opens with a retrospective overview of efforts by the Virginia Department of Education to assist low-performing schools in the Commonwealth. Subsequent segments then examine some of the issues and challenges associated with delivering technical assistance and training to low-performing schools.

LAUNCHING A STATEWIDE ASSISTANCE PROGRAM

Following the passage of the No Child Left Behind (NCLB) Act, the Virginia Department of Education (VDOE) in concert with the General Assembly and governor's office began to explore ways that the state could assist its lowest-performing schools. Virginia's governor at the time, Mark Warner, took a particular interest in education, launching his signature "Education for a Lifetime" initiative in September 2003. A Democrat with the desire to promote bipartisanship, Warner made no secret of his presidential aspirations. He hoped his new program would attract national attention.

Although many components of the "Education for a Lifetime" initiative addressed the nexus between education and the economy, several features focused specifically on struggling students and low-performing schools. One of these, Project Graduation, offered remedial instruction through special academies and online tutorials to students at risk of not earning a diploma. Project Graduation started the year before all Virginia students were required to pass state Standards of Learning (SOL) tests in order to earn a diploma.

As Virginia expanded its testing requirements, Project Graduation evolved. When state tests in selected high school subjects were added to the original SOL tests in reading and writing, online tutorials in these subjects were developed. As of 2007, Virginia high school students needed to pass SOL tests in English, mathematics, science, and history. In its first two years of operation, Project Graduation served 6,285 students. Well over two thirds of them wound up earning a diploma (Wallinger, 2006).

A second component of Warner's initiative involved leader development. "We'll also train and deploy 'Turn Around Specialists' to go into and improve the most troubled schools," Warner promised. "This concept has worked in private business. It is based on the idea of accountability, and we can measure the results" (Warner, 2003, p. 6).

Warner's promise resulted in the creation of the first state-funded training program for school turnaround specialists. The Virginia Department of Education contracted with the University of Virginia in a unique arrangement involving the Curry School of Education and the Darden Graduate School of Business Administration. The School Turnaround Specialist Program (STSP) originally focused on preparing principals for

Virginia's lowest-performing schools, but Microsoft became interested in scaling up the program nationally. By 2015 the STSP had trained turn-around specialists in dozens of states and achieved a reputation for producing results (Player & Katz, 2013).

The training model of the STSP requires that a school district commit up front to providing a support network for participating trainees. Training for turnaround specialists and members of their district and school-based support teams takes place at the University of Virginia as well as on site. Those who successfully complete the two-year program earn a credential in school turnaround management.

In light of new requirements resulting from the passage of NCLB, the VDOE recognized that local schools and districts would want help in assessing the needs of persistently low-performing schools. A school-level academic review process was created to help schools identify and analyze instructional and organizational factors affecting student achievement. The first year that a school is rated "accredited with warning," an academic review team conducts a comprehensive review. In 2005–2006, the first year of required academic reviews, 132 out of 1,862 public schools in Virginia underwent reviews (Wallinger, 2006).

Academic review teams compile data on a variety of school-based systems, processes, and practices. Use of time and scheduling practices are examined. So, too, is curriculum alignment with state standards and use of data to make planning and instructional decisions. Reviewers also collect data on professional development, instructional interventions, school culture, and resource allocation. All of this data becomes the foundation for a school's three-year improvement plan. Schools that do not exit "accredited with warning" status the year after the academic review process are assigned a school support team to provide technical assistance and monitor the implementation of an improvement plan.

The Partnership for Achieving Successful Schools (PASS) was yet another technical assistance initiative during Warner's tenure as governor. Initially targeted for 32 schools subject to sanctions under NCLB, PASS promoted partnerships between schools and businesses, community organizations, and faith-based institutions. In some cases, high-performing schools were paired with struggling schools as a means for sharing best practices. PASS schools agreed to use materials developed or approved by the VDOE, including curriculum frameworks, pacing guides, and nine-week assessments.

The early track record for PASS schools was encouraging. Between 2002 and 2006, 45 low-performing schools participated. Fourteen schools managed to exit Priority status. Students in PASS schools in 2005 achieved a pass rate in reading of 67%, compared to 47% in 2002. The pass rate in mathematics jumped from 44% to 72% (Wallinger, 2006).

Other initiatives by the VDOE focused on teacher recruitment and retention for hard-to-staff schools. Funds were appropriated to offer a one-time hiring incentive of $15,000 to teachers who met eligibility requirements and agreed to move to a hard-to-staff school. Highly qualified teachers already working in a hard-to-staff school received annual bonuses of $3,000 to stay. An additional recruitment program offered incentives for mathematics teachers with appropriate qualifications to teach in schools deemed "at risk in mathematics."

THE EVOLUTION OF PASS

Following Mark Warner's tenure as governor, Virginia's efforts to provide technical assistance and training to its lowest-performing schools continued to develop. By 2015, the combination of initiatives headquartered in the Office of School Improvement (OSI) of the VDOE achieved national recognition as one of the most comprehensive systems in the country. Now referred to collectively as the Partnership for Achieving Successful Schools (PASS), the program is driven by proven intervention strategies used in high-poverty rural and urban schools in the commonwealth.

The OSI prides itself on customizing assistance and training to meet the needs of particular schools and districts. In the early years, much of the technical assistance was delivered to principals and school leadership teams by VDOE coaches. While that work continues, other forms of assistance ranging from online webinars to regional service centers are available to school-based and district personnel. A primary goal of PASS involves developing the capacity of school districts to help their lowest-performing schools.

Partnerships still constitute an important component of PASS, but the variety of possible partners has expanded greatly. Experienced school and district administrators, including former superintendents, serve as academic review facilitators, district liaisons, lead turnaround facilitators, providers of technical assistance, and regional liaisons. The VDOE has developed a list of approved vendors as an alternative source of assistance. All Priority Schools, the lowest-performing 5% of Title I schools, are required to choose a Lead Turnaround Partner (LTP) from the VDOE list. The LTP provides assistance in implementing the school's three-year turnaround plan. The VDOE also established the Intra-agency Technical Assistance Team to coordinate the sharing of information and resources regarding how best to address the needs of low-performing schools.

Among the most important partnerships under the PASS umbrella are those with Virginia universities and professional groups. To assist schools in addressing accountability and improvement goals for students with disabilities, for example, a network of university-based Training and Technical Assistance Centers (TTAC) has been created. Recognizing that low-performing schools often fail to meet the needs of many students requiring special education services, the VDOE has charged the TTACs with implementing effective instructional practices and improvement strategies to boost the achievement of students with special needs. Any low-performing school not meeting the annual measurable objectives of Virginia's federal No Child Left Behind waiver also is eligible to receive assistance from its regional center.

According to Cherish Skinker, a team leader at the James Madison University TTAC, the center's first priority is to assist schools in Year 3 of school improvement, followed by schools just beginning the improvement process. TTAC teams conduct on-site observations and provide feedback to schools on the kinds of supports and professional development that are best suited to the school's needs. Skinker's TTAC promotes several well-established programs, including the Strategic Instruction Model, the I'm Determined Project, Positive Behavioral Interventions and Supports, and the Virginia Tiered Systems of Support (a form of Response to Intervention).

A major focus for technical assistance from the VDOE involves the collection, analysis, and sharing of data to help low-performing schools identify areas for improvement and assess progress in addressing them. The Virginia Dashboard offers schools a web-based data analysis and reporting tool that provides a single platform for compiling various types of student achievement, attendance, and discipline data.

To help school personnel identify students at risk for dropping out of high school, the VDOE implemented the Virginia Early Warning System (VEWS). VEWS focuses on ninth-grade students, tracking their progress (or lack of progress) toward graduation.

To assist low-performing schools with the planning needed to raise student achievement, the VDOE provides access to a web-based tool called Indistar. Indistar entails a six-step process for organizing and customizing planning information. Training videos help school-based personnel learn how to develop improvement plans and use Indistar to monitor progress. Wise Ways research briefs offer research-based strategies that can be used in conjunction with Indistar to accomplish planning goals. Indistar must be used to create School Improvement Plans for all Virginia Title I schools designated "accredited with warning."

Yet another useful tool is a set of school indicators called Support for School Improvement (SSI). Indicators can be employed by planners to help determine areas in need of improvement and by coaches to identify training needs. SSI indicators cover all aspects of school operations, from leadership teams to data-driven decision making to classroom instruction. A sampling of indicators for classroom instruction is provided in box 5.1 (Virginia/Support for School Improvement, n.d.).

BOX 5.1: CLASSROOM INSTRUCTION—EXPECTING AND
MONITORING SOUND INSTRUCTION IN A VARIETY OF
MODES—PREPARATION

- All teachers are guided by a document that aligns standards, curriculum, instruction, and assessment.
- All teachers develop weekly lesson plans based on aligned units of instruction.
- All teachers maintain a record of each student's mastery of specific learning objectives.
- All teachers test frequently using a variety of evaluation methods and maintain a record of the results.
- All teachers differentiate assignments (individualize instruction) in response to individual student performance on pretests and other methods of assessment.

Virginia provides its low-performing schools with as comprehensive a program of technical assistance and training as any state in the United States. Offerings continue to be adjusted in light of new research and feedback from local educators. Such flexibility and responsiveness are important because the conditions within and beyond low-performing schools are constantly changing.

TECHNICAL ASSISTANCE AND TRAINING CHALLENGES

When states deliver technical assistance and training to their lowest-performing schools, they are just as likely to encounter conflict, complexity, and local differences as they are when they initiate school and district takeovers. Educators do not always embrace help from outside. Issues arise concerning who provides help and how it is provided. There are concerns when assistance becomes too prescriptive as well as not prescriptive enough. The training of leaders to turn around schools also can be problematic.

Resistance to Help

Resistance to technical assistance actually may be resistance to change, and the reasons for such resistance are numerous (Duke, 2004). Cherish Skinker, the TTAC team leader from Virginia, reported that her group encountered opposition from some school administrators who blamed the Virginia Department of Education and its accountability system for creating their problems in the first place. In one case study of school turnaround (Duke & Landahl, 2011), the principal complained about technical assistance from the state because members of the team providing guidance could not agree among themselves on the best way to proceed.

Resistance in some instances is the result of disillusionment. Veteran teachers who once got excited about the prospects of reform become jaded after seeing their efforts frequently abandoned because of a change in administration or a shift in priorities. Then there is the inertial force of complacency. Teachers strive to create routines for handling the various tasks associated with teaching, evaluating students, and managing classrooms. Being compelled to change these routines is unlikely to be welcomed, even when the effectiveness of the routines is debatable.

Add to these reasons the fact that change can be stressful and it's easy to understand why well-intentioned individuals offering technical assistance and training often encounter resistance. Not only are educators called upon to invest precious time in learning new practices and processes, but the possibility of doing poorly is ever present. For some adults, the embarrassment of trying something new and failing in front of colleagues can lead to change aversion. Examples abound of such opposition when veteran teachers are asked to embrace new technology. Also contributing to the stress associated with technical assistance and training is the very real possibility that those who fail to change can lose their jobs.

Besides the aforementioned reasons, some educators are resistant to changes that they associate with policies perceived to be hurting the children left behind. These professionals—along with an increasing number of parents—question, for instance, the heavy contemporary emphasis on preparing students to pass standardized tests. They attribute the trend toward test-driven schooling to the politicization of education, and they blame elected officials for continually raising the requirements for promotion and graduation while millions of students grapple with the pressures of poverty, prejudice, and poor parenting.

Sources of Help

When it comes to delivering technical assistance and training to low-performing schools, various providers have been tapped by state agencies. Each type of provider comes with potential benefits and costs.

Consider the use of specialists from a state department of education. Local educators are known to question how well such individuals can relate to the daily demands of schools and classrooms. Specialists may be years removed from the front lines, and they may have little experience in persistently low-performing schools. Besides possible issues regarding the credibility of helpers, many state departments of education scaled back technical assistance when the recession hit in 2008. State officials have been slow to rebuild staffs in some states. When surveyed, 38 states reported significant gaps in the expertise needed to assist their lowest-performing schools (*State capacity*, 2015).

Principal Keith Look of Shawnee High School in Jefferson County, Kentucky, was skeptical after the state education department arranged for three specialists to be stationed in his school (Klein, 2011). When teachers saw that the specialists were not there to tell them what to do, however, they embraced the new arrivals and what they had to offer. Funding for the technical assistance team unfortunately ran out shortly after the team took up residence at Shawnee.

Kentucky's effort to provide technical assistance seems marginal compared to the action taken by Alabama's state superintendent. Faced with districtwide low performance in Montgomery, Tommy Bice dispatched a turnaround team of 30 individuals to work with teachers, students, and parents to "reinvigorate" the school system (Turnaround team, October 8, 2013). Bice warned that he would compel uncooperative district officials to leave the district.

Several states have assigned retired principals to mentor newly appointed turnaround principals. These efforts have not been evaluated in any systematic way. As might be assumed, though, reactions seem to vary widely, depending on the perceived credibility of the mentor and the relationship that mentor and mentee are able to establish.

The original PASS program in Virginia included a school pairing arrangement. The VDOE matched a high-performing school with a low-performing school with the expectation that teams from the former would advise faculty from the latter on ways to boost student achievement. Anecdotal reports suggest that teachers in the low-performing schools did not always appreciate or value the advice they received. The pairings eventually were abandoned.

The California Office to Reform Education, as part of its ESEA Waiver proposal, has implemented a variation on school pairing. Participating school districts commit to collecting a wide range of data on student achievement, teacher effectiveness, and school performance. When data reveals that a particular school is achieving impressive results, information regarding its efforts is shared with less successful schools. A new role, school pairing facilitator, has been created to coordinate the exchange of information between participating schools.

Drawing on the experience and expertise of fellow educators and state department of education specialists are two sources of technical assistance and training, but many low-performing schools and districts prefer to engage the services of independent providers. In some states, they actually are required to do so. There long has been a market for educational consulting and professional development in failing schools, but demand surged following the allocation of billions of federal dollars for Race to the Top and School Improvement Grants. Hundreds of vendors from corporate giants like Pearson to university-based nonprofit groups to tiny local outfits with a few employees began to compete for contracts to help persistently low-performing schools and districts. In addition, dozens of educational management organizations vied for opportunities to operate schools.

With so much money at stake, it was probably inevitable that controversy and corruption would follow. Some providers, like Johns Hopkins in Buffalo, found it impossible to navigate local politics and still assist failing schools. In other cases, school board members grew impatient with outsiders and the slow pace of school improvement (Slayton, 2011). Accusations of collusion between district leaders and service providers have not been uncommon. Reference was made in chapter 4 to John Covington's expensive and questionable experiment with an online learning system. In chapter 2, Buffalo superintendent Pamela Brown got into trouble for hiring a consulting firm without the school board's knowledge. The firm employed two former Buffalo administrators who had been fired from the troubled school system.

In Chicago, Barbara Byrd-Bennett's tenure as chief of Chicago Public Schools ended amidst allegations that she had violated the law by signing a $20.5 million no-bid principal-training contract with an organization that once employed her (Rogers, 2015). Byrd-Bennett also failed to file state-required ethics statements in which she was supposed to list all sources of outside income and possible conflicts of interest.

Corruption in the delivery of sorely needed services to failing schools is bad enough, but in some cases the groups providing the services actually are ill-equipped to do so. Soon after the Obama administration committed huge sums of money to turning around low-performing schools, the *New York Times* ran an article exposing the inexperience and inadequacy of some of the organizations competing for federal funds (Dillon, 2010). In the article, former New York City schools chancellor Rudy Crew, himself a consulting firm head, likened the proliferation of technical assistance and training outfits to the "carpetbaggers and charlatans" that descended on the South after the Civil War.

It certainly is not illegal for corporate conglomerates to compete for technical assistance and training money, but questions can be raised when a huge company like Pearson contracts to assist schools in which students have used its textbooks to prepare to take its standardized tests. Since Race to the Top, Pearson and other large vendors also have been purchasing well-regarded professional developers and technical assistance programs to help low-performing schools when their students continue to struggle.

Some schools and school districts have learned to insist on performance guarantees when contracting with vendors for services. If the vendor's help fails to yield improvements in student achievement or other desired outcomes, the vendor forfeits a portion or all of its fee. State departments of education also have tried to help by vetting potential providers and publishing lists of approved vendors. State officials only allocate funds to local districts for vendors on these lists.

Such cautionary steps are prudent, given how much money is involved and the negative consequences of retaining the services of an ineffective consulting group. When the *Denver Post* investigated how federal funds were being spent to help Colorado's lowest-performing schools, it found that outside consultants were receiving 35%, or $9.4 million, of the state's $26.6 million allocation (Brown, 2012). A list of seemingly excessive expenditures was given, including $185,748 a year for a "change leader" and $267,000 a year for two leadership coaches for Pueblo city schools. The article went on to decry the fact that no national effort was being made to track how federal funds are being spent by local schools and districts or to determine the return on taxpayers' investment.

The delivery of effective technical assistance and training is not just a matter of who or what group provides it but also the timing of help. It is likely that there are certain points in the turnaround process, depending on the local context, when assistance is especially critical. Providing training *before* a plan is implemented, not afterward, is one lesson many schools had to learn the hard way. Giving technical assistance first, before local planners develop a school improvement plan, instead of having them develop a draft and then critiquing it and requiring multiple revisions is another such lesson, one that Buffalo educators took a while to learn

The intensity of assistance also can become an issue. Just as there can be too little help, there can be too much. Overwhelming school personnel with teams of experts can lead to mixed messages, confusion, and ultimately to a loss of focus. Technical assistance, regardless of who provides it, should be carefully and thoughtfully coordinated. Experts must realize that schools may lack the capacity to address every identified need for improvement at the same time.

Requirements versus Options

One of the greatest challenges facing state officials in the post-NCLB era has been finding ways to hold educators accountable for student outcomes without creating so many mandates and forms to fill out that the process becomes self-defeating. Most observers probably would agree that educators' time is better spent working with the children left behind than completing forms and reports. Compliance is no substitute for professional competence and caring.

Various aspects of the school turnaround process have been subject, depending on the state, to exacting specifications without leeway for professional judgment and local customization. Among these are the format for school turnaround plans and the strategies that must be implemented in an effort to reverse a pattern of persistent failure.

Consider the example of Florida's School Improvement Plan template, the heart of the Sunshine State's differentiated accountability system. The 2012–2013 version ran 70 pages and was required for all low-performing schools. Below is a partial list of the information required for those completing the annual plan:

- Names, degrees, certifications, number of years at current school, number of years as an administrator, and prior performance record for all school administrators and instructional coaches
- School-based strategies used to recruit and retain high-quality, effective teachers
- Number of instructional staff and paraprofessionals who are teaching out-of-field and/or received less than an effective rating
- Description of teacher mentoring program
- Description of how federal, state, and local services and programs are coordinated and integrated in the school
- Description of state-mandated Multi-tiered System of Supports (RtI) and how it functions
- Description of state-mandated Literacy Leadership Team and how it functions
- Description of plans to assist preschool children in transition from early childhood programs to local elementary schools (if applicable)
- Description of how the school ensures that every teacher contributes to the reading improvement of every student (for grades 6–12 only)
- Description of how the school incorporates students' academic and career planning, as well as course selections, so that students' course of study is personally meaningful

All of the above information was called for in Part I of the Florida School Improvement Plan. Part II included 61 pages for improvement goals in specified areas. For each goal, planners had to list anticipated barriers to achieving the goal, strategies for overcoming barriers and achieving the goal, the person or position responsible for monitoring the improvement effort, the process used to determine the effectiveness of the strategy, and the evaluation tool. For each content area, space was provided for multiple goals. In reading, for example, possible goals ranged from increasing the percentage of students scoring at Achievement Level 4 or better on the Florida Comprehensive Assessment Test (FCAT) to increasing the percentage of students in the lowest quartile making learning gains in reading. Additionally, room was provided for reading goals for various student subgroups.

The School Improvement Plan, once completed, had to be reviewed by a state-mandated School Advisory Council (SAC). A majority of the SAC members could not be employed by the school district. Every School Improvement Plan then needed to be approved by the school board of the district.

Periodically, Florida officials have added other requirements for schools. Lesson Study and Professional Learning Communities, for instance, have been pushed by the Florida Department of Education. In 2014, Florida legislators mandated that the 300 lowest-performing elementary schools in the state had to expand their school day by one hour and use that time for reading.

The Florida Department of Education eventually realized that its School Improvement Plan template had grown too cumbersome for educators. In December 2014, the FDOE rolled out a significantly streamlined set of guidelines for School Improvement Plans (Form SIP-1, 2014). The heart of Form SIP-1, as the new plan is called, is an eight-step planning and problem-solving process for implementing school improvement. Not only did the FDOE provide for greater flexibility in how low-performing schools can tackle the challenge of raising student achievement, but it also recognized that plans often benefit from midcourse corrections. School personnel are encouraged to revisit their plans after midyear assessment data have been compiled and consider appropriate adjustments in light of the data.

Along with the modified form for School Improvement Plans, the FDOE introduced an expanded set of turnaround options for low-performing schools. The options include the following:

- Option 1: District-Managed Turnaround—The district will manage the implementation of the turnaround plan in the school. A school that earns a grade of "D" for three consecutive years must implement the district-managed turnaround option.
- Option 2: Closure—The district will reassign students to another school or schools and monitor progress of each reassigned student.
- Option 3: Charter—The district will close and reopen the school as one or more charter schools, each with a governing board that has a demonstrated record of effectiveness.
- Option 4: External Operator—The district will contract with an outside entity that has a demonstrated record of effectiveness to operate a school.
- Option 5: Hybrid—The district will implement a hybrid of turnaround Options 1–4 or other reform models that have a demonstrated record of effectiveness.

When a Florida school district opts for a district-managed turnaround, the FDOE also requires a second step, referred to as Turnaround Option Plan—Phase 2 (TOP-2). This process involves a set of assurances that the district is ready and willing to support a school turnaround (Form TOP-2, 2014). The six assurances are listed in box 5.2.

BOX 5.2: AREAS OF ASSURANCE

The district shall use the District Improvement and Assistance Plan (DIAP) to document compliance with the following assurances:

Assurance 1: The district shall ensure the district-based leadership team includes the superintendent; associate superintendent(s) of curriculum, general and special education leaders, curriculum specialists, behavior specialists, student services personnel, human resources directors, professional development leaders, and specialists in other areas relevant to the school's circumstances, such as assessment, English-language learners, and gifted learners.

Assurance 2: The district leadership team shall develop, support, and facilitate the implementation of policies and procedures that guide the school-based leadership team and provide direct support systems.

Assurance 3: The district shall adopt a new governance structure for the school, which may include, but is not limited to, requiring the school to report to a new "turnaround office" in the district or appointing a "turnaround lead" at the district level who reports directly to the superintendent and directly supervises the principal.

Assurance 4: The district shall give the school sufficient operating flexibility in areas such as staffing, scheduling, and budgeting, to fully implement a comprehensive approach to substantially improve student achievement outcomes and increase graduation rates in high schools.

Assurance 5: The district shall employ a reliable system to reassign or replace the majority of the instructional staff whose students' failure to improve can be attributed to the faculty.

Assurance 6: The district shall ensure teachers are not rehired at the school, unless they are effective or highly effective instructors, as defined in the district's approved evaluation system, pursuant to section 1012.34, Florida Statutes.

Florida's willingness to provide schools and districts with greater flexibility than originally allowed under the stipulations of Race to the Top is reminiscent of Indiana's adoption of transformation zones. Other states as well have sought or are seeking to create additional turnaround options that allow local educational leaders more room for innovation.

Another aspect of technical assistance where states can choose to be more or less prescriptive is improvement strategies. Rhode Island offers an interesting example in this regard. As part of its request for a waiver from certain NCLB requirements, the Rhode Island Department of Elementary and Secondary Education (RIDESE) proposed a system based on three options for low-performing schools. The first option involved school closure. Restart, the second option, entailed converting an existing school or shutting it down and reopening as a new school. The third option, called the flex model, requires districts "to select a comprehensive package of intervention strategies from a RIDESE-developed and managed list of 28 empirically proven intervention strategies" (*ESEA Flexibility Request*, 2012, p. 85).

Guidelines for the flex model explain that it reflects the basic principles of response to intervention (RtI) by classifying the 28 intervention strategies into three tiers based on their intensity and scope. Priority Schools, the lowest-performing schools in the state, must select and implement no fewer than nine intervention strategies. Guidelines specify how many strategies should be chosen from particular categories or tiers. A sample from the "Menu of Interventions" is provided in table 5.1.

Rhode Island's flex model is another illustration of how state departments of education are trying to provide greater latitude for local educators while maintaining some degree of structured accountability. The counterposition to such hybrid models holds that students in the lowest-performing schools may be put at even greater risk by allowing local educators to make choices when they already had a chance to prove themselves and fell short of the mark.

A Comprehensive Approach

Massachusetts's Office of District and School Turnaround (ODST) has established one of the nation's most comprehensive technical assistance programs. Focusing on the state's Commissioner's Districts—the 10 largest school districts—the ODST has implemented three primary strategies for helping low-performing schools (LiCalsi, Citkowicz, Friedman, & Brown, 2015):

- District Liaisons. Liaisons include ODST staff members who serve as project managers and coordinate support to the districts.
- Priority Partners. Partners include external organizations that support turnaround efforts in four areas of support: maximizing learning time; the effective use of data; social, emotional, and health needs; and district systems of support.

Table 5.1.   Menu of Interventions

Flex Model Intervention Strategy Option

Leadership	*Support*	*Infrastructure*	*Content*
Intervention III Strategies: Priority Schools select one from each area. Focus Schools select two strategies from areas of their choice.			
L-III. 1: Removal of building principal and replacement with a leader with experience and/or training in turnaround environments	S-III. 1: Require at least 30 hours of focused professional development with a focus on instructional strategies to support students with disabilities and English learners	I-III. 1: Implement staff recommitment process to substantially different working conditions, including definition of school hours, job assignment, and job duties	C-III. 1: Implement comprehensive improvement of instructional approaches for struggling students, including focused professional development and a system for student progress monitoring
L-III. 2: Restructure building leadership team to dramatically increase time available for instructional leadership	S-III. 2: Hire building-level instructional specialists to support educators to serve English learners, students with disabilities, and other students at risk for failure	I-III. 2: Dramatically increase common planning time and implement a system for its effective utilization, both horizontally and vertically	C-III. 2: Review student course-taking patterns and make substantial changes to school schedule and student placement to ensure access to rigorous academic core

Source: *ESEA Flexibility Request*, May 23, 2012 (Washington, DC: U.S. Department of Education), p. 88.

- School Redesign Grants (SRGs). SRGs are competitive funds that support turnaround efforts in persistently underperforming schools.

The American Institutes for Research (AIR) was commissioned to evaluate the ODST program (LiCalsi et al., 2015). Outcomes for schools that received SRGs were compared to outcomes of similar non-SRG schools over the same time period. Students in SRG schools performed better on the English and mathematics sections of the Massachusetts Comprehensive Assessment System (MCAS) than their counterparts in non-SRG schools. The effects were statistically significant after the first, second, and third years of SRG funding and support.

Additional analysis indicated that receipt of an SRG was associated with a decrease in the achievement gap between English-language learners and non-English-language learners. The achievement gap also narrowed between students from low-income homes and students whose homes were not designated as low-income. The gap in school attendance between students in special education versus students who were not in special education also decreased in SRG schools. AIR researchers concluded that the disbursement of SRG grants along with state-directed technical assistance yielded generally positive effects on student achievement.

Besides the ODST assistance program, the Massachusetts Department of Elementary and Secondary Education also has implemented the Wraparound Zones (WAZ) initiative in order to create coordinated district systems "that allow schools to proactively and systematically address students' nonacademic needs" (Gandhi et al., 2015, p. ix). Participating schools receive help identifying student needs and addressing them, improving school climate and culture, building community coalitions, and establishing district systems of support. An AIR evaluation of the WAZ initiative found that students in WAZ schools performed better on the MCAS English and mathematics assessments than students in comparison schools (Gandhi et al., 2015). The impact of state assistance was greatest for third- and fourth-grade students.

The Need for Leadership

If there is one thing that turnaround experts agree on, it is the crucial importance of school leadership. Where differences of opinion arise, they concern how best to ensure that capable turnaround leaders are trained and available to direct school improvement. Some organizations such as New Leaders for New Schools believe in locating talented prospective principals outside of conventional principal preparation programs. Most states, however, still require public school principals to possess an appropriate administrative credential from an accredited institution.

The question then arises: What do turnaround leaders need to know beyond what they learned in their principal preparation program? The University of Virginia's School Turnaround Specialist Program (STSP), mentioned earlier in this chapter, bases its curriculum on seven tenets derived from sound business practices as well as research on effective school leadership. The tenets include:

1. Understanding the school turnaround context and the fundamentals of successful turnarounds
2. Developing and communicating a vision that includes the need for urgent change
3. Establishing a culture of high expectations
4. Building effective coalitions and implementing shared decision making
5. Using data to drive decisions and to monitor/measure the need for midcourse corrections

6. Identifying innovation opportunities and developing strategic plans
7. Teaching state/district/school administrators to think like leaders, not simply managers (Darden Curry PLE, 2011)

The individuals chosen to participate in the Virginia program are, for the most part, experienced school administrators who already possess an administrative credential and successful experience in a leadership role.

An alternative approach was taken by the Florida Department of Education. Using Race to the Top funds, the FDOE collaborated with the Southern Regional Education Board to design and implement a leader development program for promising educators who were still teachers. The Florida Turnaround Leaders Program (FTLP) identified over 100 educators committed to leading the improvement process in low-performing Florida schools (Duke, 2014).

The FTLP's theory of action for turnaround leaders consists of five critical components:

1. Awareness of the problems that must be addressed and the obstacles that must be overcome in order to raise performance
2. Understanding why the problems and obstacles exist
3. Planning that provides the focus and direction necessary to guide action and maximize impact
4. Competence to lead staff members in addressing the problems and overcoming the obstacles
5. Commitment to lead staff members in addressing problems and overcoming obstacles (Duke, 2014, p. 81)

FTLP trainees spent two and a half years attending seminars, completing online modules, undertaking a yearlong, team-based practicum in a low-performing school, and finally tackling a semester-long internship as an assistant principal in a low-performing school. The FDOE hoped that the unique program would create a model for how other states can develop a turnaround leader pipeline. Based on Florida's experience, South Carolina has implemented a similar program.

Besides full-blown preparation programs like the STSP and the FTLP, efforts to provide capable leadership for low-performing schools include various mentoring and coaching arrangements. Mentors and coaches typically are experienced school leaders hired by state departments of education, regional service centers, and private vendors to provide on-site guidance and support to turnaround principals.

No one disputes the value of specialized training and ongoing coaching for turnaround leaders. Case studies of effective turnaround leaders suggest, however, that there is more to leadership than mastery of a set of advanced skills. Leadership is also a function of certain attributes and personality traits, including the desire to make a difference, the discipline to focus, the creativity to plan effectively, the flexibility to adjust when necessary, and the patience to persist in the face of disappointment (Duke, 2015, pp. 18–21). Acknowledging the importance of these qualities means that attention must be paid to the selection as well as the training of turnaround leaders.

This chapter has reviewed various kinds of technical assistance and training that states have made available to help low-performing schools improve. The record so far suggests that technical assistance and training, in and of itself, does not guarantee improvement, however. Much has to do with who provides assistance and training, how it is provided, whether or not it is coordinated and supported by school and district leaders, and the extent to which educators on the front lines accept or resist it.

REFERENCES

Brown, J. 2012, February 19. Cost doesn't spell success for Colorado schools using consultants to improve achievement. *Denver Post.* Retrieved from http://www.denverpost.com/investigations/ci_19997418.

Christie, K. 2007. *The state role in accelerating student growth in low-performing high schools.* Denver, CO: Education Commission of the States.

Darden Curry PLE. 2011. *University of Virginia.* Retrieved from http://www.darden.virginia.edu/web/Darden-Curry-PLE/UVA-School-Turnaround/Curriculum.

Dillon, S. 2010, August 9. Inexperienced companies chase U.S. school funds. *New York Times.* Retrieved from http://www.nytimes.com/2010/08/10/education/10schools.html?_r=4&hp=&pagewanted=.

Duke, D. L. 2004. *The Challenges of Educational Change.* Boston: Pearson.

———. 2014. A bold approach to developing leaders for low-performing schools. *Management in Education, 28*(3), 80–85.

———. 2015. *Leadership for Low-Performing Schools.* Lanham, MD: Rowman & Littlefield.

Duke, D. L., & Landahl, M. 2011. "Raising test scores was the easy part": A case study of the third year of school turnaround. *International Studies in Educational Administration, 39*(3), 91–114.

ESEA Flexibility Request. 2012, May 23. OMB No. 1810-0708. Washington, DC: U.S. Department of Education.

Form SIP-1. 2014. *Florida Department of Education.* Retrieved from https://www.floridaCIMS.org.

Form TOP-2. 2014. *Florida Department of Education.* Retrieved from https://www.floridaCIMS.org.

Gandhi, A., Slama, R., Park, S., Russo, P., Bzura, R., & Williamson, S. 2015. *Focusing on the whole student: Final report on the Massachusetts Wraparound Zones.* Washington, DC: American Institutes for Research.

Klein, A. 2011, February 23. State specialists' team offers aid in turnaround. *Education Week, 21.*

LiCalsi, C., Citkowicz, M., Friedman, L. B., & Brown, M. 2015. *Evaluation of Massachusetts Office of District and School Turnaround assistance to Commissioner's Districts and Schools.* Washington, DC: American Institutes for Research.

Player, D., & Katz, V. 2013. *School improvement in Ohio and Missouri. An evaluation of the School Turnaround Specialist Program.* CEPWC Working Paper Series. Curry School of Education, University of Virginia.

Rogers, P. 2015, June 1. Departing schools chief failed to file required ethics statements. *NBC Chicago*. Retrieved from http://www.nbcchicago.com/investigations/barbara-byrd-bennett-305759911.html.

Slayton, J. 2011, February 18. Schools turnaround company questioned. *Richmond Times-Dispatch*. Retrieved from http://www.richmond.com/news/article_759ae51b-b603-5a74-91e1-0884eb9ca370.html.

State capacity to support school turnaround. 2015. Washington, DC: Institute on Education Sciences, U.S. Department of Education.

Turnaround team sent to Ala. school district. 2013, October 8. *WFSA* [Montgomery, AL]. Retrieved from http://www.wsfa.com/story/23644846/turnaround-team-sent-to-ala-school-district.

Virginia/support for school improvement. n.d. *Virginia Department of Education.* Retrieved from http://www.doe.virginia.gov/support/school_improvement/training/teacher_leader/session_2/session_2.ppt.

Wallinger, L. M. 2006. *Virginia's role in turning around low-performing schools.* Presentation at the National Forum on Education Policy, Education Commission of the States, Minneapolis, MN.

Warner, M. September 2, 2003. Education for a lifetime. *Virginia Tech School of Education.* Retrieved from http://www.soe.vt.edu/highered/files/Perspectives_PolicyNews/09-03/Governor_Mark_Warner.pdf.

SIX

Choice, Community Action, and Closure

Technical assistance and training are the most common ways that states have intervened in the lowest-performing schools on behalf of the children left behind. School takeovers and assignment to special state districts meanwhile have grabbed the most headlines. There are other measures as well that some states have implemented in an effort to address the needs of students stuck in failing schools.

Expanding the choices available to parents of children in persistently low-performing schools is one popular measure. Arguments for greater choice frequently note that well-to-do parents always have had the opportunity to choose schools that perform well. Extending such choice to less affluent parents is only fair, advocates contend.

Some states have gone one step further and created so-called parent trigger laws that empower parents to insist that failing schools undertake the turnaround process. When turnarounds also fail, the last resort may be to close failing schools. Although districts are most likely to initiate school closures, some states also have chosen to do so — as was seen when Indiana decided to shut down a Gary school. When a school is closed, it may remain closed or it can be reconstituted and opened as an entirely new entity. Officially referred to as the *restart option*, reconstitution may involve reopening a closed school under a charter school operator, a charter management organization, or an educational management organization. Restart schools must enroll, within the grades they serve, any former student who wishes to attend the school (*State capacity to support*, 2015). Chapter 6 examines each of these additional measures.

EXPANDED CHOICES

When many people think about expanded choices in schooling, charter schools immediately come to mind. Although charter schools certainly were created with parental choice in mind, they were not necessarily targeted for parents of the children left behind—just the opposite in certain cases, in fact. Charter schools are seen by some as an alternative for parents who have given up on public schools. Diane Ravitch (2010, p. 145) characterizes charter schools as "havens for the motivated."

In chapter 4, the discussion of both Tennessee's Achievement School District and Michigan's Education Achievement Authority pointed out that charter operators were reluctant to take over persistently low-performing schools. They preferred to start new schools from scratch, often growing the schools one grade at a time. The notable exception, of course, is Louisiana's Recovery School District, which fostered charter schools for the express purpose of serving the neediest children in Orleans Parish.

Given this book's focus on the lowest-performing schools, the most appropriate place to mention charter schools comes later in the chapter, when the issue of school closure and reconstitution is discussed. It is the case in many states that some reconstituted schools become charter schools. In the present segment of the chapter, other choice-based strategies are examined. They include state policies on open enrollment, vouchers, and tax credits.

Open Enrollment

The policy of allowing students access to schools on a citywide basis, once known as "freedom of choice," has a curious history. In Richmond, Virginia, and other southern cities, "this policy was intended to slow the progress of school integration by refraining from assigning students to schools for the purpose of racial mixing" (Duke, 1995, p. 208). School officials opposed to integration reasoned that most parents, both black and white, if given the choice of schools, would opt to send their children to schools close to home. As long as Realtors practiced "red-lining" and neighborhoods remained mostly segregated by race, "freedom of choice" therefore posed little threat to the existing order.

Freedom of choice plans were struck down by the courts, but eventually they resurfaced as open enrollment policies intended for a completely different purpose: to allow low-income families greater access to high-performing schools and to promote desegregation. Although open enrollment policies typically are associated with school district actions, many actually are grounded in state law and federal initiatives such as magnet schools.

According to a report published by the Education Commission of the States (*Open enrollment 50-state report*, 2013), there are two basic types of open-enrollment policies: intradistrict and interdistrict. The former allows students to transfer to another school within their school district, while the latter permits students to transfer to a school outside their home district. Some of these policies are mandatory for districts, while others are voluntary.

The No Child Left Behind (NCLB) Act provided a boost to intradistrict open enrollment by giving parents the option to transfer their children to another district school if the home school failed to make Adequate Yearly Progress for two consecutive years. By 2013, schools were required to allow within-district transfers in 23 states (*Open enrollment 50-state report*, 2013). Mikulecky (2013) pointed out, however, that relatively few parents have taken advantage of this option. In states where studies were conducted after the passage of NCLB, the percentage of eligible students whose parents elected to transfer them from failing schools rarely exceeded 1% (Ravitch, 2010, p. 99).

The first interdistrict open-enrollment policy was passed into law in Minnesota in 1988. By 2013, 21 states had laws requiring districts to permit students to cross boundaries in order to attend school (*Open enrollment 50-state report*, 2013). When researchers studied the impact of interdistrict open enrollment in the Twin Cities region (Minneapolis and St. Paul metropolitan area), they found that racial segregation had increased (Mikulecky, 2013). White students were more likely to take advantage of the transfer option, and they tended to move to districts with greater percentages of white students than the districts they left (*Open enrollment and racial*, 2012). The same phenomenon also was found in interdistrict open-enrollment programs in Rochester, New York, and Omaha, Nebraska, leading the researchers to conclude that open enrollment on a regional basis leads to a shift from within-district segregation to between-district segregation (Finnigan et al., 2015).

Perhaps the most illuminating study of open enrollment on an interdistrict basis was conducted in Colorado (Lavery & Carlson, 2015). The researchers began by pointing out that interdistrict open enrollment is the nation's largest school choice program, surpassing charter schools, voucher schemes, and other efforts to provide students with more educational options. The study investigated five years of student data (2005–2006 to 2009–2010) from the entire population of students attending public schools in Colorado. Of 832,368 public school and charter school students enrolled in 2009–2010, 60,916 were involved in interdistrict open enrollment programs and 66,556 attended charter schools.

Dating from 1994, Colorado's open enrollment law encourages but does not require districts to give interdistrict enrollment priority to applicants from low-performing schools (Lavery & Carlson, 2015, p. 750). Advocates of open enrollment as a strategy to help the children left behind cannot be anything but disappointed by the findings of the present study. Lavery and Carlson reported that socioeconomically disadvantaged students were significantly less likely to open enroll than their more affluent peers (p. 771). Rather than increasing diversity across districts, Colorado's open enrollment policy appears to have contributed to greater concentrations of disadvantaged students in certain school districts. The researchers concluded that interdistrict open enrollment in Colorado constituted a "public school voucher program for middle-class and upper-middle-class families" (p. 771).

While open-enrollment policies vary from state to state, most share some common features (Mikulecky, 2013). State and local funding, for example, typically follow transferring students. Districts and schools are ensured a "space available" opt-out option. States, in most cases, are prohibited from accepting or denying student transfers based on such factors as prior achievement, disabilities, and/or English-language proficiency. California's Open Enrollment Act is unusual in that it allows students to enroll in a higher-performing school, assuming there are seats available, if their current school is identified by the state education department as one of the 1,000 lowest-achieving schools in the state (Reid, March 18, 2015).

Compelling evidence that open enrollment benefits the children left behind is hard to come by. Proponents argue that open enrollment contributes to constructive competition between schools and districts and greater accountability, both of which can improve schooling for all students. Critics counter that open enrollment leads to increased economic and racial segregation. The most highly motivated students are "creamed off," leaving low-performing schools with greater concentrations of struggling and unmotivated students (Mikulecky, 2013).

Vouchers

The use of vouchers to give students an opportunity to attend nonpublic schools predated the passage of NCLB by more than a decade. Milwaukee's program was launched in 1990, followed by programs in Cleveland and Washington, D.C. Interest in voucher schemes waned in the wake of charter school legislation but revived in several states in the new century. It is worth noting that, when John Boehner gave his last radio address before stepping down as Speaker of the House in October of 2015, he called for an expansion of voucher programs.

One of the most expansive voucher schemes was approved by the Indiana legislature in 2011. Unlike some other schemes, students do not have to attend a failing public school in order to be eligible for a voucher (So you want to go, 2013). Indiana's voucher program has been praised by choice advocates because it allows middle-income parents to take advantage of state funds. Indiana legislators eventually removed the cap on the number of students who can participate in the voucher program and made vouchers available to students already enrolled in private schools

(Prothero, 2015). Clearly, legislators were not thinking only of the children left behind when they approved these voucher measures.

In the first year of the program, 3,919 students received vouchers. By 2014, 29,000 students were taking advantage of vouchers to attend 316 nonpublic schools in Indiana (School choice programs, 2015). By 2015, about half of Indiana's 1.1 million school-age children qualified for the voucher program. Participating nonpublic schools are required to be accredited, administer the Indiana Statewide Testing for Educational Progress (ISTEP), and refrain from discriminating on the basis of race and national origin. Nonpublic schools in Indiana along with public schools are subject to the state's A–F school accountability rating system. Nonpublic schools that receive a D or F rating for two consecutive years are ineligible to receive new voucher students.

The Center for Tax and Budget Accountability produced a report in 2015 in which the following question was addressed: Can Indiana expect its school choice program to enhance student performance or help build a better public education system statewide (*Analysis of Indiana School Choice*, 2015)? The report's conclusions were not very encouraging. Consider the first finding: "None of the independent studies performed on the most lauded and long-standing voucher programs extant in the U.S.—Milwaukee, Wisconsin; Cleveland, Ohio; and Washington, D.C.— found any statistical evidence that children who utilized vouchers performed better than children who did not and remained in public schools" (*Analysis of Indiana School Choice*, 2015, p. 3).

When the investigators looked at a demographic breakdown of voucher recipients in 2011–2012 and 2014–2015, they found that the percentage of white recipients had climbed from 46.4% to 61.1%, while the percentages of black and Latino recipients fell from 24.1% and 20.3% to 14.4.% and 16.7% respectively (p. 21). A disturbing conclusion in the report was that the diversion of tax dollars away from Indiana's public schools could have the effect of diminishing student achievement statewide (p. 3).

At least one study found evidence that vouchers have been beneficial (Witte et al., 2014). In 2009 Wisconsin Act 28 was signed into law. It required private schools participating in the Milwaukee Parental Choice Program (MPCP), which provided vouchers for students to attend private schools, to test all voucher students in grades 3 to 8 and 10 in reading and mathematics. The tests were the same required of public school students, thereby allowing researchers to compare the achievement of voucher students with students attending Milwaukee Public Schools. The results for the first testing year (2010–2011) showed substantial growth for voucher students, particularly in mathematics. Students with higher levels of earlier academic achievement, not surprisingly, also performed significantly better.

The scarcity of evidence that voucher schemes benefit students in general or the children left behind in particular has not caused existing programs to disappear or stopped new programs from emerging. In 2015 Nevada became the newest state to permit tax dollars to be used so students can attend nonpublic schools. What alarms advocates for students in failing schools is the fact that programs like Nevada's and Indiana's are not designed exclusively for the neediest students. In Nevada's case, all students, regardless of family income, are eligible for vouchers. Eskelsen Garcia, president of the National Education Association, expressed the fear held by many of those committed to public education: "Vouchers will exacerbate the gap between rich and poor by giving a public subsidy to affluent families that choose elite private schools, which are unlikely to admit students who struggle academically or cannot afford tuition even with a voucher" (Layton & Brown, 2015).

Tax Credits

Yet another way that some states have increased the educational choices available to parents are tax credit programs that encourage corporations and other entities to donate funds to scholarship-funding organizations (SFOs). In return for donations, donors receive tax credits. Indiana's program, for example, allows corporate and individual donors to receive a 50% state tax credit.

One of the oldest and largest programs is the Florida Tax Credit Scholarship Program (FTCSP). Created in 2001, the FTCSP has provided a voluntary means for expanding educational options for children from families of limited means. Students are eligible for a scholarship if they qualify for free or reduced-price school lunches under the National School Lunch Act or they have been placed in foster care. The maximum amount allowed for a private school scholarship in 2014–2015 was $5,272. Students electing to attend a Florida public school located outside their home district can receive a $500 scholarship.

The state exercises various controls over the FTCSP. The Florida Department of Education, for instance, must annually verify the eligibility of SFOs, private schools, and expenditures for scholarships. Students receiving scholarships must maintain good attendance and take whatever norm-referenced assessment is offered by their private schools.

Pennsylvania's Opportunity Scholarship Tax Credit (OSTC) is unusual in that it specifically targets students in failing schools. To qualify for a scholarship to attend a private or parochial school, a student must reside in the catchment area of the lowest-performing 15% of public schools in the state. More than $17 million in scholarships were awarded to needy students in 2013–2014 (Real accountability, 2015).

According to the National Conference of State Legislatures (School choice, 2015), 14 states offer some form of tax credit to those donating scholarship funds. All of the programs target students from low-income families, but not necessarily those stuck in failing public schools. Some programs place a cap on the amount that can be awarded in tax credits in a given year.

Little data exists on the impact of tax credit programs. Some participating states do not require nonpublic schools to administer annual standardized tests, making it difficult to determine if scholarship recipients have transferred to schools performing less well than the schools they left. This point gives rise to an interesting question: Should a parent whose child qualifies for a scholarship be permitted to choose a nonpublic school with a poor track record or no data on student achievement? Public school advocates argue that nonpublic schools should be as accountable for measured student achievement as public schools.

COMMUNITY ACTION

Efforts by states to ensure that parents have a voice in the operation of their children's schools are not a new phenomenon. In 1988, Illinois legislators passed a bill intended to transform the struggling Chicago school system. A key element of the legislation required elected local school councils (LSCs) for every Chicago school. Each LSC had to consist of 11 teachers, parents, and other community members, but parents and community members had to constitute a majority. LSCs were granted the authority to (1) hire and fire principals, (2) control academic programs through approval of mandated annual School Improvement Plans, (3) oversee the school's share of state Title I funds, and (4) contract for support services (Duke, 2010, p. 56).

The Kentucky Education Reform Act of 1990, an omnibus reform bill that altered everything from school finance to accountability measures, included a provision for school councils in order to decentralize school policy making and planning. Each council consisted of the principal, three teachers, and two parents. Teachers and parents had to be elected. Councils were given the authority to make decisions regarding curriculum, instruction, discipline, extracurricular programs, and the school budget. Councils also had to be consulted when principals hired teachers. When the principal's position became vacant, school councils were charged with hiring a new principal.

Measures involving parents and community members, such as those for Chicago and Kentucky, applied to all public schools. In 2010, however, a new type of community action bill was passed in California. The Parent Empowerment Act targeted low-performing schools. Dubbed the "parent trigger" law, this bill empowered parents to petition school districts for sweeping educational improvements and staffing changes in struggling schools. Within two years of the Parent Empowerment Act's passage, six other states had followed suit: Connecticut, Indiana, Louisiana, Mississippi, Ohio, and Texas. A national advocacy group—Parent Revolution—with support from several major foundations initiated a campaign to promote parent trigger laws across the United States.

In order to press for drastic changes in a local school, parents in California must obtain support from 50% of students' parents, plus one. Changes range from hiring a new principal and replacing staff to converting the school to a charter. Most of the small number of schools where parents have used the law serve predominantly Hispanic and African American students from low-income families (Reid, March 18, 2015). There has not been a lot of hard evidence on the impact of parent trigger reforms; although Parent Revolution claimed that state tests in science revealed impressive gains in several California schools that underwent reforms following community action (Positive early indications, 2014).

Controversy has characterized the parent trigger process since it first was initiated in California. Parents may decide that sweeping changes are needed but disagree on the nature of the changes to be made. School districts also have rejected petitions from parents. Parent Revolution has been accused of self-promotion and unethical practices (Reid, March 18, 2015).

Although there have been few reports of sustained turnarounds in schools where the parent trigger law has been exercised, there may be some unexpected benefits to the legislation. The existence of a parent trigger law can serve as an inducement for school district officials to negotiate with disgruntled parents. Such may have been the case when a partnership agreement was brokered between parents at West Athens Elementary School and the Los Angeles Unified School District. Parents were able to acquire $300,000 in additional funding for the school without resorting to a parent trigger petition.

Parent trigger laws are not the only steps being taken by states to ensure that parents with children in low-performing schools have a voice. Connecticut's Public Act 10-111, for example, empowers the commissioner of education and state board of education to create parent–teacher school governance councils with the authority to petition local boards of education to reconstitute failing schools. Utah's Senate Bill 235 requires a local school board of a low-performing school to establish a school turnaround committee composed of a board member, the principal, two teachers, and three parents. The committee is charged with partnering with an independent school turnaround expert to develop an improvement plan for the school.

SCHOOL CLOSURE AND RECONSTITUTION

Among the most drastic actions that a state can take in order to help the children left behind are (1) closing a persistently low-performing school and transferring students to other schools and (2) school closure followed by the opening of a new school on site (restart option). It is important to note that school districts have closed schools for various reasons for many years, but state-initiated school closures involving failing schools are relatively recent and rare actions.

The experience of Houston's Sam Houston High School offers an interesting example of what can happen when a state acts to close a school with deep roots in the local community (Duke, 2012). In 2008 Texas Education Agency commissioner Robert Scott ordered the closure of Sam Houston High School because of persistent low academic performance and a high dropout rate. The action required that the school's name be changed, that the principal and a significant number of faculty members be replaced, and that half the students be transferred to other schools.

There was one major problem with this plan. The local community served by the high school had grown very attached to the school. Many of the students in the mostly Hispanic high school lived nearby and walked to school. In order to placate the community, officials with the Houston school district worked out an ingenious plan.

The existing campus of Sam Houston High School would be divided into a separate ninth-grade center and an upper school focused on math, science, and technology. Houston officials argued that this arrangement met the Texas Education's Agency's requirement that half of the existing student body be moved because a quarter of Sam Houston's students would be assigned to the ninth grade center (operated as a separate school) while another quarter of the students (seniors) graduated and would no longer attend Sam Houston.

The fall of 2008 saw the opening of Sam Houston Math, Science and Technology Center and the adjacent Ninth Grade College Preparatory Academy. Both schools had new principals, and three quarters of the teachers were new. Within a year the new arrangement resulted in an "acceptable" rating from the state. The local community was pleased that its teenagers could continue to attend "their" school.

Preserving neighborhood schools, even when they struggle academically, can be important, argues Diane Ravitch. As she puts it,

> Our schools will not improve if we continue to close neighborhood schools in the name of reform. Neighborhood schools are often the anchors of their communities, a steady presence that helps to cement the bonds of community among neighbors. Most are places with a history, laden with traditions and memories that help individuals resist fragmentation in their lives. (2010, p. 227)

Not everyone, however, would agree with Ravitch. Drawing on several studies of low-performing schools, Smarick (2010, p. 21), for instance, arrives at the following conclusion: "Looking back on the history of school turnaround efforts, the first and most important lesson is the 'Law of Incessant Inertia.' Once persistently low performing, the majority of schools will remain low performing despite being acted upon in innumerable ways." Going with the odds and discounting disruptions to established communities and students' lives, Smarick contends that the best course of action is to close the lowest-performing schools.

Support for this position comes from a study of low-performing schools in 10 states (Stuit, 2010). Out of 2,025 low-performing district schools and charter schools, only 26 schools moved into the top half of their states' proficiency rankings within five years. While attaining this level of success in a relatively brief period of time might seem an unfair basis for judging turnarounds, the dramatically low figure is at least an indication of the challenges presented by the lowest-performing schools.

The fact that charter schools did not fare better than regular public schools in Stuit's study is worth noting, since school closures often are followed by the opening of a charter school, one of the options under the Department of Education's reconstitution provision. Charter schools in the study actually were likelier to be closed for low performance than district schools (Stuit, 2010, p. 30).

Advocates for closing persistently failing schools are apt to regard this finding as yet another reason to support charter schools. If a charter school continues to record poor marks, it is less likely to linger. As of 2013, 11 states had established laws *requiring* failing charter schools to close (Carlson & Lavertu, 2015a).

Not all states have laws that allow them to close schools or reconstitute schools after closures. A report published by the Education Commission of the States (Christie, 2007) indicated that 16 states had the authority to close low-performing schools and reopen them as charter schools. Thirty states permitted reconstitution of failing schools' staffs.

Just because some states have the authority to close and reconstitute low-performing schools does not mean they exercise this authority very frequently. A 2013 report by the Center on Reinventing Public Education (Jochim & Murphy, 2013) examined actions taken in 10 states: Colorado, Connecticut, Florida, Kentucky, Maryland, Michigan, Nevada, New Jersey, South Carolina, and Washington. Only three states closed at least one school—Colorado (3), South Carolina (1), and Washington (1). Three states ordered at least one reconstitution—Maryland (5), Colorado (1), and Connecticut (1).

School closures and reconstitutions have been more common in large urban school systems, particularly New York and Chicago. It should be noted, however, that these actions have been taken by mayors and/or their city school administrations, not by state authorities.

Between 2001 and 2006, for example, Chicago Public Schools closed 44 public schools because of poor academic performance or underutilization (de la Torre & Gwynne, 2009). Then in 2006, the school system shifted policy and focused on turning around academically weak schools instead of closing them. Parent and community opposition prompted this move. When researchers at the Consortium on Chicago School Research studied the impact of the prior school closures on Chicago students, they found little evidence to justify the drastic action. Among their findings were the following:

- Most students who transferred out of closing schools reenrolled in schools that were academically weak.
- Once students left schools slated for closing, on average the additional effects on their learning were neither negative nor positive.
- When displaced students reached high school, their on-track rates to graduate were no different than the rates of students who attended schools similar to those that closed (de la Torre & Gwynne, 2009, p. 2).

When Rahm Emanuel was elected mayor of Chicago in 2011, school closures were resumed, despite the lack of convincing evidence that the children left behind benefitted from these measures. Community activists brought suit against the city to stop the threatened closure of 50 schools. The suit alleged that the process by which schools were closed and students transferred violated federal law by not providing parents of disabled students with adequate opportunity to negotiate Individual Education Plans (IEPs) to ease the transition to new schools (Perlstein, 2013). The federal judge who handled the case ruled against the plaintiffs, however, holding that there was no proof that children "would suffer substantial harm as a result of the school closures" (Perlstein, 2013, p. 6).

The Emanuel administration went ahead and closed 49 schools, all of them serving poor black and Hispanic children. The closures later became an issue when Emanuel ran for reelection in 2015. His opponents claimed that the school closures disrupted the very neighborhoods that depended on their schools for stability and a sense of identity (Amin & Putzel, 2015). Emanuel countered that the closures were paying off because suspensions in Chicago schools had fallen and graduation rates were up.

New York City's Department of Education closed 91 schools between 2002 and 2010 for reasons similar to those in Chicago. When school system officials proposed closing 19 more schools in January 2010, parents affected by the action sought redress in the courts, and a state court placed the closures on hold. Robert Jackson, chair of the City Council Education Committee, voiced the misgivings held by many: "School closures displace many of the students most at risk. There is a 'domino effect' from school closings, leading to surrounding schools becoming overcrowded, then being targeted for closure themselves" (Zelon, 2010, p. 2).

Jackson and 18 city council members proposed an alternative to closing schools. A School Transformation Zone (STZ) would be created to oversee improvement efforts in low-performing schools. Schools would have three years to implement a range of strategies, including smaller classes, longer school days, academic tutoring, and targeted professional development for teachers and principals. Parents applauded the proposal, which was passed by the city council in May 2010. The New York City Department of Education, however, decided not to implement the STZ because the measures were judged to be insufficient to raise student achievement significantly.

A modified version of the STZ resurfaced following the election of Mayor Bill de Blasio. Dubbed the School Renewal Plan, the $150 million initiative targeting 94 of New York City's lowest-performing schools launched in the spring of 2015. An "executive superintendent" was appointed to oversee the project. De Blasio hoped that the School Renewal Plan would preempt efforts by New York governor Andrew Cuomo to assign failing schools in New York City to outside organizations. Under de Blasio's plan, schools receive intensive assistance for three years. Failure to improve after three years will result in closure.

TO CLOSE OR NOT TO CLOSE

School closure for the lowest-performing schools has emerged as one of the most contentious strategies to help the children left behind. Those most directly affected—students, parents, and teachers in schools designated for closure—tend to oppose the drastic measure. Proponents of closure include some politicians and policy makers as well as a few researchers who doubt that examples of successful turnarounds can be taken to scale. Supporters of charter schools also line up in favor of closing low-performing schools. Arguments on both sides range from the pragmatic to the emotional.

The irony of these arguments is that advocates for and against closure justify their positions in terms of protecting the interests of the children left behind.

Consider the position taken by some civil rights groups. In July 2010, the National Association for the Advancement of Colored People (NAACP), the National Urban League, and five other civil rights groups urged Secretary of Education Arne Duncan to "dismantle core pieces of his education agenda, arguing that his emphases on expanding charter schools, closing low-performing schools, and using competitive rather than formula funding are detrimental to low-income and minority children" (McNeil, 2010). When schools are closed, it is the lives of poor families that invariably are disrupted and the neighborhoods in which they live whose stability is threatened.

Hard evidence on the academic impact of school closures is scarce. What findings exist are mixed. Mention already has been made of the Chicago study (de la Torre & Gwynne, 2009) that reported most students from closing schools transferred to other academically weak schools and failed to experience positive effects from the switch. A follow-up study published six years later (de la Torre, Gordon, Moore, & Cowhy, 2015) sought to understand why families made particular choices of schools when their home schools were closed.

Recognizing the possible problems associated with school closure, Chicago Public Schools (CPS) created a policy that assigned displaced students to a "welcoming school" that was rated higher performing than their closed school. Because CPS has an open enrollment policy as well, students were not required to attend a welcoming school if they wished to attend another school and space was available. Researchers from the Consortium on Chicago School Research interviewed families in order to determine why they chose to attend a school other than an assigned school. In some cases, the chosen school actually performed below the level of the assigned school.

The study found that school choices often were made based on school proximity to home and the perceived safety of the school and its surroundings. Students also were more likely to attend an assigned welcoming school if it had been relocated to the site of the closed school, again demonstrating the importance of proximity to home. One of the most intriguing findings from the study concerned the way many families thought about the academic quality of a school. Rather than relying on a school's official rating by CPS, they defined quality in terms of "having after-school programs, certain curricula and courses, small class sizes, positive and welcoming school environments, and/or one-on-one attention from teachers in classes" (de la Torre et al., 2015, p. 3).

Researchers who studied the impact of school closures on student achievement in urban Ohio district and charter schools, however, reported findings quite different from the first Chicago study (Carlson & Lavertu, 2015b). A sophisticated research design was used to analyze the pre- and post-closure trends in reading and math achievement of 22,722 students in grades 3–8 who attended one of 198 schools that closed between 2006 and 2012. The findings indicated that closing a district-run school "increased the reading and math achievement of displaced students by 0.073 and 0.065 standard deviations, respectively—corresponding to 49 and 34 extra days of learning—by the third year after closure" (p. 9). Achievement gains for students displaced by charter school closures were greater in math, but negligible in reading.

The researchers credit achievement gains to the fact that higher quality schools were available in most cases for displaced students in Ohio.

The determination that a receiving school was higher quality was based on the fact that its students had higher average reading scores than the closing school. Should higher quality schools be unavailable for displaced students, the efficacy of school closure becomes questionable, according to the researchers.

When school closure is followed by reconstitution rather than transfer to another school, other issues may come into play. Rice and Malen (2010), for example, recognized that reconstitution depends on the availability of a capable replacement principal and a large number of replacement teachers. In many parts of the United States, such availability is anything but assured. Capable educators also may be reluctant to move to a reconstituted school because of the possibility of damaging their reputations and careers (Hamilton, Heilig, & Pazey, 2013).

If reconstitution is to be turned over to an outside provider, availability once again becomes a concern. Mention already has been made of the reluctance of charter organizations to take over an existing school and all of its students. When Colorado attempted to develop a list of approved restart providers, it failed to locate any providers willing to manage the full operation of a school (Kowal & Ableidinger, n.d.).

States can promulgate policies that expand the choices available to the children left behind. They can pass laws enabling parents to force low-performing schools to improve. They can insist that persistently low-performing schools be reconstituted or closed. The success of these and other initiatives discussed in this section, however, ultimately depends on the capacity for and commitment to improvement of local school districts. It is to the local realm of action that we now turn.

REFERENCES

Amin, S., & Putzel, C. 2015, May 27. School debate threatens Rahm Emanuel's re-election. *Al Jazeera America*. Retrieved from http://america.aljazeera.com/watch/shows/america-tonight/articles/2015/3/27/rahm-emanuel-chuy-garcia-chicago-run-off-schools.html.

Analysis of Indiana School Choice Scholarship Program. 2015. Chicago, IL: Center for Tax and Budget Accountability.

Carlson, D., & Lavertu, S. 2015a. *School closures and student achievement.* Washington, DC: Thomas B. Fordham Institute.

————. 2015b. The effect of school closure on student achievement: Regression discontinuity evidence from Ohio's automatic school closure law. Unpublished paper.

Christie, K. 2007. *The state role in accelerating student growth in low-performing high schools.* Denver, CO: Education Commission of the States.

de la Torre, M., Gordon, M. F., Moore, P., & Cowhy, J. 2015. *School closings in Chicago: Understanding families' choices and constraints for new school enrollment.* Chicago, IL: Consortium on Chicago School Research.

de la Torre, M., & Gwynne, J. 2009. *When schools close: Effects on displaced students in Chicago Public Schools.* Chicago, IL: Consortium on Chicago School Research.

Duke, D. L. 1995. *The school that refused to die.* Albany: State University of New York Press.

————. 2010. *The challenges of school district leadership.* New York: Routledge.

————. 2012. Tinkering and turnarounds: Understanding the contemporary campaign to improve low-performing schools. *Journal of Education for Students Placed at Risk, 17*(1), 9–24.

Finnigan, K. S., Holme, J. J., Orfield, M., Luce, T., Diem, S., Mattheis, A., & Hylton, N. D. 2015. Regional educational policy analysis: Rochester, Omaha, and Minneapolis' interdistrict arrangements. *Education Policy, 29*(5), 780–814.

Hamilton, M. P., Heilig, J. V., & Pazey, B. L. 2013. A nostrum of school reform? Turning around reconstituted urban Texas high schools. *Urban Education, 48*(1), 1–34.

Jochim, A., & Murphy, P. 2013. *The capacity challenge: What it takes for state education agencies to support school improvement.* Seattle, WA: Center for Reinventing Public Education.

Kowal, J., & Ableidinger, J. n.d. *School turnarounds in Colorado.* Denver, CO: Donnell-Kay Foundation.

Lavery, L., & Carlson, D. 2015. Dynamic participation in interdistrict open enrollment. *Educational Policy, 29*(5), 746–79.

Layton, L., & Brown, E. 2015, June 3. The ultimate in school choice or school as a commodity? *Washington Post.* Retrieved from https://www.washingtonpost.com/local/education/in-nevada-school-choice-on-steroids-and-a-breakthrough-for-conservatives/2015/06/03/3cdd2300-09ff-11e5-95fd-d580f1c5d44e_story.html.

McNeil, M. 2010, July 26. Civil rights groups call for new federal education agenda. *Education Week.* Retrieved from http://blogs.edweek.org/edweek/campaign-k-12/2010/07/civil_rights_groups_call_for_n.html.

Mikulecky, M. T. 2013. *Open enrollment is on the menu—but can you order it?* Denver, CO: Education Commission of the States.

Open enrollment and racial segregation in the twin cities. 2012. Minneapolis: Institute on Metropolitan Opportunity, University of Minnesota Law School.

Open enrollment 50-state report. 2013. Denver, CO: Education Commission of the States.

Perlstein, R. 2013, August 26. Rahm Emanuel's minority-bashing school closings go forward. *Nation.* Retrieved from http://www.thenation.com/article/school-daze-rahm-emanuels-minority-bashing-school-closings-go-forward/.

Positive early indications continue at first parent trigger schools. 2014, October 7. *Parent Revolution.* Retrieved from http://parentrevolution.org/press-releases/2014/10/7/positive-early-indications-continue-at-first-parent-trigger-schools.

Prothero, A. 2015, March 25. Eligibility rules fuel growth of Indiana's voucher program. *Education Week,* 6.

Ravitch, D. 2010. *The death and life of the great American school system.* New York: Basic Books.

Real accountability, real results. 2015. *PennCAN: The Pennsylvania Campaign for Achievement Now.* Retrieved from http://www.penncan.org/research/real-accountability-real-results.

Reid, K. S. 2015, March 18. Parent-trigger law used in new ways. *Education Week,* 1, 20.

Rice, J. K., and Malen, B. 2010. *School reconstitution as an education reform strategy: A synopsis of the evidence.* Washington, DC: National Education Association.

School choice programs. 2015. *Institute for Quality Education.* Retrieved from http://www.i4qed.org/participate.

Smarick, A. 2010. The turnaround fallacy. *Education Next,* 21–26.

So you want to go to private school? An Indiana school voucher guide. 2015. *Indiana Public Media.* Retrieved from indianapublicmedia.org/stateimpact/tag/school-vouchers.

State capacity to support school turnaround. 2015. Washington, DC: NCEE Evaluation Brief, Institute of Education Sciences.

Stuit, D. A. 2010. *Are bad schools immortal?* Washington, DC: Thomas B. Fordham Institute.

Witte, J. F., Wolf, P. J., Cowen, J. M., Carlson, D. E., & Fleming, D. J. 2014. High-stakes choice: Achievement and accountability in the nation's oldest urban voucher program. *Educational Evaluation and Policy Analysis, 36*(4), 437–56.

Zelon, H. 2010, May 6. Parents, pols push alternative to school closings. *City Limits* [New York City]. Retrieved from http://citylimits.org/2010/05/06/parents-pols-push-alternative-to-school-closings/.

Part III

Local Responses to State and Federal Pressure to Help the Children Left Behind

Part II provided examples of the many ways in which states have responded to the federal government's drive to aid the lowest-performing schools. With the possible exception of special state districts, however, states have not gotten directly involved in the day-to-day operation of these schools. For the vast majority of low-performing schools, it is the local school district that assumes primary responsibility for school improvement.

The Buffalo case illustrated how challenging school improvement at the local level can be. We have seen how policies and practices with regard to the school turnaround process can vary from state to state, depending on contextual differences ranging from which political party is in power to the state's financial condition. This section provides some examples of the variability of district approaches to failing schools.

Federal policy, of course, endorsed variability by offering school districts four options for addressing the lowest-performing schools: transformation, turnaround, restart, and closure. Other options emerged in the wake of federal waivers for No Child Left Behind. These "official" options, however, fail to capture the rich variety of approaches that have been undertaken by particular school districts.

Part III focuses on three of these approaches. The first approach, *standardization*, involves the specification of requirements for *all* failing schools. Standardization presumes that there are certain tried and true ways to address the needs of struggling students and that all low-performing schools should employ them. *Innovation* represents the second approach. Unlike the first approach, innovation relies on original thinking, new ideas, and novel ways to provide learning opportunities. The third approach is based on *choice*. It calls for the creation of a variety of options for the students left behind. Presumably, no single option is best suited to the needs of all these students.

These approaches are not necessarily mutually exclusive. Schools that follow a standardized model of learning, for instance, might be offered as one of several options. Some very large school systems such as New York City and Chicago take advantage of all three approaches. Becoming familiar with how these three approaches are being implemented in several local districts, however, should provide a useful foundation for thinking about possible next steps in the campaign to leave no child behind.

SEVEN

One Best Way to
Leave No Child Behind

One of the central tenets of bureaucratic organization is the standardization of production. The guiding assumption is that at any given time there is one approach to production that is more efficient and effective than any other. The rational course of action, therefore, is to pick this approach and require it of all production units.

For better or worse, school districts are bureaucratic organizations. It is not surprising then that school districts faced with a number of low-performing schools should consider a standardized approach to school improvement. Standardization can take several forms in this regard.

A school district, for example, can decide to standardize academic programs across all low-performing schools. Such action may be justified for different reasons. If student within-district mobility is high, as it often is in districts with large numbers of students from poor families, standardized academic programs can ensure that students are exposed to the same curriculum content regardless of which school they attend. There also may be economies of scale associated with standardized programs. Publishers may discount materials purchased in large quantities, and professional development related to the materials can be offered more efficiently.

Another possibility is the standardization of organizational processes. It has become vogue for consulting groups to analyze case studies of successful school turnarounds and extrapolate a set of common organizational processes. These processes are then purveyed as keys to school improvement. Processes that frequently are mentioned include curriculum alignment, continuous analysis of student data, team planning, and parent engagement.

Yet another form of standardization concerns classroom practices, including the delivery of instruction, classroom management, and assessment of student learning. The past few decades have witnessed the emergence of a large body of carefully conducted research on effective teaching. This research has yielded a collection of "best practices" associated with efforts to raise student achievement. Advocates for best practices argue that it is professionally irresponsible to use anything but proven methods with students in low-performing schools.

The remainder of this chapter examines examples of two school districts that opted for standardization in their efforts to help the children left behind.

IMPROVING READING IN RICHMOND

If there is one ubiquitous characteristic of America's lowest-performing schools, it involves literacy deficits. There, of course, can be other serious problems—low math achievement, unsafe conditions, high dropout rates, chronic absenteeism. But the main reason why many schools are failing can be traced to fundamental weaknesses in students' vocabulary, reading comprehension, and other dimensions of literacy.

When Deborah Jewell-Sherman accepted the position of superintendent of Richmond Public Schools in 2002, she understood what needed to be done.[1] Reading achievement had to improve. Only one of Virginia's school divisions had a lower level of student achievement than Richmond. There were 55 schools under her leadership, but only five schools had attained full accreditation based on Virginia's accountability system. With No Child Left Behind going into effect, Jewell-Sherman understood that accreditation benchmarks would only get tougher in the future.

In order to achieve full accreditation in 2002, a school needed to have at least 70% of its students pass Virginia's Standards of Learning tests in reading and mathematics. Tests were given in the third, fifth, and eighth grades. Twenty-nine Richmond schools were in the lowest accountability category—accredited with warning. This meant that their passing rates on state tests fell 20 or more percentage points below the 70% benchmark.

Other challenges also needed to be addressed, including a dropout rate of 2.7% a year and a truancy rate of 22%, both among the highest in the state. High school students took few advanced courses, and students performed poorly on the Scholastic Aptitude Tests. To make matters worse, many aging schools were in desperate need of repair and renovation, district finances were in a perpetually precarious position, and school violence was a constant concern. In the 2001–2002 school year, Richmond principals reported 10,961 disciplinary actions, including almost 9,000 suspensions. There were only 27,000 students in the school system!

Having previously served as Richmond's associate superintendent for accountability and instruction, Jewell-Sherman understood the steps that needed to be taken before significant improvements in student achievement could be made. She also understood that these improvements had to be made quickly. The school board had tied Jewell-Sherman's tenure to one of the first performance-based contracts for a U.S. superintendent. Unless she accomplished three goals, Jewell-Sherman could be fired the following summer. First, at least 20 of Richmond's 55 schools had to be fully accredited, based on 2003 state tests. Second, no more than 12 schools could be accredited with warning. Third, at least 16 of the city's elementary schools had to achieve passing rates of 70% or higher on the third-grade reading test. At the time she signed her contract, only three elementary schools had reached this benchmark.

In her former position as associate superintendent, Jewell-Sherman already had begun to implement measures intended to address Richmond's academic problems. She contracted with the Voyager reading program in order to provide students with summer reading instruction. She also tested a commercial benchmark assessment service that tracked student progress on the state Standards of Learning.

Jewell-Sherman knew that the focus of her energies had to be on raising student achievement, especially in reading. But knowing and doing are not one in the same. No sooner did she assume office than a variety of distractions emerged to deflect her efforts. Concern over transportation costs prompted the school board, for example, to extend the residential zone within which students were expected to walk to school. Parents who worried about the safety of their children inundated the district office with complaints. It took months of negotiations for Jewell-Sherman to resolve the matter.

In the midst of the transportation maelstrom, the possible presence of the Washington, D.C.–area sniper in Richmond caused widespread panic. Schools were closed as a precautionary measure. No sooner had the sniper been captured than a local architectural firm's report on the deteriorating conditions of many Richmond schools gave parents something new to worry about. School board members were shaken by the estimated $350 million price tag for renovation and replacement of facilities.

Then came Governor Mark Warner's announcement that Virginia faced a $1.1 billion revenue shortfall. Not only would state assistance for capital improvements be unavailable, but the prospects for Jewell-Sherman to receive supplementary funding for literacy programs, alternative education, teacher salary increases, and school security appeared dim.

Jewell-Sherman and the school board spent the winter of 2003 deciding how to cut the budget. Proposals ranged from school closings to curtailing the district's early retirement incentive program. As the discussions of retrenchment proceeded, Jewell-Sherman received more bad news. The school system received a strongly worded report from the state on the inadequacies of its special education program. Many children who were eligible for special education services, the report indicated, failed to receive these services. The Virginia Department of Education demanded that a plan to fix the problem be submitted by March 21. Correcting the problem doubtless would require additional funding at a time when the school system was struggling to reduce expenditures. The head of Richmond's special education department, not surprisingly, resigned in early March.

Problems continued into the spring. On March 27, Jewell-Sherman and the school board learned that its proposal for budget reductions had been rejected by city council. School divisions in Virginia cannot raise their own revenues but must depend on elected officials to provide the funds to operate. City council members expressed concern that administrative costs for the division kept rising while school enrollment declined. They pointed to other Virginia school districts that operated much more efficiently than Richmond Public Schools.

On June 2, 2003, the city council finally agreed on its funding for the upcoming year. The amount was $3.2 million less than had been requested, but it was sufficient to fund a small raise for teachers and to allow Jewell-Sherman to move forward with her plans to turn around Richmond's lowest-achieving schools.

Despite the abundance of serious issues and unexpected distractions, Jewell-Sherman somehow managed to press on with efforts to improve instruction in core subjects. More importantly, she began to build a coalition of supporters who believed in her mission. Skeptical board members rallied behind her, along with parents and district employees.

As has been indicated elsewhere in this book, it is not uncommon for turnaround initiatives to begin with the replacement of principals. Jewell-Sherman, however, opted to give sitting principals another chance. She explained her decision as follows:

> The principals never received the training they needed to be effective. So we trained them to understand data, to use data to lead their staff. But I don't believe in just working with principals. I believe in working with a school's entire leadership team. We work really hard at getting information out to a team—empower the principal to lead, but to lead an instructional or leadership team at the school.

Jewell-Sherman did make one key personnel move, however. She promoted Yvonne Brandon to her former position, associate superintendent of accountability and instruction. Highly regarded as a principal and director of instruction, Brandon understood curriculum and instruction. In their early discussions of a turnaround strategy for Richmond, Jewell-Sherman and Brandon agreed that the popular practice of site-based management, where key decisions concerning curriculum programs and instructional methods were left to the discretion of principals, had to go. Brandon put it this way:

> We were working hard, but we weren't working hard on the right things. We had an extremely dedicated staff of teachers, instructional staff, principals, but we did not have a clear definition of how to connect the pieces. We had no centralized curriculum alignment. We did not have any means of assessing our children to determine where they were and what they needed to do to get to the next level. The first step that we took was to look at an inventory of reading and mathematics products throughout the schools. We had previously been experimenting with site-based management. As a result, instruction became very, very varied. Each principal did what they wanted—it was varied in intensity and in product, which didn't quite match with having a 44 percent mobility rate.

Students in Richmond frequently moved around the city, often switching schools in the process. To ensure that no student was placed at a disadvantage because of between-school differences in academic programs, site-based management would have to give way to greater standardization of curriculum content, instructional methods, and assessment practices. Jewell-Sherman and Brandon expected pushback from principals who had grown accustomed to doing their own thing, but they understood that turning around Richmond's lowest-performing schools depended on a unified strategy.

One of Brandon's first acts as associate superintendent was to inventory reading programs in Richmond schools. She found elements of 29 different programs. Not only was program consistency from school to school lacking, but often there was no consistency from one grade level to another in the same school! Principals were persuaded by vendors to try new reading programs without insisting on evidence that the programs worked. Brandon let it be known that this practice would end.

> So one of the things that we started to do was to research products. We developed a list of critical criteria that a product must have, which included being scientifically based, having embedded assessments, having professional development, and having provisions for training central office and lead administrative staff on a regular basis so that we could monitor the implementation and use of the product. Fidelity to implementation was a big, big issue because, of course, teachers are sometimes territorial. So, when the classroom door was shut, we had to be sure that what needed to be taught was being taught.

Inventorying and assessing reading and mathematics programs were major accomplishments, but Jewell-Sherman and Brandon did not stop there. Curriculum inconsistency was just the tip of the iceberg. Instructional practice also varied greatly, from school to school and teacher to teacher. They determined that a standardized model of instruction, based on research, needed to be implemented. Once again, they expected to encounter resistance, but they recognized that curriculum consistency without high-quality instructional practices was unlikely to boost achievement. By the end of the 2002–2003 school year, Brandon had identified a proven instructional model and mandated it for the entire school system. She described the model as follows:

> The model follows some of the more respected instructional strategies. You have a snapshot in the beginning of the class. You do direct instruction based on the children's level of understanding. You give guided practice. You give homework. You take the children through some of the steps of the homework. You give them an opportunity to ask questions. And then you do a maintenance moment to conclude the lesson. That's a question that ties the current instruction to previous learning.

The ultimate determination of whether Jewell-Sherman's and Brandon's efforts at turning around Richmond's lowest-performing schools had worked would be student performance on Virginia's Standards of Learning (SOL) tests. Success on the tests, in turn, required that Richmond teachers actually knew the standards for their grade level and content area. Being familiar with Richmond's teachers, Jewell-Sherman and Brandon realized that teacher knowledge of the standards could not be assumed.

To ensure that the standards were known and taught, Brandon hit upon the idea of developing model lessons for every standard. Each lesson would be based on the new standardized instructional model. Model lessons to guide every teacher constituted yet another layer of standardization. The task was enormous, but Brandon reasoned that engaging Richmond teachers in helping to develop the model lessons would accomplish two goals at one time. Through the act of creating model lessons, teachers also would learn the standards. Teachers were paid stipends to work with instructional specialists over the summer to create the model lessons. Brandon described the process thusly:

> Lesson plans for each SOL include a breakdown of the objective—spiraling objectives. And those were objectives that perhaps were taught in the previous grade that were related to this objective. We have vocabulary terms, technology integration such as Web sites that the teacher could go to. We have field trips that were related to SOL objectives. We have critical terms that the teacher needed to concentrate on. Basically we created a well-organized book of lesson plans for each SOL objective in each subject, K–12.

Their first year had been a busy one, but Jewell-Sherman and Brandon could take pride in having set the stage for the turnaround process. The next few years demonstrated the benefits of their efforts. By 2005, 39 of Richmond's 51 schools achieved full accreditation by the state. The following year, 42 out of 49 schools (two schools were closed) achieved full accreditation. The Richmond turnaround reached a special milestone in March of 2007 when the Virginia Board of Education formally released the school system from a state review process required for low-performing school divisions.

How had Jewell-Sherman and Brandon been able to achieve such impressive results in a relatively brief period of time? The short answer is that they were willing to lead. They understood the risk of curtailing the discretionary authority of principals by standardizing Richmond's reading programs. They knew that many teachers would resent having to follow a particular instructional approach and teach model lessons. Such measures were essential starting places, they reasoned, if students in the lowest-performing schools were to be ensured a quality education.

Brandon took a pragmatic position regarding standardization, maintaining that "it is easier to loosen up than tighten up." If student achievement improved, then principals and teachers would be accorded greater latitude.

Brandon was pragmatic in other ways as well. Consider her reasoning regarding the decision to use the Voyager reading program in all low-performing schools:

> We had used Voyager products in summer school. We understood that some of our children needed to have intense assessments very quickly and a response from the instructor at the same level of urgency. That's what attracted us to Voyager. And we saw how our children got excited during the summer with the Voyager materials. But then they went back to the normal school program in the fall and had the same "4 across, 5 in a row" kind of classroom arrangement. And the teachers weren't able to do flexible reading groups. When they did what they thought were flexible reading groups, kids were stuck in the same group all year! You had the redbirds, the bluebirds, and the buzzards, just like when I was in school. That doesn't work for children. They need to be able to mingle into groups, move in and out, work with their peers, have concrete content, but have the instruction of that content differentiated. And Voyager allows this. We started out by piloting Voyager, then we looked at the results and saw that it was working. We didn't go full-district, though. What we did was use Voyager for our very lowest-performing schools.

Brandon and Jewell-Sherman had enough experience with vendors like Voyager to know that an initial training of teachers to launch the program would be insufficient. To prevent the rollout of Voyager from becoming another reform that ran out of steam, they insisted that Voyager become an active "partner" with Richmond Public Schools. This meant that Voyager would have to provide ongoing training of teachers and monitoring of program progress.

Knowing that some students would encounter difficulties with reading, despite differentiated instruction using well-designed lessons, Brandon worked with principals and teacher leaders to make certain that timely and targeted interventions were available. Regular testing tied to state standards ensured that teachers were able to pinpoint areas where particular students needed help. By eliminating early release Wednesdays for elementary students, Jewell-Sherman created additional time for struggling students to receive remediation.

In another move to help the children left behind, Jewell-Sherman got the school board to approve Twilight School. Operating from 2:00 to 4:30 p.m. on Mondays through Thursdays, Twilight School provided an opportunity for older students with credit deficiencies to make up credits and eventually earn a diploma.

Jewell-Sherman and Brandon took an additional step toward standardizing procedures when they addressed special education. Traditionally, building principals and faculty members exercised considerable discretion when it came to deciding how to operate services for special needs students. This often led to self-contained classes and the isolation of special education students from mainstream learning opportunities. Brandon described the new approach as follows:

> We stopped dealing with special education students in a separate mode. We blended our efforts by having our special education specialists train with our content specialists so they could get a better handle on content versus compliance and regulations. We stopped thinking of special education children as a separate group of children in Richmond Public Schools. All of our efforts were toward training all of the teachers, whether special education teachers or non-special education teachers. And I think it helped because the special ed teachers could no longer say that something was the academic teacher's issue. It became every teacher's responsibility to teach.

The story of Richmond's turnaround reveals the power of a focused mission. Jewell-Sherman and Brandon managed to address various distractions without losing momentum on their central concerns—literacy and instructional improvement. By standardizing curriculum content, instruction, and assessment, they were able to build a foundation for turning around Richmond's lowest-performing schools.

CINCINNATI—A POSTER DISTRICT FOR TURNAROUNDS

While inspiring, Richmond's success story was short-lived. Persistent meddling in school district affairs by Richmond's mayor, Doug Wilder, resulted in Deborah Jewell-Sherman's departure and the erosion of many of the gains achieved under her leadership. The Cincinnati story, on the other hand, is more encouraging because the turnaround of the district's elementary schools has been sustained.[2] It is no coincidence that Cincinnati's superintendent, Mary Ronan, has been able to remain in office, providing the stability at the top that can be so critical to prolonged progress.

A veteran educator with Cincinnati Public Schools (CPS), Ronan was chosen to lead the district in 2008. Soon thereafter, she and her central office team determined that improvement efforts in the low-performing school system should focus on K–8 schools, the goal being to get every student ready for high school. At the time, CPS enrolled around 34,000 students, 73% of whom qualified for free and reduced-price lunch. More than half of the students lived below the federal government's poverty line, the second-highest percentage of any school district in the United States. Seven out of 10 students were African American, and 4% were English-language learners.

Elementary schools in Cincinnati, as in Richmond, were highly decentralized when Ronan took office. There was no common curriculum or set of practices that cut across all elementary schools. Thirteen elementary schools were in "academic emergency," according to Ohio's system for ranking schools.

In what has become the signature program of Ronan's administration, the Elementary Initiative was launched with Race to the Top funds in the fall of 2008 in Cincinnati's 16 lowest-performing elementary schools, including the 13 in "academic emergency." Deputy Superintendent Laura Mitchell was chosen to oversee the initiative. After assessing conditions and staffing in the 16 schools, Ronan and Mitchell decided that the principal and all staff members needed to be replaced in four schools. The remaining 12 schools proceeded with their existing personnel.

The strategy guiding school turnaround in the Elementary Initiative schools consisted of 14 elements, and every school was expected to implement all 14 elements. The elements included:

- Principal training and development
- Data and analysis to support evidence-based decision making
- Realignment of resources to support turnaround instructional support teams
- On-site core academic content specialists
- School-based learning teams
- Model reading structure in grades 4 through 8
- Essentials-focused and multisensory reading instruction
- Differentiated instruction expert cadre
- Expanded learning time
- Individual student success plans
- Targeted and effective district support
- Family and community engagement
- Targeted and effective external support and resources

Ronan and Mitchell's program aimed for nothing less than whole-school reform. Although the heart of the Elementary Initiative involved improvements in reading instruction, the two leaders understood that short-term gains in reading achievement could soon be lost if schools were unable to build the capacity to support and sustain gains over time. They also knew that the district had a key role to play in developing that school-based capacity.

Just because the Elementary Initiative entailed a standardized reform program dictated by district leadership did not mean that school principals were expected to be managers instead of leaders. Ronan and Mitchell realized that nothing less than energetic and inspired leadership would be required if the 14 reform strategies were to be implemented successfully. Principals of the 16 schools were enrolled in the University of Virginia's School Turnaround Specialist Program to equip them with a variety of leadership skills, including data-driven decision making, strategic planning, and project management. Mitchell made certain that the relationships among the principals that were established during the two-year training program continued afterward through a carefully planned networking program.

To help principals with some of their routine responsibilities, the district provided a resource coordinator for each school. This individual worked with the principal using a district-created worksheet to examine how effectively people, time, and money were being used. The resource coordinator also helped to manage partnerships with external service providers.

Everyone appreciated the fact that even the most talented principal could not turn around a school singlehandedly. For this reason, great emphasis was placed on team building at the school and district levels. Each of the 16 schools established grade-level and content-teaching teams charged with analyzing data and planning. Teams also were expected to develop individual assistance plans for struggling students. On alternating weeks, teachers met in grade-level and content-based teams for 50 to 60 minutes. In addition, every teacher was allotted 200 minutes a week for individual planning. Teams also worked with coaches and content specialists to hone skills and receive team-specific training.

Teams of central office specialists also had key roles to play. Coaches assisted teachers in assessing student performance data, instructional grouping, differentiated instruction, and regrouping of students to address individual needs. Special measures were taken, however, to ensure that school-based personnel were not subjected to too many district specialists. Ronan and Mitchell understood that an overabundance of "helpers" increased the possibility of mixed messages and confusion.

Like Richmond, Cincinnati standardized its reading program and approach to reading instruction in the 16 schools. All reading classes consisted of whole-group instruction, small-group centers, and whole-group closure at the end of a lesson. Language Essentials for Teaching Reading and Spelling (LETRS) was selected as the common reading program for grades 4 through 8. A minimum of 90 minutes of reading instruction was provided on a daily basis. In addition, a "fifth quarter" was added to the school calendar in the summer. Students in the monthlong fifth quarter received instruction in core content in the morning and enrichment activities with community partners in the afternoon.

Partnerships with local businesses and community organizations were another cornerstone of the Elementary Initiative as well as CPS efforts to raise student achievement in high school. Under the auspices of the Strive Partnership, for example, Procter & Gamble used its influence to recruit Microsoft to develop a data management system for CPS. The system integrated early childhood, K–12, higher education, and social services data and enabled CPS to track student progress as well as district performance. Many Cincinnati businesses provided volunteers to work in schools and mentor students.

Another outreach component of the Elementary Initiative involved the creation of Community Learning Centers (CLCs) in the participating schools. The CLCs served a number of functions, ranging from parent access to technology to family reviews of "student success plans." Some CLCs offered health and dental services to needy students as well as after-school programs and child care for working parents.

Elementary Initiative schools operated full-day early childhood programs. The preschool curriculum in these programs was aligned to state standards and designed to provide children with the prerequisites needed to succeed in elementary school. A major focus of the early childhood programs was the identification of at-risk youngsters who require special assistance in order to make a successful transition to elementary school.

In the case study of the Elementary Initiative that was commissioned by CPS, the importance of standardization is clearly noted:

> The approach is highly standardized, with schools receiving the same general resources and sharing similar curricula, day-to-day routines, schedules, and structures. Principals note that this makes sense, not only because the district has tightly linked its strategies to a strong research base, but also because of the high mobility of students. (School turnaround in Cincinnati Public Schools, n.d., p. 7)

The Elementary Initiative has evolved since its inception in order to address new needs and incorporate additional components. With the increasing population of English-language learners, teachers have earned TESOL endorsement at no cost through a program with Xavier University. The district also has provided all teachers with Sheltered Instruction Observation Protocol (SIOP) training to equip them with proven strategies for teaching English-language learners.

The heavy emphasis on literacy has led to the hiring of 43 additional reading specialists to work with struggling students. Elementary schools have expanded departmentalization, meaning that greater emphasis is placed on assigning teachers to particular content areas rather than having each teacher teach all the content areas. CPS mandated that Response to Intervention (tiered instruction) be implemented as well. Graduate students from the University of Cincinnati have been enlisted to assist with the assessment of student progress and tutoring.

As a result of all these efforts, Cincinnati has achieved national prominence as a model turnaround district. The gap in achievement between African American and white students has narrowed considerably. The overall graduation rate has climbed from 50% to 80%. In some years, the graduation rate for African American students exceeds the rate for white students. In 2009–2010 and 2010–2011, CPS earned an "effective" rating on the Ohio Report Card, the highest rating ever achieved by an urban district in Ohio. Educators in Cincinnati are especially proud of the fact that local public school students are outperforming charter school students on the Ohio Performance Index (Brown, 2014).

IS STANDARDIZATION THE ANSWER?

The answer to this question would seem to be "yes" if the examples of Cincinnati and Richmond are taken as representative of all turnaround efforts. Even without controlled studies of turnaround practices in low-performing schools that achieved quick and dramatic improvements, the U.S. Department of Education has encouraged, and in some cases required, that a host of "best practices" be implemented in schools receiving School Improvement Grants (SIGs) (Are low-performing schools, 2014).

Table 7.1 presents the 32 practices endorsed by the Department of Education and the percentage of 320 low-performing schools receiving SIG funds that reported using each practice. While no practice was reported by principals to have been adopted at every school, the first seven were reported for very high percentages of schools. It would appear, based on this data, that federal efforts to standardize at least some practices in low-performing schools have succeeded. It is worth noting that four of the seven most popular practices involve data collection and utilization.

When Greg Anrig (2015) examined some of the most successful SIG-funded turnarounds for the Century Foundation, he found that five practices were common across all the schools:

1. An intense focus on improving classroom instruction through ongoing, data-driven collaboration

Table 7.1.   Adoption Rates for SIG Practices, Overall

Practices, Sorted by the Percentage of SIG Schools That Reported Adopting Them	Schools Implementing a SIG Intervention Model, 2012–2013 Percentage of Schools That Adopted:	
	This Practice	This Practice and All Practices in the Rows Above
1. Use data to inform and differentiate instruction	99.7	99.7
2. Increase technology access for teachers or use computer-assisted instruction	97.8	97.8
3. Provide ongoing professional development that involves working collaboratively or is facilitated by school leaders	98.1*	96.9*
4. Provide professional development on student learning needs	98.1*	95.6*
5. Use benchmark or interim assessments at least annually	96.9	94.7*
6. Use data to evaluate instructional programs	95.3	90.6*
7. Use data to guide nonacademic supports	92.8*	85.6*
8. Use data to evaluate the success of professional development	85.9*	76.2*
9. Provide professional development on Common Core State Standards, state standards, or turnaround	83.1*	66.5*
10. State or district provides professional development on budgets or turnaround strategies	79.6*	57.4*
11. State or district provides professional development on working with parents or creating a safe school environment	78.4*	51.4*
12. Use evaluation results to inform reductions in force or have policies that allow principal authority to hire staff	69.6	34.8
13. Implement strategies to ensure English Language Learners master academic content	66.8	24.5
14. Use multiple performance measures for principal evaluations	68.7	16.6

15. State or district provides professional development on aligning professional development with evaluation results	69.9	13.8
16. Establish schedules and implement strategies to increase learning time	70.5*	11.0
17. Replace the principal	71.5*	7.2
18. State or district provides training or technical assistance to support school improvement or the use of data to improve instruction	71.2*	6.6
19. Change parent or community involvement strategies	67.4*	5.6
20. Change discipline policies	63.6	5.6
21. State or district provides professional development on identifying staff for leadership positions	60.2	5.6
22. Provide multiple-session professional development events	58.6*	3.1
23. Require student achievement growth as a component of teacher evaluations	50.2	0.9*
24. Design professional development with school staff	53.0*	0.6*
25. Use multiple performance measures for teacher evaluations	48.9*	0.6
26. Use student achievement growth as a component of principal evaluations	40.8	0.6
27. Review competencies of staff or replace instructional staff	41.1*	0.3
28. Use teacher evaluation results to inform compensation	26.3	0.0
29. Have autonomy on budgeting, hiring, discipline, or school year length	25.4	0.0
30. Use principal evaluation results to inform compensation	22.9	0.0
31. Use financial incentives and other strategies to recruit and retain effective teachers	17.2*	0.0
32. Use financial incentives to recruit and retain effective principals	7.8	0.0

Number of schools: 320

*Significantly different from schools not implementing a School Improvement Grant (SIG) intervention model in 2012–2013 at the 0.05 level, two-tailed test.

Source: *Are low-performing schools adopting practices promoted by School Improvement Grants?* 2014. Washington, DC: Institute of Education Sciences, National Center for Education Evaluation and Regional Assistance.

2. A concerted, systematic effort to create a safe and orderly school environment through implementation of research-supported practices that all staff members can adopt
3. An expansion of both classroom and nonclassroom time throughout the school week dedicated to instruction and tutoring in core academic subjects
4. A strengthening of connections to parents, community groups, and local service providers
5. A limited reliance on expert consultants to jump-start changes that school leaders and teachers sustain on their own

Low-performing schools might be adopting common practices in order to obtain generous government grants, but that does not necessarily mean that states and school districts wholeheartedly embrace federally sponsored standardization. Many state applications for waivers to NCLB and Race to the Top guidelines have included provisions for alternatives to mandated federal reforms. State and local leaders have expressed a desire for more flexibility in addressing the needs of the lowest-performing schools. It is worth noting that the successful prescriptions for school improvement in Richmond and Cincinnati were home-grown, not imposed by Washington. The next chapter explores some of the ways that school districts are moving beyond standardization in an effort to help the children left behind.

NOTES

1. Much of the information about Richmond Public Schools comes from a case study conducted by the author and reported in his book *Leadership for Low-Performing Schools*, published in 2015 by Rowman & Littlefield.
2. Much of the background on Cincinnati's turnaround initiative was gathered from the school district website (http://www.cps-k12.org/academics/district-initiatives/elementary-initiative) and a case study entitled *School Turnaround in Cincinnati Public Schools* (http://www.erstrategies.org/cms/files/1492-cincinnati-case-study.pdf).

REFERENCES

Anrig, G. 2015. *Lessons from School Improvement Grants that worked.* New York: Century Foundation.
Are low-performing schools adopting practices promoted by School Improvement Grants? 2014. *National Center for Education and Evaluation.* Washington, DC: Institute of Education Sciences, National Center for Education Evaluation and Regional Assistance.
Brown, J. 2014, September 16. Charter schools still lagging. Retrieved from http://www.cincinnati.com/story/news/education/2014/09/16/charter-schools-still-lagging/15714433/.
School turnaround in Cincinnati Public Schools. n.d. *Education Resource Strategies.* Retrieved from http://www.erstrategies.org/cms/files/1492-cincinnati-case-study.pdf.

EIGHT

Local Innovation and Options

A Better Prescription?

If standardization is the mantra of the bureaucrat, then innovation is the entrepreneur's watchword. Some contemporary critics of public education are calling on educational leaders to become more entrepreneurial, and many educational leaders have responded by embracing innovation as the key to addressing a variety of concerns. Evidence of interest in new educational ideas can be found at all levels—federal, state, and local.

The U.S. Department of Education, for example, has allocated millions of dollars in American Recovery and Reinvestment Act (ARRA) funds to Investing in Innovation (i3) grants in an effort to stimulate new thinking about teaching and learning. The program's purpose, according to its website, is to provide competitive grants to applicants "with a record of improving student achievement and attainment in order to expand the implementation of, and investment in, innovative practices that are demonstrated to have an impact on improving student achievement or student growth, closing achievement gaps, decreasing dropout rates, increasing high school graduation rates, or increasing college enrollment and completion rates" (*What's new*, 2015).

The White House has joined the cause in the form of the Turnaround Arts initiative, a signature program of the President's Committee on the Arts and Humanities. Turnaround Arts represents a public–private partnership that employs the arts as a tool to help turn around the nation's lowest-performing schools. Schools receive arts education resources, professional development, leadership coaching, and strategic planning assistance in order to stimulate novel approaches to the improvement of school climate and culture, instruction, and student and parent engagement.

137

Some states also have gotten behind the push for innovation in education. Kentucky, for example, has identified seven school districts as centers of innovation. According to one report, most of these districts have chosen to explore competency-based learning, new uses of classroom technology, and different ways to extend learning time (Herold, 2015).

Local school districts are initiating educational innovations as well. Some of these efforts have been small-scale tests, such as Coshocton (Ohio) City Schools' experiment with paying elementary students for successful completion of their standardized testing (Bettinger, 2010). Other efforts are massive endeavors involving many schools and large investments. Several of these large-scale initiatives are highlighted in this chapter.

As a result of the increasing interest in educational innovation, "education innovation clusters" have begun to emerge across the United States (Molnar, 2015). These regional networks consist of school districts, research organizations, and private companies. Although the focus of these groups is not exclusively on the needs of the children left behind, they share a concern for discovering new ways to improve schools and learning.

Frequently coupled with innovation is an interest in expanding the range of choices available to students. Choice, like innovation, is presented by its advocates as a panacea for the ills of education. Once again, measures to promote choice have been taken by the federal government, state governments, and local school districts. The federal government, for example, has promoted magnet schools as a vehicle for facilitating desegregation. By creating a variety of schools with special themes and course offerings, districts presumably encourage students to make selections that take them beyond their neighborhoods into more diverse settings.

States have done their bit to expand educational choice by creating legislation that allows public funds to be used to support charter schools.[1] In response to competition from charter organizations, school districts have sought to expand the variety of district-based choices available to students. These options range from within-school programs like the International Baccalaureate to career academies and alternative schools. Not all of these choices, of course, are aimed at helping students in the lowest-performing schools. In this chapter, we examine how local school systems are employing innovation and choice to help the children left behind.

DUVAL COUNTY EMBRACES CHOICE

There was a time in the not too distant past when the primary response to low performance in the Duval County (Florida) Public Schools was standardization. Supovitz (2006) has provided an extensive account of Superintendent John Fryer's efforts to address pervasive academic problems in the nation's 20th-largest school district. From 1999 to 2006, Supovitz tracked the steps that were taken by district staff and school-based leaders to implement Fryer's "Framework for Implementation of Standards in Duval County Public Schools" (FISDCPS).

The FISDCPS was a complex program of reforms tied to the district's strategic plan. Five "targets" made up the framework and included academic performance, safe schools, high-performance management, learning communities, and accountability (Supovitz, 2006, p. 41). Each target consisted of specific programs and strategies that all schools were expected to implement. The academic performance target, for example, required schools to adopt common assessments, connect student work to district and state standards, and integrate technology with course content, among other mandates.

After tracking efforts to implement the FISDCPS for seven years, Supovitz concluded that there was "extensive variability in the extent to which schools were implementing the district's reforms" (p. 111). Furthermore, there was little relationship between a school's reform adoption and its performance. Low-performing schools sometimes exhibited high fidelity to the FISDCPS, while some high-performing schools were spotty implementers.

Duval County continued to work on elements of the Framework for Implementation of Standards, but increasingly the focus shifted to expanding the range of choices available to students, including those stuck in low-performing schools. By the 2013–2014 school year, the district website (http://www.duvalchoice.com/about-duval-choice) listed eight categories of school options. Four of the options targeted high-achievers and included Early College, the International Baccalaureate, the Advanced International Certificate of Education, and Advanced Placement programs.

The centerpiece of Duval's choice offerings and one of the options most likely to attract students from low-performing schools is the magnet-school program. Located in 62 different schools, magnet options focus on a particular theme or career cluster, such as culinary arts or computer science. To enter a magnet program and remain in good standing, students are required to pass all courses in grades 6 and 7 and maintain an unweighted grade point average of 2.0 throughout middle and high school.

Career academies also are available to Duval high school students. Operated as schools-within-schools, the career academies are managed by small teams of teachers. According to the district website, "This business-driven model incorporates a number of innovative features, including a family-like atmosphere, integration of academic and career-related curriculum, and involvement of employers in a number of roles." Students applying to career academies outside of their school's attendance area have to submit their application to the district's School Choice Office.

Charter schools constitute another component of Duval Choice. Operating as public schools on performance contracts with Duval County Public Schools, charter schools are not subject to many of the regulations governing traditional public schools. They have to hire certified teachers, however, and they are evaluated and assigned a school grade using the same standards and criteria as traditional public schools. In 2013–2014, Duval County had 31 charter schools operated by independent contractors, educational management organizations, and Florida State College at Jacksonville. Charter schools are required to see that transportation is not a barrier to equal access for all students residing within a reasonable distance of the school.

The newest addition to Duval's portfolio of options is the choice school. All traditional middle and high schools became choice schools in 2013. This designation means that every secondary school has to offer one or more "special programs" designed to attract students to the school.

The various options that comprise Duval Choice cater to all students, of course, not just those in low-performing schools. The district has added several other alternatives more in line with the special needs of the children left behind, though these programs are not part of Duval Choice per se.

Duval has implemented "over-age academies" at seven high schools and four middle schools ostensibly to help students who are two or more years over age for their grade to complete high school. Initially underresourced and perceived by many as a way to remove struggling students from mainstream classes, the district has made an effort to upgrade the academies. Teachers working at the academies now qualify for a $3,000 bump in salary, and appropriate instructional materials finally are available at the academies (Thompson, 2014). As of 2014, about 1,200 students attended the over-age academies.

A year after launching the over-age academies, Duval piloted single-gender academies at Eugene J. Butler Middle School (now known as the Leadership Schools at Eugene J. Butler), a perennially low-performing school. Girls are on the first floor in the Young Women's Leadership Academy, while boys are on the second floor in the Young Men's Leadership Academy (Duvall, 2015). If the program succeeds, the district plans to expand single-gender schooling.

INNOVATION AND CHOICE IN DENVER

Few school systems have done as much to promote both innovation and choice as Denver Public Schools (DPS). The impetus for much of this work has been concern for students in the Mile High City's low-performing schools. As of September 2014, Denver Public Schools enrolled 87,382 students, three quarters of whom were eligible for free and reduced-price lunch. Only about half of Denver's minority students were performing on grade level across all subjects, and the achievement gap between low-income and non–low-income students was almost 40% across all subjects (*Denver Public Schools*, 2014).[2]

For more than a decade, DPS has been developing and refining a comprehensive strategy for turning around low-performing schools. Early on in this process, DPS's chief officer of innovation and reform, Alyssa Whitehead-Bust, explained that the district was "systematically looking at schools and deciding whether to turnaround, replace, phase out, or close down. Next, we determine which schools should be district-run Innovation—a district-run school with much more flexibility in programming and staffing—or charter" (School turnaround in Denver Public Schools, 2011, p. 1).

Drawing largely on federal School Improvement Grant funds, DPS created a tiered intervention system that differentiated the improvement needs of low-performing schools. Plans for district-run Innovation schools and charter schools are developed by two regional support networks, one covering Denver's "near northeast" area and the other covering the city's southwest quadrant. These two "clusters," as they are called, represent the highest rates of poverty and English-language learners in Denver (*The 2015 Call*, 2015).

The two regional networks are each staffed by four or five individuals trained to support school turnaround initiatives. They assist with data collection and analysis, school websites, and communication about choices to parents. Denver Public Schools, like Louisiana's Recovery School District, also has established a universal enrollment system that provides parents with access to all of the city's public schools through a single online or paper application. The regional networks are responsible for monitoring schools and identifying areas in need of improvement. They are supported in this work by the district's Office of School Innovation and Reform.

Each year since 2008, the call has gone out from DPS for new school proposals. By 2015, 80 new schools had been approved for SchoolChoice: 21 Innovation schools, 11 district-run schools not designated as Innovation schools, and 48 charter schools (*The 2015 Call*, 2015). Regardless of a new school's status, it must operate within DPS's "three equities":

1. Equity of Opportunity means that the schools have access to equitable per pupil funding, support services from the district, and available facilities.
2. Equity of Responsibility and Access means that the schools must offer equitable and open access to all students—regardless of socioeconomic status, disability, home language, or other status—and

share an equal obligation in districtwide responsibilities, such as the cost of districtwide special education services.

3. Equity of Accountability means that all schools have the same accountability system under our School Performance Framework and that standards of performance are applied evenly across all school types. (*The 2015 Call*, 2015, pp. 12–13)

An example of one of Denver's Innovation schools provides an idea of what the district is trying to do for its neediest students. The Collegiate Prep Academy (CPA) is one of several new schools colocated at the site of Montbello High School, formerly one of Denver's lowest-performing high schools. CPA was launched in 2012 as a ninth-grade academy, and a grade was added each year until it became a full-fledged high school. This process of growing a new school occurred as Montbello High School was winding down, dropping one grade level each year from 2012 through 2015.

Many of the key features of CPA may not sound especially innovative to those familiar with other high school turnaround initiatives. They include the recruitment of talented school administrators and teachers, a longer school day and year, a culture of high expectations, frequent assessments, and daily small-group tutoring. To students used to mediocre instruction and low expectations, however, CPA is anything but routine.

Perhaps the most innovative feature of CPA is its small size. The starting ninth-grade class enrolled just over 100 students. The designers of CPA reasoned that a small high school would offer a safer, more supportive environment for students. Later in this chapter more information is provided on the move to downsize large schools in order to help the children left behind.

One of the most important components of the CPA program is the time set aside for tutoring in reading and mathematics. The majority of CPA's students entered the school below grade level in these core areas. By adding two extra periods to the traditional seven-period day, CPA ensures that all students spend additional time catching up to their higher-achieving peers. More time for tutoring also is available after school and on Saturdays.

Denver students looking for a nontraditional school have other options besides CPA. Among the other 20 Innovation schools are the Noel Community Arts School, offering an integrated arts focus; the Swigert International School with a curricular emphasis on international affairs; and the Denver Public Montessori Junior/Senior High School, one of the few Montessori secondary schools in the United States. Each year applications for new Innovation schools are solicited and received by Denver Public Schools.

One of the challenges of operating a district-based choice program like Denver's SchoolChoice is ensuring that applicants receive one of their top selections. An evaluation of the Denver program during the period 2012–2014 found that more than a quarter of Denver Public School students were participating in SchoolChoice and that between 76% and 89% (depending on the year) of all participants were matched to one of their choices (Gross & Denice, 2015).

The SchoolChoice evaluation contained some disturbing findings for advocates for the children left behind, however. Lower proportions of students eligible for free or reduced-price lunch participated in School-Choice than their more well-to-do counterparts (Gross & Denice, 2015). Furthermore, white students participated at higher rates than minority students. An encouraging finding, though, was the high participation rate for English-language learners. Also noteworthy was the lack of evidence that special needs students were purposely being excluded from participation or were choosing not to participate in SchoolChoice. Proximity to residence was not found to be the primary factor in school selection in many cases. One fifth of SchoolChoice participants indicated a first-choice school outside of their region.

Whether student achievement has been improved by SchoolChoice depends, to some extent, on the particular school. Among the 80 schools involved in the program, some are "distinguished," some "meet expectations," some are "on watch," and some are "on probation" (DPS designations). From 2009 to 2014, overall achievement in Denver schools improved by seven percentage points and gains were made by African American and Latino students in reading and mathematics (*Denver Public Schools progress report*, 2014). These figures are based, however, on all Denver schools, not just those participating in the SchoolChoice program.

THE ALLURE OF SMALL SCHOOLS

A century and a half ago, virtually all public schools in the United States were small schools. Urbanization led to higher concentrations of children in smaller geographical areas and hence larger schools, especially high schools. Interest in large schools eventually was accelerated by post–World War II concerns about the burgeoning baby boomer population and about fear that small high schools did not offer a sufficient range of challenging, advanced courses. Harvard's James Bryant Conant (1959), among others, insisted on the necessity of consolidating small high schools so that there would be a large enough group of talented students to justify the creation of advanced academic tracks.

Another boost to large schools came with school desegregation in the 1960s and 1970s. Small neighborhood schools were associated with racial homogeneity, based in part on discriminatory housing practices. The larger the school, the more likely it would enroll a diverse student body.

Fast forward to the early years of the 21st century and large urban schools are seen as part of public education's problems, not as educational panaceas. Large schools are characterized as impersonal and unsafe "warehouses" for students with no other options (Duke, DeRoberto, & Trautvetter, 2009). Overcrowded conditions mean that teachers struggle to manage classrooms and students wait for long periods before getting needed assistance. Managing these schools—what one researcher termed "dropout factories"—is a nightmare that scares off capable teachers and administrators.

To encourage small-school innovation, the Bill and Melinda Gates Foundation initiated a massive funding program. Denver was one of the first school districts, along with New York City and Chicago, to take advantage of the grants.

Efforts to downsize schools took various forms. Mention of charter schools already has been noted. Other efforts included building new schools that were small, reorganizing and reallocating space in existing schools, and renovating and redesigning existing schools. Given the expense of building small schools from scratch, many districts focused on the last two alternatives.

As far back as the late 1980s, New York City, for example, undertook a major initiative to subdivide large high schools into houses and schools-within-schools (Duke, DeRoberto, & Trautvetter, 2009). To help with the transition to high school, a large high school might create a separate house for ninth graders. A house was a largely self-contained unit with a cohort of students, one or more teams of teachers and counselors, and at least one administrator. Protected from the distractions of upperclassmen, students got to know their classmates and teachers.

One of the most popular approaches to downsizing involves the creation of so-called multiplex schools. A large high school, for instance, is redesigned to accommodate a variety of small, self-contained schools, each with a different focus and clientele. One such multiplex conversion about which much has been written is the Julia Richman High School in New York City (Duke et al., 2009). Built in 1922, the massive, five-story structure and its annex occupies an entire city block. Over the years, the aging school's reputation declined, its dropout rate grew, and vandalism and violence increased. In an effort to reverse this downward spiral, the school district invested in the redesign of the entire facility in order to accommodate six smaller entities, each enrolling approximately 300 students. The schools included:

- Vanguard High School: a high school offering a typical course of study and organizational structure.
- Manhattan International School: designed for students with limited fluency in English.

- Talent Unlimited Performing Arts High School. A specialty school that also offers basic courses.
- Urban Academy: a high school for transfer students that is organized around multiage classes.
- P226M: a special education junior high school designed for severely autistic children.
- Ella Baker Elementary School: an elementary school for children of employees of hospitals in the neighborhood.

Although the small size and self-contained nature of these schools is innovative for a large urban school system like New York's, the programs offered in the schools are not necessarily so. The six schools share some space, such as gymnasiums, library, and cafeteria. Their location in the midst of the city enables students to take advantage of various cultural opportunities, work experiences, and courses offered at local community colleges. Accessibility to these additional learning environments may be one of the small schools' greatest benefits (though, of course, the same access would be available to students in large schools as well).

Several efforts have been made to assess the impact of small schools. The focus of one study was Chicago's program for converting large high schools into several small schools (Kahne, Sporte, de la Torre, & Easton, 2008). As of 2005, approximately 106,000 students attended 107 Chicago high schools, including 30 small schools and charter schools. Drawing on data from the biannual surveys of students, teachers, and principals conducted by the Consortium for Chicago School Research and test data from 2002–2003 to 2005–2006, the study focused on 11th graders and their teachers. The schools chosen for conversion to small schools were among the lowest-performing high schools in Chicago. The study compared student outcomes in conversion schools to outcomes for students in Chicago's nonalternative high schools.

Researchers found some evidence of decreased dropout rates and increased graduation rates for the first cohort of students to attend the small schools, but not for the succeeding year's cohort. Student achievement did not improve in the conversion schools nor was instruction found to be stronger. There were indications, however, that teachers preferred working conditions in the small schools. The researchers questioned why these improved working conditions—greater teacher-to-teacher trust, a sense of collective responsibility, openness to innovation, and greater teacher influence—failed to produce higher-quality instruction or student academic gains on standardized tests.

Like Chicago, New York City used Gates Foundation funds to embark on a program to create academically nonselective small schools in 2002. Researchers undertook a large-scale study of the program's impact and found results that were much more encouraging than those from Chicago. The central question of the study was "By how much does attending an SSC [small school of choice] improve academic outcomes for students who attend them, relative to what these outcomes would have been if these students had not attended an SSC?" (Bloom & Unterman, 2013). Because access to the small schools was determined by lottery, the researchers were able to conduct a randomized control study with students who "won" their school choice in the lottery compared to students who tried but were not picked (and therefore had to attend a traditional high school). The study involved more than 21,000 students, including students enrolled in 105 of 123 small schools and students who wanted to enroll but were lotteried into one of 200 other New York high schools.

Students in the New York study fit the profile of students attending low-performing schools. Almost 94% were black or Hispanic, 84% were eligible for free or reduced-price lunch, 22% were over age in the eighth grade, and nearly 71% were reading below grade level in eighth grade.

The findings provide evidence that small schools can be an effective innovation for at least some of the children left behind. Small schools accounted for nearly nine more graduates per 100 entering ninth graders than the traditional high schools. Positive graduation effects were recorded for virtually every subgroup, including students with low entering proficiency in English and math, males and females, blacks and Hispanics, and students eligible for free and reduced-price lunch. Small-school students also were more likely to score 75 or higher on the English Regents exam, a measure of college readiness.

When the two researchers from the above study and a colleague examined the cost effectiveness of the small-schools initiative, they found more good news (Bifulco, Unterman, & Bloom, 2014). After conducting an "experimental" comparison of per pupil operating costs for the small high schools and the control group's traditional high schools, they found that the cost per high school graduate was substantially lower for the small-school enrollees than for their control-group counterparts.

An important cautionary note regarding New York's small-school initiative was sounded by Bruce Fuller (2014), however. While acknowledging the impressive graduation findings, Fuller pointed out that small schools have contributed to greater racial and ethnic segregation. Three fifths of all black and Hispanic teenagers in New York City attend small high schools, according to Fuller. In contrast, less than one fourth of all white and Asian American ninth graders enter a small school. These students are more likely to attend a selective high school. The question for educational policy makers is a perplexing one: Is higher achievement and attainment for the children left behind worth the price of greater racial and ethnic segregation?

NEW YORK CITY'S IZONE

As the nation's largest school system, New York City always has provided innovative educational choices, at least for some students. In recent years, however, the range of innovations has mushroomed. When city schools opened in September 2015, there were 130 new community schools, each providing wraparound services such as counseling and health care: 94 "renewal" schools supplied with lots of extra resources to boost academic achievement, and 40 new dual-language programs designed to mix native English speakers with those who speak other languages (Disare, 2015). There also were the small high schools mentioned earlier and the select schools for high-achieving students.

Perhaps New York City's boldest effort to innovate, though, has been the Innovation Zone (iZone) launched in 2010. The iZone requires schools to reinvent themselves in order to meet students' learning needs. "Rather than prescribing a standardized approach to curriculum, staffing, school schedule, and testing, the iZone schools are supposed to explore and innovate with student-centered mastery designs that are characterized by the following five core principles:

1. Performance assessment and mastery-based grading
2. Personalized learning plans
3. Multiple learning modalities (e.g., a combination of independent student work, small group instruction, one-on-one instruction, student collaborative activities, online instruction)
4. New staff and student roles
5. Globally competitive standards" (Lake & Gross, 2011, p. 1)

The iZone assigns a small number of schools "Lab" status, thereby freeing them to explore new ways to provide learning opportunities, especially for students who have struggled to succeed in school. Online and blended learning play a significant role in the designs implemented by many Lab schools. To equip teachers with the skills necessary to implement blended learning, the iZone also created the Blended Learning Institute. By 2014, more than 250 city schools were using some form of blended learning.

One of the best known programs offered under the iZone rubric is the School of One, a unique math program for middle schoolers. Five teachers along with several assistant teachers work with roughly 150 students gathered in a single large room. The room is organized into various learning stations, including computer stations. Students are assigned to modules involving virtual exercises with off-site tutors, peer-to-peer activities, and teacher-led instruction. At the end of each class period, students are assessed on their mastery of the lesson's content. According to the School of One website, students receive "personalized lessons based on their precise academic level every day" (FAQ, n.d.).

By using digital technology to develop individualized, daily adjusted math curricula that students access using an online portal, School of One offers a powerful model for customizing learning. New York's Office of Innovation is hopeful that the model eventually can be applied to other content areas besides mathematics. It should be noted that the New York City school district is able to support a technology-dependent program like School of One because of its Achievement Reporting and Innovation System (ARIS), a sophisticated data and knowledge management system that provides detailed information about student performance and progress.

The iZone has taken the initiative to invite providers of educational services, particularly online programs, to work with the Office of Innovation to develop new learning opportunities for both students and teachers. The iZone also participates in the Portfolio Network, a national consortium of districts offering students a range of innovative options. The Portfolio Network enables districts to share their experiences with new models of learning.

In the preceding chapter, we saw that standardized approaches to school turnaround have their merits. They also have their drawbacks. Too much emphasis on standardization can obscure important local variations in schools and their clientele. Highly qualified teachers may resent having to follow prescribed guidelines and set protocols.

Innovative approaches to teaching the children left behind and programs that give students educational choices also have strengths and possible weaknesses. Choice, for instance, can be very appealing to poor parents who feel that only the well-to-do typically get their pick of schools. Innovative programs and instructional methods also can be an antidote to uninspiring teaching and provide a motivational boost for struggling students.

The downside of innovation, however, is that new approaches may not necessarily have been tested adequately. The educational landscape is littered with failed experiments once deemed panaceas. Students, especially students stuck in the lowest-performing schools, are not guinea pigs with whom educators should try unproven practices and programs.

As for choice-based programs, they can be helpful, but only if all parents (1) have equal access to information so that they can make well-informed choices for their children, and (2) actually have equal access to *all* the schools and programs involved. Without adequate provisions for transportation, for example, some students from poor families may be unable to take advantage of a full range of educational options.

The majority of Americans nonetheless remain supportive of school choice. In the 2015 Phi Delta Kappa/Gallup Poll of the Public's Attitudes toward the Public Schools, for example, 64% of respondents favored charter schools as well as allowing students and their parents to choose which public schools to attend, regardless of where they live (*The 47th annual PDK/Gallup Poll*, 2015, p. 18).

Whether innovative learning environments and multiple options prove to be better turnaround strategies than standardized models based on "best practices" remains to be determined. In the final analysis, both probably have their place in the struggle to serve the children left behind. One thing is certain, though: Local school districts must be able to support school-based improvement efforts, whatever their focus. It is to the matter of district support that we turn in the next chapter.

NOTES

1. In September 2015, Washington State's Supreme Court decided that taxpayer-funded charter schools were unconstitutional. The court reasoned that charters are not truly public schools because they are not governed by elected boards and therefore are not accountable to voters. See Emma Brown, "Washington state ruling highlights charter-school debate," *Washington Post*, September 10, 2015, p. A8.

2. Much of the background materials on Denver Public Schools' efforts to innovate and expand choice for students is derived from a case study, "School turnarounds in Denver Public Schools," that was retrieved from http://www.erstrategies.org/cms/files/1496-denver-case-study.pdf.

REFERENCES

Bettinger, E. P. 2010. *Paying to learn: The effect of financial incentives on elementary test scores*. National Bureau of Economic Research Working Paper Series. Cambridge, MA: National Bureau of Economic Research.

Bifulco, R., Unterman, R., & Bloom, H. S. 2014. *The relative costs of New York City's new small public schools of choice*. New York: MDRC.

Bloom, H. S., & Unterman, R. 2013. *Sustained progress*. New York: MDRC.

Conant, J. B. 1959. *The comprehensive high school*. New York: McGraw-Hill.

Denver Public Schools progress report. 2014. Denver, CO: A+ Denver.

Disare, M. 2015, September 9. On her 50th first day, New York City chancellor tours schools carrying out her vision. *Chalkbeat*. Retrieved from http://ny.chalkbeat.org/2015/09/09/on-her-50th-first-day-new-york-city-chancellor-tours-schools-carrying-out-her-vision/#.VnAd60orLIU.

Duke, D. L., DeRoberto, T., & Trautvetter, S. 2009. *Reducing the negative effects of school size*. Washington, DC: National Clearinghouse for Educational Facilities.

Duvall, T. 2015, May 29. Transforming Butler: A bold plan to turn around a struggling middle school meets with challenges and successes. *Florida Times-Union* [Jacksonville]. Retrieved from http://jacksonville.suntimes.com/jax-news/7/115/194312/transforming-butler-a-bold-plan-to-turn-around-a-struggling-middle-school-meets-with-challenges-and-successes.

FAQ. n.d. *iZone, New York City Department of Education*. Retrieved from http://izone-nyc.org/faqs/category/school-of-one.

Fuller, B. 2014, January 22. Is small beautiful? *Education Week*, 24.

Gross, B., & Denice, P. 2015. *An evaluation of Denver's SchoolChoice process, 2012–2014*. Denver, CO: A+ Denver.

Herold, B. 2015, August 5. Innovation networks need both autonomy, support. *Education Week*, 10.

Kahne, J. E., Sporte, S. E., de la Torre, M., & Easton, J. Q. 2008. Small high schools on a larger scale: The impact of school conversations in Chicago. *Educational Evaluation and Policy Analysis, 30*(3), 281–315.

Lake, R., & Gross, B. 2011. *New York City's iZone.* Bothell, WA: Center on Reinventing Public Education.

Molnar, M. 2015, March 18. "Education innovation clusters" aim to improve schools. *Education Week,* 12.

School turnarounds in Denver Public Schools. 2011. *Education Resource Strategies.* Retrieved from http://www.erstrategies.org/cms/files/1496-denver-case-study.pdf.

Supovitz, J. A. 2006. *The case for district-based reform.* Cambridge, MA: Harvard Education Press.

The 47th annual PDK/Gallup poll. 2015. Bloomington, IN: Phi Delta Kappa.

The 2015 call for new quality schools. 2015. Denver, CO: Denver Public Schools.

Thompson, R. 2014, June 19. Bridge to Success sees mixed results in first year. *WJCT* [Jacksonville, Florida]. Retrieved from http://news.wjct.org/post/bridge-success-sees-mixed-results-first-year.

What's new. FY 2015 development competition. 2015. Retrieved from http://www2.ed.gov/programs/innovation/2015competition.html.

NINE

Developing District Capacity to Support School Turnarounds

Buffalo's struggles to provide the guidance and support needed to effect turnarounds in its lowest-performing schools were recounted in chapter 2. Later we learned of Cincinnati's impressive initiative to improve its lowest-performing elementary schools. Why did one school system succeed while the other faltered? The simple answer is that Cincinnati possessed the leadership at all levels—community, school board, superintendent, teachers union, and school—needed to promote, plan, implement, and sustain the turnaround process.

Buffalo, meanwhile, descended into a pattern of petty squabbles among stakeholder groups. Agreement could not be reached on such important matters as teacher replacement, teacher evaluation, principal replacement, school closure, student transfers to selective schools, or even whose outside help to accept. Eventually the school board split over whether to invite the state to take over the school district. Meanwhile, the schooling of thousands of children continued to be placed in jeopardy.

In the campaign to raise up the lowest-performing schools, local leadership clearly is necessary. It is not sufficient by itself, however. Too often, too much faith is put in a change of leadership. What is required in addition includes an organizational structure to support school-based improvement, adequate financing, a strategy that seeks out talented principals and teachers to staff troubled schools, and, in many cases, an adaptable transportation system. These key elements are discussed in the pages that follow.

RESTRUCTURING WITH TURNAROUND IN MIND

School districts, as noted earlier, are bureaucracies, and the bureaucratic form of organization—characterized by hierarchy of authority, division of labor, regulations, and an orientation to compliance—has come to be associated with such undesirable features as red tape, rigidity, and resistance to change. Created to promote efficiency, bureaucracy to many observers connotes the very opposite.

Bureaucracy, however, does not have to be an obstacle in the path to better schooling for the children left behind. Some organization theorists, for example, differentiate between "enabling" and "coercive" bureaucracies (Duke, 2010, p. 84). Specialization and regulations can serve useful purposes under the right conditions. So how can restructuring district operations help to improve low-performing schools?

Among the purposes for which restructuring has been justified is the signaling of a new focus on turning around failing schools, expediting the planning process, coordinating the allocation of resources and targeted assistance, and facilitating the monitoring of improvement efforts. The particular form of restructuring is likely to vary with such factors as the existing organizational structure, the district's size, and the number of low-performing schools.

Fairfax County's Project Excel

Fairfax County (Virginia) Public Schools, under the leadership of Dan Domenech, made an effort to address the needs of its lowest-performing elementary schools several years before the advent of No Child Left Behind (NCLB) (Duke, 2005). Titled Project Excel, the initiative targeted 20 elementary schools with low test scores, high poverty and mobility rates, and high numbers of English-language learners. To support improvement efforts, the district allocated an extra $8 million in the first year. Each school was required to choose one of several approved curriculum models, and each was allowed to offer full-day kindergarten (other Fairfax elementary schools were limited to half-day kindergarten). The 20 schools were given three years to raise their test scores on state tests. Achieving performance goals resulted in a substantial bonus for school faculty members.

Project Excel schools, for the most part, accomplished their goal of boosting student achievement, but the process of delivering district assistance to the schools had its shortcomings. Domenech had attempted to turn around the 20 schools without any significant restructuring of district operations (Duke, 2005, pp. 142–43). The district continued to be divided into three enormous "areas," each as large as a midsize city's school district. Project Excel schools were located in each of these areas, and each area was led by a powerful area superintendent.

Over the years, each area superintendent had developed a distinct office culture and way of handling issues in area schools. Overlapping responsibilities for low-performing schools between the area offices and the central administration resulted in mixed messages and confusion for Project Excel principals. They complained about uncertainty regarding whom to contact when a problem arose. Given the span of control for each area superintendent, the close monitoring and supervision of Project Excel schools expected by state authorities became difficult.

To avoid these kinds of problems, large school systems with many low-performing schools have engaged in various kinds of restructuring efforts, ranging from establishing a special office of school turnaround to clustering low-performing schools into separate subdistricts. In the case of Fairfax County, the decision recently was made to pair low-performing schools with high-performing schools as a means of sharing expertise and raising student achievement.

Miami-Dade's School Improvement Zone

Mention has been made in previous chapters of special district units comprised of low-performing schools. One of the largest of these entities was the School Improvement Zone (SIZ) in Miami-Dade County Public Schools. The SIZ was one of Superintendent Rudy Crew's first initiatives when he arrived in Miami in 2004. Previously during his stint as chancellor of the New York City Department of Education, Crew had created a similar subdivision of low-performing schools. The New York City Chancellor's District served as the model for Miami-Dade's SIZ.

The two special units shared a focus on literacy, extended school day and academic year, small-group tutoring for struggling students, district-mandated schedule and curriculum, intensive professional development and coaching requirements for teachers, and efforts to improve school leadership through principal replacement and mentoring (*Meeting the turnaround challenge*, 2009, p. 7). The SIZ initially consisted of 39 elementary, middle, and high schools. Principals of these schools, unlike their colleagues in non-SIZ schools, were constrained in their discretionary authority. Decisions regarding SIZ schools were highly centralized within a small group of district office staff members led by an associate superintendent.

Teachers in SIZ schools worked under a separately negotiated collective bargaining agreement that included a voluntary transfer process. Teachers received a 20% pay increase for working in SIZ schools because of the extended school day and school year. At each SIZ school, teachers elected a Professional Development Team to plan and coordinate in-service training to address student needs.

By clustering together the 39 low-performing schools in a single district subdivision, Miami-Dade avoided the logistical and coordination problems that Fairfax County experienced with Project Excel. Centralized decision making meant that the confusion resulting from schools being located in three Fairfax "areas," each under an area superintendent, were avoided.

Schools in the SIZ were given three years in which to achieve significant improvements in student performance. According to a case study of the SIZ undertaken by Mass Insight (*Meeting the turnaround challenge,* 2009, p. 4), SIZ schools demonstrated inconsistent growth. Florida's state report card showed eight elementary and three middle schools experiencing improvement in student achievement over the course of three years. The other 28 schools either recorded no improvement or declined. Rudy Crew's efforts in New York City had netted much more impressive results, with 56% of Chancellor's District schools exiting "underperforming" status. It is worth noting, however, that it took six years for these schools to improve.

The School Improvement Zone was abandoned in 2008, less because of its disappointing outcomes than funding issues. Facing an enormous deficit and unable to secure sufficient bailout funds from the state or private funders, Crew was compelled to discontinue the experiment.

In Mass Insight's case study (*Meeting the turnaround challenge,* 2009, p. 3), several suggestions are made as to why the SIZ failed to live up to expectations. Tight central control by the district office may have inhibited the actions of principals. Additionally, SIZ schools were not allowed to develop relationships with external lead partners or to build partnerships with local community and business organizations. Such partnerships could have produced supplementary support when the district faced the need to retrench.

District Turnaround Offices

Not all school systems are large enough to consider creating a subdivision or zone made up entirely of low-performing schools. Smaller districts with a handful of low-performing schools may consider establishing a district turnaround office, however. The potential benefits of such an office are numerous.

Central office personnel with the expertise to assist low-performing schools, for example, can be assigned to the special office. Individuals might include reading specialists, math specialists, instructional coaches, special education and English-language learner experts, and data analysts. Combining this talent in one unit facilitates turnaround planning and the delivery of comprehensive assistance. Principals in need of help are able to make a single contact with the turnaround office instead of getting in touch with resource people scattered across various district offices.

A district turnaround office can handle special sources of funding such as federal grants and contributions from donors. Responsibilities range from writing grants to monitoring and managing them. Principals of low-performing schools are spared these duties as well as the tasks of preparing reports required by funders. District turnaround office personnel compile the pertinent information from principals and prepare the reports. Since state education authorities typically monitor district efforts to improve low-performing schools, the district turnaround office also can maintain contact with state officials and apprise them of progress.

Other functions best assigned to a district turnaround office include expediting the procurement of curriculum and assessment materials, recruiting and developing personnel for low-performing schools, and keeping the superintendent and school board informed about school improvement efforts. In situations where external consultants and lead partners are involved, turnaround office administrators assist with vetting possible partners, negotiating contracts, and managing contracts.

Professional development for principals and teachers typically is a major component of school turnaround efforts. When training needs are similar for different schools, district turnaround office specialists coordinate professional development, thereby ensuring consistency and likely saving money in the process. Districts that have implemented turnaround offices often assign responsibility for principal supervision and mentoring to office administrators as well.

Mass Insight has played a major role in helping school districts set up turnaround offices. According to the Boston-based consulting firm, the purpose of such offices is "to support failing schools and partner organizations and, at the same time, hold them accountable for student performance" (Mass Insight, 2010, p. 10). To accomplish this purpose, the consulting firm recommends that district turnaround offices:

- streamline supports from multiple offices rather than create additional bureaucracy
- create a "club you want to join" for low-performing schools rather than punitive framework
- ensure that low-performing schools are prioritized in not only talk but also action
- protect school and lead partner level authority to deliver results (Mass Insight, 2010, p. 4)

The size of district turnaround offices, based on Mass Insight's investigations, can range from two to eight professionals, depending on the district's size, number of low-performing schools, and available funds. The annual cost of operation can run $1 million or more.

After tracking the operation of five turnaround offices in very large urban districts, Mass Insight (2010, p. 45–46) noted a number of challenges associated with them. Four of the five offices experienced periodic realignment and reorganization, especially when changes occurred in outside funding and state and local politics. Needless to say, these events can have a disruptive effect on service delivery and other functions. The Mass Insight report also warned that turnaround office staff should "expect high workloads and competing priorities, and may find it challenging to continue/scale up initiatives without diluting the level of support provided" (p. 46).

In supporting the turnaround efforts of school principals, overzealous turnaround office personnel sometimes can undermine principals' authority. When this happens, principals hesitate to exercise the strong leadership needed to provide direction to and inspire commitment from school staff. It is vital that school personnel and community members regard principals as the individuals in charge of the school improvement process.

Project Management

Turnaround offices may not be viable options for districts that are very small or that lack adequate resources. For these districts, project management offers a useful approach to supporting the improvement of low-performing schools.

The Roswell Independent School District (RISD) in New Mexico serves a student population of approximately 10,000 students. When Michael Gottlieb became superintendent in 2005, 11 of Roswell's 20 schools failed to meet Adequate Yearly Progress under NCLB (Gottlieb, Duke, & Smalley, 2011). Gottlieb decided that the keys to improving Roswell's low-performing schools involved access to quality data and a structure for linking data to the turnaround process.

"Data Day" was initiated in order for the school year to begin with training for all instructional staff in how to interpret and use student achievement data to guide instruction. Benchmark assessments were put in place so that teachers would periodically assess student progress on state standards. Eventually Gottlieb launched a classroom walk-through project so principals could gather observational data on how well teachers were using formative assessment data to address student needs.

To support these and other improvement efforts, Gottlieb implemented project management. A project manager was assigned to oversee each new initiative. To track project progress, the Project Management Oversight Committee (PMOC) was established. The members of the PMOC included the assistant superintendents for finance, instruction, human resources, and testing and technology; the directors of construction and maintenance; a computer programmer; a principal; and two teachers. Gottlieb chaired the PMOC.

Meeting once a month, the PMOC heard progress reports from each project manager. Each project manager assembled a project team to handle the specific tasks associated with accomplishing the project. When a team encountered difficulties or needed additional resources, the project manager appealed to the PMOC for assistance. Because representatives of all the major central office departments sat on the PMOC, the project manager was able to receive responses to requests for help at one meeting. Time was not wasted trying to contact department heads individually.

Among the first projects to be launched during Gottlieb's tenure were a reading comprehension improvement program, a math-skills across-the-curriculum project, and the aforementioned classroom walk-through initiative. The open and honest discussions between project managers and PMOC members enabled each project to be fine-tuned and adjusted over time. These discussions continued until the project was completed.

By 2008, the number of Roswell schools meeting Adequate Yearly Progress benchmarks had jumped to 15, an increase of six schools. Gottlieb credited the gains, in part, to the intense focus on data-driven decision making and the implementation of project management and the PMOC (Gottlieb et al., 2011).

A team of researchers from the Center for the Study of Teaching and Policy at the University of Washington found that project management also is being employed in large school systems, including Atlanta, New York City, and Oakland (Honig, Copland, Rainey, Lorton, & Newton, 2010). According to the research team, central office administrators started to shift the focus of their work from delivering services that they controlled to assuming responsibility for work projects and gathering resources from throughout and sometimes beyond the central office to address them. As an Atlanta administrator reported, "when a central office shifts its focus from delivering services to truly solving problems, staff begin to see that they have to work with their colleagues in more integrated and collaborative ways" (Honig et al., 2010, p. 74).

Besides the examples just cited, there is an additional way, albeit a more indirect one, that districts can reorganize to support school turnarounds. When support services associated with helping low-performing schools are scattered across various central office units, consolidating these units under one umbrella department can encourage data sharing and coordination of interventions and resourcing.

Fairfax County Public Schools took such a step in 2001 when Superintendent Dan Domenech launched the Department of Educational Accountability (Duke, 2005). Previously, problems arose anytime it became necessary to pull together data from various sources in order to facilitate analysis, planning, and action. Data on special education students, for example, resided in one "silo," while minority student achievement data was located elsewhere.

Domenech considered the various units that handled data for the school system. They included the Office of Educational Planning, the

Office of Program Evaluation, the Office of Student Testing, and the Office of Minority Student Achievement. The last office had been created in the 1980s after African American parents complained about the achievement gap between black and white students in Fairfax County.

By placing the four offices in one department, it was possible to develop a comprehensive data management system and expedite responses to requests for data from school board members, the superintendent, and school principals. Furthermore, student test data could be linked quickly to program evaluations in order to determine whether programs were addressing student needs effectively. Colocating the four offices also made it easier to support principals engaged in developing school improvement plans.

FINANCING SCHOOL IMPROVEMENT

It is generally assumed that turning around the lowest-performing schools requires supplementary funding. When the funding of school turnarounds has been discussed so far in this book, it usually has involved federal and state support. Such support, however, cannot be taken for granted. Shifts in political priorities and economic conditions may result in the reduction or elimination of special funds targeting low-performing schools. In these circumstances, the financial burden falls on local school systems.

In cases such as federal School Improvement Grants, the additional funds only are allocated for a three-year period. Consider what happened in a suburban St. Louis middle school when its $6 million SIG ran out (Duke, Barbour, & Dolby, 2015). Programs and personnel that were added as a result of the SIG had to be eliminated. Losses included a reading teacher, reading interventionist, math interventionist, parent/community coordinator, and an assistant principal. In addition, the extended school day was canceled along with an after-school program, and professional development was scaled back. With the state of Missouri introducing new state curriculum standards and standardized tests, the timing could not have been worse. The school system lacked the resources to preserve any of these add-ons.

What is unfortunate about the example of the Missouri middle school is that student achievement had begun to improve just as SIG funding ended. Sometimes additional resources can be secured by tapping local community organizations, philanthropies, and businesses. Cincinnati benefitted from such local support. In other instances, taxpayers are willing to accept a tax hike in order to bolster school turnarounds. Neither strategy worked for the Missouri middle school, however.

How school districts choose to allocate available funds can have a significant impact on turnaround efforts. In chapter 3, for example, it was noted that achievement gains in low-performing Massachusetts schools were greater when higher percentages of special funds were spent on instruction and job-embedded professional development for teachers rather than on programs to address students' social-emotional and behavioral concerns (Lane, Unger, & Rhim, 2013).

Montgomery County (Maryland) Public Schools was chastised in a state report in 2015 for failing to allocate more than a third of its state aid for low-income students to programs specifically aimed at their needs (St. George, 2015). The school district instead used $47 million of its $128.6 million allocation for "broader operating-budget functions." The report went on, however, to applaud Montgomery County's commitment to greater staffing and lower class sizes for its high-poverty elementary schools.

San Diego, under the leadership of Alan Bersin, provides a useful example of what a large school system can do to ensure that resources are aligned effectively to support school improvement (Hightower, 2002). Bersin believed that the district office was not organized to facilitate the efficient delivery of assistance to San Diego's schools. In 1998 he launched, with the help of Chancellor of Instruction Anthony Alvarado, a restructuring initiative designed to focus resources on teaching and learning and bring coherence to the proliferation of special programs that had been implemented over the years to address the needs of low-performing schools.

New programs in San Diego typically were created when the district received a grant or responded to a government mandate. As the number of separate programs grew, so too did operational complexity and coordination problems. By consolidating all programs under Alvarado's leadership in the newly named Institute for Learning, Bersin ensured that all programs served the same priority: improving instruction in order to raise student achievement. He also cut overhead expenses in the process by streamlining program management.

According to a study of San Diego's restructuring efforts, "budgeting and operational managers learned to collaborate with instructional administrators to specify and prioritize instructional needs and direct district dollars toward instructional priorities" (Hightower, 2002, p. 90). The result of this culture of collaboration was a "shift *away* from letting the available money guide program and policy decisions, and *toward* having districtwide, articulated, instructional needs govern the budget" (Hightower, 2002, p. 90).

To free up additional resources to support instructional improvement, Bersin downsized the central office. Central office staff members were asked how their functions supported teaching and learning. Individuals whose responses revealed a weak link to these priorities lost their jobs. Cost savings were passed on to the district's neediest schools.

San Diego's efforts to align finances and district priorities, as might be expected, generated considerable controversy and pushback from affected groups. Educators in high-performing schools in affluent neighborhoods, for instance, questioned why they had to be part of the restructuring initiative. Hightower (2002, p. 76) suggests in her case study, however, that "systemic change in a large urban district may require strong, even bureaucratic, methods to transition the system into supporting a culture focused on instruction and learning."

Some districts are taking a very different tack regarding the financing of school improvements. Rather than a top-down approach, they are moving to Student-based Budgeting (SBB), a funding system that increases the discretionary authority of school principals. Metropolitan Nashville Public Schools (MNPS) is one of the districts making the move to SBB, in large part to enable principals of low-performing schools to address better the needs of their students. As Director of Schools Jesse Register (2015, p. 9) noted in his 2015 State of the Schools remarks, "This model allows principals to hire the staff they need for the school environments they design. School budgets are set based on the characteristics of the students they serve—so schools get resources to match the increased needs of EL students, students with disabilities, or low-performing students."

Conventional approaches to school budgeting rely on preset staffing formulas. One teacher, for instance, is allocated for every 25 students. When the 26th student shows up, the school gets another teaching position. Similar formulas also apply to guidance counselors and school administrators. The specific needs of the particular students at a certain school are not taken into account when these formulas are applied.

Student-based Budgeting, like most systemic approaches to school improvement, has potential problems as well as benefits. Calvo (2011) points out, for example, that developing a formula of what factors to weigh and by how much can be a very complex and contentious matter. She goes on to note that funding may be thrown off when enrollment projections miss the mark. To guard against the misallocation of funds by principals, districts also may need to create fiscal oversight systems.

A benefit of SBB is that principals are not constrained by fixed staffing formulas that treat all schools the same. Principals are accorded the flexibility to hire staff based on the needs of their school's student population. They can make adjustments as enrollments shift. Calvo (2011) goes on to point out that SBB is compatible with programs to expand school choice. "Since schools receive dollars for every additional child," she writes, "they have an incentive to reach out to the community and be responsive to parents in order to attract their target number of students" (p. 2).

STAFFING SCHOOL IMPROVEMENT

Student-based Budgeting is not only a new approach to school finance, it also is a new approach to school staffing, one that replaces staffing formulas with school-based hiring decisions linked directly to student needs. It is difficult to imagine a more important domain of district policy than staffing when it comes to helping the children left behind.

Many school districts face an uphill struggle when it comes to staffing their lowest-performing schools. A study of staffing in four school districts (Atlanta; New York City; Portland, Oregon; and Eugene, Oregon) identified four interrelated challenges that need to be addressed:

> maximizing the quality and longevity of teaching staff in high-needs schools, which are typically hard to staff; deploying and supporting the generally high proportions of novice teachers; managing and minimizing the often high rates of teacher mobility and attrition; and matching the ethnic, racial, and linguistic diversity of the student population with corresponding diversity in the teacher ranks. (Plecki et al., 2009, p. iii)

In order to deal effectively with the staffing of low-performing schools, district leaders need a multifaceted strategy encompassing recruitment, selection, placement, development, and retention of teachers. Piecemeal approaches are not likely to make much of a difference. It does little long-term good to attract talented black, Hispanic, and Asian American teachers, for example, if they leave within a few years of being hired. This appears to be exactly what is happening in many school systems, however (Layton, 2015).

Recruitment of capable teachers is the first order of business. Without them, little can be done to turn around low-performing schools. When Paul Vallas became CEO of the School District of Philadelphia in 2002, he pursued a novel approach to teacher recruitment (Duke, 2010). The colleges attended by teachers who remained for long periods of time in the school district were identified. Most of the colleges were located in the metropolitan Philadelphia area. District recruiters thus were able to target a relatively small number of institutions for some of their most intensive recruitment efforts.

There were several other components to Philadelphia's recruiting strategy under Vallas. In order to increase the number of African American teachers in the predominantly African American school system, recruiters visited historically black colleges and universities. They reached out to college sophomores and juniors as well as students getting ready to graduate. The district hosted weekend gatherings of college students in order for possible recruits to learn more about Philadelphia schools and the district's ambitions.

Recognizing that the competition for teachers was keen, the Vallas administration incentivized the recruitment process with signing bonuses, competitive starting salaries, and tuition reimbursement. To overcome Philadelphia's negative public image, the district hired a communications expert to advertise the positive aspects of living and working in the City of Brotherly Love.

Duval County (Florida) Public Schools also initiated an incentive program to secure talented teachers for schools in its newly formed Transformation Region. This special organizational unit contained many of the district's lowest-performing schools. Instead of only seeking newly minted teachers, however, Duval recruited teachers with proven track records at non-Transformation schools in the district (Stepzinksi, 2014). In return for making a three-year commitment to teach at a Transformation school, these veterans received a first-year incentive of $17,000. In subsequent years, they became eligible for performance incentives. Funds for Duval's incentive program came from private donations of $40 million raised by the Community Foundation for Northeast Florida.

It goes without saying that the value of recruitment strategies such as those in Philadelphia and Duval County is diminished if capable teachers cannot be retained. Ingersoll (2001) challenged the notion that improved recruiting alone can solve staffing problems in low-performing schools. He found that the early departure of large numbers of qualified teachers was more likely to account for staffing problems than a shortage of qualified applicants. Job dissatisfaction was a major reason why many teachers chose to leave. Besides concern over low salaries, teachers noted lack of administrative support, student discipline problems, poor student motivation, and lack of faculty influence.

Efforts to retain teachers must begin as soon as they are hired, since a significant percentage of teachers depart early in their careers. Assigning new teachers to teach the toughest classes, greater numbers of students, and multiple preparations contributes to job dissatisfaction, as does the lack of guidance, encouragement, and support. Providing new teachers with mentors, coaching, and induction classes can help to ease the transition to a new job. District leaders must work with principals to make certain that new teachers are given reasonable assignments as well as continuing support.

Once teachers have survived the induction period and gained the competence and confidence to be effective teachers, other measures may be required to ensure their continued employment. Competitive salaries certainly are an important element in a district teacher retention policy, but money alone may not be sufficient, especially in persistently low-performing schools. Efforts to promote teacher collaboration, teaming, and professional learning communities can enhance job satisfaction and reduce feelings of isolation and alienation. Opportunities for experienced teachers to exercise leadership and share responsibility for such matters as mentoring novice teachers, conducting professional development, and assisting with school improvement serve as visible forms of teacher recognition, thereby lessening the likelihood of premature exits.

The quality of school leadership has been found to be a key factor in teachers' decisions to remain at a school or leave (Duke, 2010, pp. 190–91). Teachers appreciate principals who value their opinions and consult them before embarking on a new initiative. On the other hand, when principals ignore what teachers have to say, fail to recognize teacher contributions, and do not treat teachers like professionals, they have no one to blame but themselves when teachers decide to depart. Over one third of the teachers in one large study (Luekens, Lyter, Fox, & Chandler, 2004) reported that they transferred to another school because of dissatisfaction with school leadership.

A study of teacher retention commissioned by the District of Columbia Public Schools confirmed the role of school leaders in determining whether teachers—especially high-performing teachers—leave or stay (Keeping irreplaceables, 2012). The authors of the study went on to point out that school districts should not be concerned about retaining weak teachers. As a result of a new performance-based teacher evaluation system launched by Michelle Rhee in the D.C. system, fewer weak teachers are able to hang on to their jobs. Interestingly, the study concluded that getting rid of low-performing teachers seemed to have a positive impact on the retention of high-performing teachers. In the 2010–2011 school year, for instance, D.C. Public Schools kept 88% of its high-performing teachers compared to 45% of its low performers.

While many teacher organizations have criticized performance-based teacher evaluation and compensation systems, often for legitimate methodological reasons, it is worth noting that the D.C. study found that high-performing teachers in the District of Columbia were less likely to be critical than their counterparts in three other large school systems. While D.C. seemed to be holding on to a significant percentage of its high-performers, it should be pointed out that these highly rated teachers were much less likely to teach in schools with high concentrations of students from low-income homes.

In districts where capable teachers who start out in low-performing schools tend to transfer to higher-performing schools, district leaders can try to limit the number of transfers in a given year. They also can offer incentives to stay, as was the case in Duval County.

Teacher retention may be somewhat less of an issue in many rural schools than in urban and suburban schools, where attractive employment options are generally greater. Because teacher turnover typically is less great in rural districts, as is their ability to recruit teachers, rural districts with low-performing schools may need to place greater emphasis on helping the existing faculty improve their skills than on replacing mediocre teachers.

Many of the points that have been made regarding the recruitment and retention of teachers apply as well to principals. Without capable principals, the lowest-performing schools are unlikely to turn around. Mention was made in chapter 5 of efforts by states such as Virginia, Florida, and Texas to train turnaround principals. Leader development also has been a primary focus for many consulting groups and lead partners working with struggling schools. Some larger school systems have created their own training programs for prospective and incumbent turnaround principals.

The Charlotte-Mecklenburg School District decided in 2008 that low-performing schools needed veteran district principals with proven track records (NC: Putting the best leaders, 2012). Being assigned to turn around a low-performing school was touted as an honor, a placement reserved for the district's most highly regarded leaders. Those principals chosen to take the helm of failing schools were allowed to bring a team of up to seven staff members with them from their former school. The transfer team received additional compensation—a 10% salary supplement for administrators and a $10,000 bonus for teachers in the first year. Transfer team members were expected to make at least a three-year commitment to their assigned school. Although the Strategic Staffing Initiative no longer is in place, it suggests one approach to securing the leadership and teaching talent needed to help the children left behind.

In 2015, the Denver Public Schools implemented a new program to attract capable leaders for low-performing schools. Dubbed "Year Zero," the initiative called for hiring prospective turnaround principals a year before they were to take over as principals (Zubrzycki, 2015). During their "year zero," these individuals have an opportunity to meet the staff of their school and develop a turnaround plan. The hope is that giving turnaround principals time to build relationships and prepare a plan before taking over will lead to sustainable improvements in school culture and student achievement.

"Year Zero" is a step in the right direction, given horror stories about turnaround principals who were appointed mere days before the beginning of school, but it is not a substitute for ongoing support from district leaders. As noted earlier in the chapter, a district turnaround office can be instrumental in coordinating support for principals and their efforts to improve schools. When a fully staffed district office is not possible, a central office administrator can be designated to assist and support each turnaround principal.

DISTRICT TRANSPORTATION

Although it may not be discussed very much by turnaround scholars, a school district's efforts to transport students to schools can be a key component of plans to boost student achievement. Busing students to school as a strategy for addressing problems, of course, has a long history. Busing to achieve desegregation and provide African American students access to high-quality schooling began in the 1960s and continues to this day. More recently, busing has been used to support district efforts to expand the range of school choices available to students, especially students stuck in low-performing schools.

One of the most highly touted of the choice-based initiatives followed the merger of school systems in Raleigh, North Carolina, and adjoining Wake County (Grant, 2009). Nearly a third of Raleigh's schools were converted to magnet schools. In a shrewd move, district leaders located the magnets in schools along the border between the city and the county. As a result, no student from either the city or the suburbs had to endure a long bus ride. The magnet program quickly won the support of local parents.

In the late 1990s, the Raleigh-Wake County school system took another bold step to address diversity and the needs of the children left behind. Because court rulings for school systems that had been declared free of racial discrimination prohibited school assignment based on race, the school board opted to base school assignments on socioeconomic status (Grant, 2009). The U.S. Department of Education's Office of Civil Rights challenged the policy on the grounds that income-based assignment of students was just a proxy for race-based assignment and therefore discriminated against whites by giving preferential treatment to blacks. The Raleigh-Wake County system, however, was able to make a successful case for maintaining the new policy because socioeconomic status clearly was linked to academic achievement for all racial and ethnic groups.

Student achievement steadily improved as a result of efforts in Raleigh-Wake County to balance school enrollments between students from low-income and more affluent homes. The district aimed to limit a school's low-income enrollment to 40% or less. Eventually, however, assigning students based on socioeconomic status had to be abandoned, in part due to an increase in the overall percentage of students from low-income families and in part because of parent objections to expanding the assignment policy.

As long as we are looking at North Carolina, it is worth noting how transportation to and from school surfaced as an issue with regard to the state's charter schools. Unlike Florida, where charter schools are obliged to make certain that transportation is available to all students living within a reasonable distance of a charter school, no such provision exists in North Carolina. This omission helps to reinforce the perception that North Carolina charter schools cater primarily to well-to-do white parents who do not want their children in public schools (Guo, 2015). These parents have the time and resources to see that their children get to school without relying on publicly funded transportation.

Researchers studying the effects of school closures in Chicago found that "distance and transportation costs were barriers for many families" seeking new schools for their displaced children (de la Torre, Gordon, Moore, & Cowhy, 2015, p. 29). These "barriers" prevented some parents from selecting a higher-performing school, forcing them to make do with a less desirable option.

Denver Public Schools (DPS) has done as much as any school system to ensure that its SchoolChoice program is backed up by adequate transportation (Ely & Teske, 2014). Various concerns served as the impetus for the Success Express shuttle bus service that DPS launched in August 2011. Parents objected that their children could not consider particular choice schools because transportation was not readily available. Principals engaged in turning around low-performing schools voiced frustration because their efforts to lengthen the school day and year as well as provide after-school tutoring ran into transportation problems. Charter school operators complained as well about lack of adequate transportation.

After working with parent groups and community organizations, the school board authorized the creation of a shuttle bus system to serve two fast-growing regions of Denver, the Near Northeast and the Far Northeast. The system involves circular fixed routes operating between 6:30 a.m. and 9:30 a.m. in the morning and between 2:30 p.m. and 6:30 p.m. in the afternoon. Each shuttle bus is staffed by a paraprofessional as well as the driver. Access to the bus is controlled and monitored through the use of a +Pass identification system.

A study of the Success Express shuttle bus system by the School of Public Affairs at the University of Colorado Denver (Ely & Teske, 2014) showed that the percentage of DPS students eligible for the service has steadily grown. Access to charter and Innovation schools has greatly increased for students in the two regions. Perhaps most surprising is the fact that the shuttle system lowered the transportation costs for the district. Savings are attributed, in part, to the replacement of traditional bus routes that operated below capacity with more heavily used shuttle routes.

There clearly is much that districts, as well as states, are doing to address the needs of the students left behind. The present chapter has examined ways that districts can reorganize to support the turnaround of low-performing schools. Examples of new approaches to financing and staffing turnaround efforts as well as seeing that students have transportation to and from improving schools have been described. All that remains to do is to consider the collective impact of these efforts and the lessons thus far learned in America's struggle to turn around its lowest-performing schools.

REFERENCES

Calvo, N. 2011. Opportunities and challenges of Student-based Budgeting. *District Administration.* Retrieved from http://www.districtadministration.com/article/opportunities-and-challenges-student-based-budgeting.

de la Torre, M., Gordon, M. F., Moore, P., & Cowhy, J. 2015. *School closings in Chicago.* Chicago: Consortium on Chicago School Research.

Duke, D. L. 2005. *Education empire: The evolution of an excellent suburban school system.* Albany: State University of New York Press.

———. 2010. *The challenges of school district leadership.* New York: Routledge.

Duke, D. L., Barbour, C., & Dolby, D. 2015. *The leadership challenges of school turnaround in two low-performing suburban middle schools.* Paper presented at the annual meeting of the University Council for Educational Administration, November 2015.

Ely, T., & Teske, P. 2014. *Success Express: Transportation innovation in Denver Public Schools.* Denver: Center for Education Policy Analysis, University of Colorado Denver.

Gottlieb, M. H., Duke, D. L., & Smalley, E. F. 2011. A relentless quest for useful data. In D. L. Duke and E. F. Smalley (Eds.), *Essentials for education executives.* Charlottesville, VA: Partnership for Leaders in Education, University of Virginia, 23–29.

Grant, G. 2009. *Hope and despair in the American city.* Cambridge, MA: Harvard University Press.

Guo, J. 2015, April 15. White parents in North Carolina are using charter schools to secede from the education system. *Washington Post.* Retrieved from https://www.washingtonpost.com/blogs/govbeat/wp/2015/04/15/white-parents-in-north-carolina-are-using-charter-schools-to-secede-from-the-education-system/.

Hightower, A. M. 2002. San Diego's big boom: Systemic instructional change in the central office and schools. In A. M. Hightower, M. S. Knapp, J. A. Marsh, & M. W. McLaughlin (Eds.), *School districts and instructional renewal.* New York: Teachers College Press, 76–93.

Honig, M. I., Copland, M. A., Rainey, L., Lorton, J. A., & Newton, M. 2010. *Central office transformation for district-wide teaching and learning improvement.* Seattle, WA: Center for the Study of Teaching and Policy, University of Washington.

Ingersoll, R. M. 2001. Teacher turnover and teacher shortages: An organizational analysis. *American Educational Research Journal, 38*(3), 499–534.

Keeping irreplaceables in D.C. Public Schools. 2012. *The New Teacher Project.* Available at http://tntp.org/publications/view/keeping-irreplaceables-in-d.c.-public-schools-smart-teacher-retention.

Lane, B., Unger, C., & Rhim, L. M. 2013. Emerging and sustaining practices for school turnaround. Institute for Strategic Leadership and Learning. *Massachusetts Department of Education.* Retrieved from http://sites.bu.edu/miccr/files/2015/03/Emerging-and-Sustaining-Practices-for-School-Turnaround.pdf.

Layton, L. 2015, September 16. Black teachers flee schools, leading to concerns about diversity. *Washington Post,* A-2.

Luekens, M. T., Lyter, D. M., Fox, E. E., & Chandler, K. 2004. *Teacher attrition and mobility: Results from the Teacher Follow-up Survey, 2000–2001.* Washington, DC: National Center for Education Statistics.

Mass Insight. 2010. *The district turnaround office: A comprehensive support structure for struggling schools.* Boston: Mass Insight.

Meeting the turnaround challenge: District case study, Miami-Dade County Public Schools. 2009. Boston: Mass Insight.

NC: Putting the best leaders in the neediest schools. 2012, August 1. *Center for Public Education.* Retrieved from http://www.centerforpubliceducation.org/Main-Menu/Success-stories/Success-Stories-By-State/North-Carolina/Putting-the-best-leaders-in-the-neediest-schools.html.

Plecki, M. L., Knapp, M. S., Casteneda, T., Halverson, T., LaSota, R., & Lochmiller, C. 2009. How leaders invest staffing resources for learning improvement. Seattle, WA: Center for the Study of Teaching and Policy, University of Washington.

Register, J. 2015, April 15. *State of the schools address*. Retrieved from http://www.mnps.org/files/_CfDtg_/81c699cd85520ebd3745a49013852ec4/State_of_the_Schools_Address.pdf.

St. George, D. 2015, September 25. Some aid for needy students redirected. *Washington Post*, B-1–B-2.

Stepzinski, T. 2014, June 14. Study: Duval County Public Schools losing effective teachers. *Florida Times-Union* [Jacksonville]. Retrieved from http://jacksonville.com/news/metro/2014-06-14/story/study-duval-county-public-schools-losing-effective-teachers.

Zubrzycki, J. 2015, June 18. Why Denver Public Schools thinks "Year Zero" may be the answer to rocky turnarounds. *Chalkbeat*. Retrieved from http://co.chalkbeat.org/2015/06/18/why-denver-public-schools-thinks-year-zero-may-be-the-answer-to-rocky-turnarounds/#.VnC4sEorLIU.

Part IV

Reflections on America's Struggle to Improve Its Lowest-Performing Schools

The years from 2002 through 2016 represent the high-water mark for federal, state, and local efforts to improve the plight of America's lowest-performing schools. A Republican and a Democrat took advantage of their tenure in the White House to see that no child was left behind. In the process they found themselves trying to prevent the quest for educational accountability from colliding with the cause of educational equity.

This section attempts to sum up 15 years of unprecedented action on behalf of the nation's neediest children. Chapter 10 draws on previous chapters as well as additional material to assess what has been and has not been accomplished with regard to our lowest-performing schools. The chapter opens by considering three different perspectives on efforts to improve these schools and moves on to look at the results of these efforts. Chapter 11 offers a discussion of some of the lessons learned over the course of the past 15 years as well as several recommendations for future measures to strengthen efforts on behalf of the children left behind.

TEN

Reviewing an Equivocal Verdict

The problems that wind up in the lap of federal, state, and local officials rarely are resolved fully to the satisfaction of the citizenry. Efforts to improve the lowest-performing schools are no exception. If many have been disappointed with what has been accomplished in the wake of No Child Left Behind (NCLB) and Race to the Top, it is not, however, for lack of trying. No one can accuse policy makers or educational leaders of ignoring the welfare of the children left behind.

As is the case with most daunting challenges, people can look at them from different perspectives. Let us consider three perspectives on contemporary efforts to turn around our lowest-performing schools.

The Idealist. "If we can turn around just one persistently low-performing school," says the Idealist, "there's no reason why we can't turn around all persistently low-performing schools. We just need to study how the one school succeeded and scale up."

As we have seen in previous chapters, examples abound of schools and districts that have raised student achievement in low-performing schools. These success stories are heartening to the Idealist. They point to what can be accomplished by well-trained and committed principals and teachers working in concert with state and district leaders and local groups of parents and community members.

The Pragmatist. "We can turn around a significant number of low-performing schools, especially low-performing elementary and middle schools," says the Pragmatist, "but each turnaround occurs in a unique context. It is doubtful that a single turnaround prescription will cure every troubled school. What's more, some low-performing schools are unlikely ever to be turned around."

The Pragmatist is guided by past history and a realistic assessment of the world. Resources always are in short supply compared to the needs that require attention, and priorities periodically shift. Educators have taken advantage of a window of opportunity during the George W. Bush and Barack Obama administrations, but that window could close with the election of a new president in 2016.

The Pragmatist understands that the percentage of needy students in the public schools will continue to climb, thereby putting even greater pressure on educators and increasing the likelihood of more low-performing schools. Refusing to abandon the cause of improving low-performing schools, the Pragmatist nonetheless recognizes that it will always be an uphill battle. Besides, given any distribution of schools, there have to be some schools that do less well than other schools.

The Cynic. "Given the significant number of persistently low-performing schools," says the Cynic, "we are unlikely to improve more than a handful of them. What's more, there is little evidence that achievement gains can be sustained over time or that the lowest-achieving schools can ever move into the upper echelons of schools. It is better to close persistently low-performing schools than continue to waste resources on keeping them open."

One of the main reasons for the Cynic's lack of faith in school turnarounds is the dwindling number of top-notch principals and teachers willing to tackle the challenges of working in low-performing schools. The Cynic does not believe that policies improve schools. Only people do.

Further, the Cynic has little faith that federal and state government can help. Government, after all, has failed to eliminate such pervasive problems as poverty, drug abuse, smoking, obesity, and alcoholism. Overcoming low student achievement is not something government is equipped to handle. If the Cynic harbors any hope for the children left behind, it is based on expanding the educational choices available to students and allowing the educational marketplace to determine which schools survive.

What can be perplexing about these three perspectives is that the Idealist, the Pragmatist, and the Cynic have access to the same data on low-performing schools and efforts to improve them. They just arrive at different conclusions. Let us look as objectively as possible at some of this data. Readers can draw their own conclusions.

SEARCHING FOR SIGNS OF SUCCESS

The lofty goal of No Child Left Behind—to get all children to achieve proficiency in reading and math—has yet to be accomplished. Target dates were pushed back when the Obama administration permitted states to apply for waivers to NCLB. It is unclear if the reauthorization of NCLB, will continue to aim so high.

What we do know is that between 2002 and 2016 every state and the District of Columbia undertook to improve its lowest-performing schools. How did they do?

When the Government Accountability Office (GAO) assessed the progress made under NCLB as of 2006, it found that 2,790 Title I schools were in some stage of corrective action or restructuring (*No Child Left Behind*, 2007). The GAO went on to predict that the number probably would rise as state proficiency targets approached 100% in 2014. It would seem that Idealists did not author the GAO report.

In 2010 the Thomas B. Fordham Institute published a report entitled "Are Bad Schools Immortal?" (Stuit, 2010). The report was based on a study of 1,768 low-performing district-operated schools and 257 low-performing charter schools in 10 states over the period from 2003–2004 through 2008–2009. The standard for achieving school "turnaround" was set high. Schools performing below the 10th percentile at the beginning of the study period had to surpass the 50th percentile within five years in order to be considered turned around. Only 26 out of 2,025 schools achieved such an impressive gain. The report's author used this finding to justify closing low-performing schools on the grounds that improvement was unlikely.

It could be argued, though, that the bar purposely had been set too high, perhaps to support a political agenda on the part of the Thomas B. Fordham Institute. Besides, when percentile rank is used as the basis for judging when a school improves or not, there will always be schools in the lowest ranks. This mathematical fact does not necessarily mean, however, that the lowest-ranked schools are failing to improve.

Interest in improving low-performing schools understandably increased following the Obama administration's commitment of billions of dollars in Race to the Top funds to the cause. In 2013 the U.S. Department of Education released an assessment of how the first two cohorts of School Improvement Grant schools were faring (*School Improvement Grant*, 2013). Almost seven out of 10 schools that entered the three-year program in the first year (2010–2011) saw increases in math achievement after two years. Thirty percent of the schools registered declines, while 2% stayed the same. Reading achievement followed a similar pattern, with 66% of schools raising achievement, 31% experiencing declines, and 3% staying the same. Overall, Cohort 1 schools saw an 8% rise in math and a 5% rise in reading over two years. Fewer Cohort 2 schools posted gains, but they had only been involved in the SIG program for a year.

Further analysis of the SIG data revealed that rural and small town schools had bigger gains in math than their urban and suburban counterparts, but slightly lower gains in reading. Schools that adopted the Race to the Top restructuring option, including those that converted to charters, recorded greater gains than schools opting for the transformation or turnaround options.

In 2015, the Council of the Great City Schools published an assessment of School Improvement Grant schools in large urban school districts (*School Improvement Grants*, 2015). Part of the report focused on a comparison of achievement for grades 3 through 8 in both reading and math in three sets of schools: (a) SIG-award schools, (b) SIG-eligible schools that did not receive grants, and (c) non-SIG-eligible schools. Gaps in the percentages of students scoring at or above "proficient" narrowed between SIG-award schools and the other two categories of schools for years 1 and 2 of SIG funding but leveled off in year 3.

Another finding indicated that SIG-award schools reduced the percentage of students in the lowest proficiency levels on state assessments. The authors of the report keyed in on this outcome, noting that it might be the most encouraging finding of all. One out of every three students in SIG-award schools, they observed, originally was classified in the lowest performance level on state tests.

Regarding performance data for high schools, the Council of the Great City Schools report found that "school districts have improved their ability to promote students from one high school grade to the next," resulting in "less of a 'pile-up' in the ninth grade and higher percentages of students in the final two grade levels of high school" (*School Improvement Grants*, 2015, p. 3).

Not surprisingly, data on improved student outcomes varied widely between urban school districts within states as well as between states. For the 2012–2013 school year, for example, the mean percentage of students scoring proficient or above in math was 26.78% for six Los Angeles SIG-award schools and 54.89% for seven San Francisco SIG-award schools. The mean percentage scoring proficient or above in math for all 43 California SIG-award schools in 2012–2013 was 46.55%. The figure for 13 Missouri SIG-award schools was 26.11%.

Other kinds of comparative data also have been compiled on low-performing schools engaged in improvement efforts. Data already has been presented in chapter 4 comparing student achievement in special state takeover districts with student achievement elsewhere in the state. The most impressive results so far have been posted by Louisiana's Recovery District schools, all of which have become charter schools. The percentage of RSD schools at or above "basic" on state tests has risen four times as much as the statewide average, though RSD schools still trail the state average (Smith, 2015). It is important to point out that just 23% of Orleans Parish students were attaining proficient scores on state tests when the Recovery School District took over in 2003. By the 2013–2014 school year, 57% of RSD students scored proficient (Smith, 2015).

When researchers at the Center for Research on Education Outcomes (CREDO) at Stanford University compared the academic achievement of students in Ohio charter schools with students in traditional public schools, they found that overall charter school students performed worse in reading and mathematics than their traditional public school counterparts (*Charter school performance in Ohio*, 2014). Regarding the children left behind, though, it was found that students in urban charter schools outperformed the statewide average for student performance. Learning gains for charter school students in poverty and African American students outpaced equivalent students in traditional public schools.

Interpreting results such as those presented in this section poses a number of hard-to-resolve problems. Since state tests and scores required to achieve "proficiency" vary, it is difficult to compare student achievement from one state to another. Students who seemingly are improving academically based on one state's results might have done far less well had they taken another state's tests.

Another problem concerns the lack of longitudinal data on "success story" schools. Various schools have been recognized for making substantial improvements in student achievement by government agencies, educational organizations, and research groups. These entities, however, rarely follow up their initial efforts to see if gains have been sustained over time. Consequently, it is hard to tell whether school turnarounds tend to be temporary or relatively long-lived phenomena.

Furthermore, there is no consensus regarding what constitutes a turnaround. The term may be used to characterize a small jump in achievement in a particular subject area such as reading, a large change in achievement for a particular subgroup, across-the-board gains in reading and math at all grade levels, a change from missing a state benchmark to meeting a state benchmark, evidence of closing an achievement gap, and so on.

Interpreting trends in standardized test performance is all the more difficult when particular states adopt new tests or substantially modify existing tests. Such action typically is taken when states alter curriculum standards, as some states have done in response to federal pressure to endorse the Common Core State Standards (CCSS). When states make these changes, comparing prechange student achievement and postchange student achievement poses a variety of methodological challenges.

Because of data interpretation issues such as these, the Idealist, the Pragmatist, and the Cynic may all find outcomes to support their position regarding the lowest-performing schools. What constitutes sufficient improvement to justify all the effort and expense associated with turning around the lowest-performing schools, it would seem, is in the mind — and perhaps the heart — of the beholder.

Given how accountability tends to be determined these days, it is easy to overlook any accomplishment other than a boost in reading and math achievement based on state standardized tests. Such single-mindedness on the part of policy makers has led, in fact, to a growing outcry from concerned parents and educators who worry that the thing authorities care most about is test performance. It would be wrong, of course, to minimize the importance of literacy and numeracy when it comes to the future prospects of the children left behind, but it also would be a mistake to downplay other areas of academic and personal development.

LOOKING BEYOND TEST SCORES

Even if there are far too many low-performing schools and children left behind, it is unfair to argue that little of lasting worth has been accomplished during the years from 2002 to 2016. Perhaps the most important accomplishment has been the unprecedented focus of federal, state, and local policy makers on the needs and challenges of the lowest-performing schools. Although government certainly does not have all the answers, it is hard to imagine that failing schools would have been better off if government had ignored them. Of particular importance has been the intense concern for the performance of particular subgroups of students. It had been all too easy in the past to accept low expectations for students from poor homes, English-language learners, minorities, and students with special needs.

The capacity of most states to identify and monitor the performance of their lowest-performing schools expanded greatly following passage of the No Child Left Behind Act. Governors and state legislators took a keen interest in reports on the performance of schools and school districts. The educational prospects of the children left behind ceased to occupy the political backburner. The Cynic, of course, could argue that the politicization of low-performing schools did not necessarily benefit struggling students in places like Buffalo and Indiana, and there unfortunately would be some validity to the argument. Once again, however, it is hard to claim that political neglect would have been a better response.

It is one thing to improve the means for identifying and monitoring low-performing schools and calling attention to their plight. It is quite another matter to see that effective assistance is delivered. As previous chapters have shown, states have tried a variety of strategies, from taking over low-performing schools and districts to setting up special state districts to approving educational management organizations and lead partners to help schools. States also have provided a variety of direct services to failing schools. Although these efforts have been well-intentioned, they have not always yielded the desired results. The capacity of individual states to deliver effective assistance is highly variable.

The same statement, of course, can be made regarding school districts. For every Cincinnati, there is a Buffalo. Some superintendents have been able to pull together a powerful coalition of local political leaders, community organizations, district specialists, and outside service providers in order to achieve widespread school improvement. Other superintendents have been unable to overcome the divisive forces of local politics, special interest groups, and economic distress.

The federal government's efforts to deliver effective assistance have drawn criticism as well as praise. A GAO report (*Race to the Top*, 2015), subtitled "Education could better support grantees and help them address capacity challenges," noted various aspects of Race to the Top grants that lacked sufficient technical assistance. Rural districts, in particular, reported greater challenges in responding to grant requirements. The GAO's survey of grant recipients revealed a need for better coordinated technical assistance and more professional development opportunities.

When it comes to improving low-performing schools, the Bush and Obama years have been characterized by serious efforts to identify the foundational changes that failing schools need to address in order to boost achievement. This author has referred to these as First Order changes, and they include such actions as aligning curriculum to state standards and tests, focusing on instructional improvement, developing teacher teams, targeting professional development to student needs, improving attendance and student behavior, creating time in school schedules for student assistance and faculty training, and engaging families in supporting school improvement (Duke, 2015). Such measures may not be sufficient alone to raise student achievement, but they clearly are necessary.

Another accomplishment concerns teacher unions. Once criticized for blocking efforts to transform low-performing schools, many union locals have displayed a willingness in recent years to negotiate such sacred issues as seniority and teacher transfers. Union officials have accepted, in various cases, the need to replace significant numbers of teachers in failing schools. At the national level, teacher unions have advocated for the needs of the children left behind and fought for more resources and better professional development for low-performing schools.

No Child Left Behind introduced a progressive set of sanctions for persistently low-performing schools. The ultimate sanction was school closure. Faced with the prospect of losing their neighborhood school, parents and community members in many parts of the United States have rallied to prevent this drastic step. Such action on behalf of low-performing schools can be viewed as a worthy accomplishment, especially when it leads to greater parent and community involvement in the schools. One key to the school turnaround process is the active engagement of local stakeholders (Bryk, Sebring, Allensworth, Luppescu, & Easton, 2010).

As a result of No Child Left Behind and Race to the Top, the range of educational choices for many of the children left behind has expanded greatly. Some of these choices have been developed as school district options. The Denver (Colorado) and Duval County (Florida) systems provide two examples of district-sponsored choice programs. In other cases, state and local initiatives have spawned the growth of charter schools. Between the 1999–2000 school year and 2012–2013, the number of students enrolled in public charter schools increased from 0.3 to 2.3 million (Charter school enrollment, 2015).

Not everyone, of course, regards the growth of charter schools as a positive development. Critics point out that charter schools draw resources away from struggling public school systems. Besides, some charter schools are not intended as choices for the children left behind but instead for children from advantaged families who are dissatisfied with public schools. There also are many failing charter schools. It is estimated, for example, that approximately 200 charter schools that were open in 2012–2013 did not open in 2013–2014 (*Estimated number*, 2014). The reasons for closure included low enrollment, financial concerns, and low academic performance.

Other choices for the children left behind have come about as a result of state-sponsored voucher programs. Vouchers permit students to attend, depending on the state, private schools, parochial schools, and public schools in neighboring school districts. By 2015, 364,000 students were taking part in voucher programs (Prothero, 2015). Not all of these students, however, were transfers from persistently low-performing schools.

Strides clearly have been made in the campaign to improve America's lowest-performing schools. Much remains to be done, however. Advocates for the children left behind rightfully worry that their cause is unlikely to continue to be a political priority. For the focus on the nation's neediest students to have persisted for 15 years in and of itself is an accomplishment. Let us briefly look at what remains to be done.

THE UNFINISHED AGENDA

Children in large numbers are still being left behind their peers when it comes to their education. That is a fact. Why they continue to be left behind, however, is a matter of opinion, and opinions vary widely. Poverty probably is the most frequently mentioned cause of low performance because its impact is so pervasive. Poverty can affect the quality of health care, parenting, school attendance, nutrition, and educational aspirations. Poverty is a thief that robs many young people of self-esteem and hope.

Some observers also see connections between poor performance in school and community factors such as distrust of schools as institutions and negative peer culture. Others concentrate on the actions and beliefs of educators. Low expectations, tracking, and discriminatory disciplinary practices have been noted as contributors to low performance. Still others complain that low-performing schools lack adequate human and financial resources. Fingers also have been pointed at government. Politicians are accused of raising standards before educators have been able to help struggling students meet existing benchmarks. Higher standards may be fine for high-achievers, but they can ensure that the children left behind will continue to be left behind.

That the playing field has not been leveled for millions of students also could be a by-product of our culture—a culture that values competition and achievement. Policy makers want U.S. students to outperform students in other countries. One state wants its students to outperform students in other states. One school district wants its students to outperform students in other districts. So, too, with individual schools. Every parent would love for his or her child to have a leg up on the competition, whether it's in academics, sports, or access to postsecondary opportunities. When public schools are perceived to hold back high achievers, parents with the means quickly search for other options. Given this competitive cultural characteristic, one has to wonder whether "leveling the playing field" is simply politically correct rhetoric rather than a true national commitment.

All of which is to say that we still lack consensus on the causes of low-performing schools and, hence, on how best to address the problem. Politics fills the void created by the absence of consensus. Various special interest groups lobby to gain acceptance for their explanation for failing schools. As Deborah Stone (1997) has pointed out, when a group gains acceptance for its "causal story," it is in a prime position to dictate the solution to the problem. So far, however, no group has won universal acceptance.

To say that causal consensus is lacking is not to argue that there is only one reason for failing schools and all stakeholders have yet to agree on it. There are, of course, many reasons why schools fail and leave children behind. Before we can move further forward than we have in the 15 years covered in this book, it will be necessary for stakeholders to recognize the complex array of causes and share ownership in *both* the causes and their solutions. This means that responsibility must be acknowledged and shared by governing bodies, elected representatives, educational leaders, teachers and their unions, communities, parents, and, yes, students.

In lieu of such broad-based agreement, we are apt to see a continuation of the politics of disappointment. Some groups are disappointed with their local schools. Other groups are disappointed with public education in general. Yet other groups are disappointed in government. Republicans criticize the education policies of Democrats. Democrats return the criticism. The politics of disappointment, if unchecked, can lead to a kind of blindness where people refuse to recognize positive developments. Even when there are signs of educational improvement, some group can be counted on to deny or discount them.

Some people will look at all the efforts of the Bush and Obama administrations to leave no child behind and the immense sums of money given to the improvement of the lowest-performing schools and conclude that nothing more can be done. Such a conclusion could lead to tragic consequences. One cannot help but wonder how the nation can unify during a world war, a Great Depression, and a homeland attack by terrorists but remain divided in the face of millions of struggling children in need of high-quality education.

So, two elements of our unfinished agenda regarding the children left behind are: (1) the absence of agreement regarding why we have failing schools and how best to improve them, and (2) no apparent course of action to achieve consensus on these matters. When this book was being written, for instance, Congress still could not agree on the reauthorization of No Child Left Behind.

The third element of the unfinished agenda concerns the failure of states and school districts to recruit and retain sufficient numbers of talented principals and teachers to lead and staff persistently low-performing schools. This failure is especially acute when it comes to African American and Latino educators. It is difficult to imagine improving the prospects of the children left behind without an influx of committed and capable educators willing to stay the course.

Sorely needed at this time is what the military refers to as an "after-action review." A decade and a half has been spent trying to turn around our lowest-performing schools. There have been successes and failures, steps ahead and steps back. The nation's political and educational leaders need to reflect, in an open and honest way, on what lessons have been learned that can help our continuing efforts to leave no child behind. It is to this task that we turn in the final chapter.

REFERENCES

Bryk, A. S., Sebring, P. B., Allensworth, E., Luppescu, S., & Easton, J. Q. 2010. *Organizing schools for improvement.* Chicago: University of Chicago Press.
Charter school enrollment. 2015. *Institute for Education Sciences, National Center for Education Statistics.* Retrieved from http://nces.ed.gov/programs/coe/indicator_cgb.asp.
Charter school performance in Ohio. 2014. Palo Alto, CA: Center for Research on Education Outcomes, Stanford University.
Duke, D. L. 2015. *Leadership for low-performing schools.* Lanham, MD: Rowman & Littlefield.
Estimated number of public charter schools & students, 2013–2014. 2015. Washington, DC: National Alliance for Public Charter Schools.
No Child Left Behind: Education should clarify guidance and address potential compliance issues for schools in corrective action and restructuring status. 2007. Washington, DC: Government Accountability Office.
Prothero, A. September 30, 2015. Choice advocates seek expansion of private schools. *Education Week,* 1, 11.
Race to the Top. 2015. Washington, DC: Government Accountability Office.

School Improvement Grant assessment results: Cohorts 1 and 2. 2013. Washington, DC: U.S. Department of Education.

School Improvement Grants: Progress report from America's Great City Schools. 2015. Washington, DC: Council of the Great City Schools.

Smith, N. 2015. *Redefining the school district in America.* Washington, DC: Thomas B. Fordham Institute.

Stone, D. 1997. *Policy paradox.* New York: Norton.

Stuit, D. A. 2010. *Are bad schools immortal?* Washington, DC: Thomas B. Fordham Institute.

ELEVEN

Thinking About the Path Ahead

That America has struggled to turn around its lowest-performing schools is evident in the previous chapter's discussion of the various opinions concerning why such schools exist in the first place and what to do about them. The struggle also is a function of the variability within and between school district and state contexts. The steps taken during the Bush and Obama years to improve failing schools can be understood to represent a commitment to reduce this variability. A case can be made that, in trying to do so, federal, state, and local governments have added to the complexity of operating school districts and schools, thereby contributing to, rather than diminishing, the struggle.

Perhaps the struggle would not have been as great if there were precedents to study and learn from, but America never before has focused so much attention, so many policies, and so much money on improving its lowest-performing schools. Nor has any other nation. Small wonder that the process has been likened to building a bridge as it is being crossed. To put it differently, policy makers lacked a rigorous body of research on school turnarounds to guide them, so they took action based on a combination of factors: input from stakeholder groups, analyses of strategies that had not yet been tried but that seemed politically possible and affordable, and assessments of likely causes of school failure.

Only now, after 15 years of initiatives, are we in a position to begin determining what lessons have been learned. Among the lessons discussed below are the following:

- In a world of exceptions, the search for a panacea may be futile.
- Government involvement invariably leads to greater complexity.
- Locally developed solutions may stand the best chance of succeeding when it comes to the lowest-performing schools.
- Every solution has the potential to generate problems.

- Just because a school fails to reach a benchmark does not mean that it has failed.

EXCEPTIONS ARE THE RULE

If there is one conclusion that emerges from the preceding examination of state and local efforts to improve the lowest-performing schools, it is the ubiquitousness of variability. Put differently, context matters. What works in one state or district may not work in another state or district. Rudy Crew achieved impressive results in New York City with his Chancellor's District, but not with his School Improvement Zone in Miami. Louisiana's Recovery School District boosted the performance of students in New Orleans, but Michigan's efforts to do the same for Detroit students flopped. State takeovers fared reasonably well in Massachusetts but failed in Indiana. Converting low-performing public schools to charters succeeded in New Orleans but not in Memphis. Mel Riddile, a nationally acclaimed principal, accomplished an amazing turnaround at Stuart High School in Fairfax County (Virginia), but when he moved several miles east to become principal of T. C. Williams High School in Alexandria, teacher resistance nullified his efforts.

As appealing as is the notion of a panacea—a universal solution to the problem of failing schools—the evidence so far indicates that solutions are highly context-dependent. This presents a challenge for policy makers, whose grail is successfully scaling up a turnaround strategy that works in a few settings. They struggle to grasp the notion that exceptions may be the rule when it comes to improving low-performing schools.

When No Child Left Behind was passed with bipartisan support, the panacea was supposed to be greater accountability, based on student performance on state standardized tests, and sanctions for schools that failed to meet predetermined benchmarks. While there have been some benefits as a result of this prescription, low-performing schools persist. Elmore (2007, p. 328) even suggests that there may be a relationship between the accountability panacea and the persistence of low-performing schools: "Accountability measures that penalize schools for failing to improve at a constant, and arbitrary, rate simply wind up making it harder for them to sustain and build on their accomplishments."

Diane Ravitch (2010, p. 29) was even harsher in her criticism of No Child Left Behind: "No Child Left Behind . . . was bereft of any educational ideas. It was a technocratic approach to school reform that measured 'success' only in relation to standardized test scores in two skill-based subjects, with the expectation that this limited training would strengthen our nation's economic competitiveness with other nations."

A quarter century ago Lisbeth Schorr (1989, p. 268) warned that the national obsession with *proving* that improvements are being made can lead to a single-minded focus on verification: "Unfortunately, the reasonable demand for evidence that something good is happening as a result of the investment of funds often exerts unreasonable pressures to convert both program input and outcomes into whatever can be readily measured."

Confirmation of Schorr's concern over verification came from a 2015 report that indicated that the typical U.S. student takes 112 mandated standardized tests between prekindergarten and 12th grade (Layton, 2015). The average number of hours spent taking these tests exceeded 257. Shouldn't policy makers and educators be asking themselves whether there are other important measures or indicators of school improvement besides student achievement on standardized tests?

Besides measurement issues, there are other reasons why the search for "the one best solution" has been so frustrating. Variability is the norm when it comes to state and local politics, school board competence, available resources, district capacity to support school improvement, and school-based talent. What's more, economic conditions change. Turnover produces new casts of characters. What worked last year fails this year for want of capable leadership.

Then there's the challenge of competing priorities. Do we seek the most effective solution to the problem of failing schools? Or the most efficient solution? Or the most equitable solution? Or the most acceptable solution? Consider this. Over the past decade we have been trying to improve the lowest-performing schools while simultaneously raising standards and promoting greater academic rigor. Both are important aims, but are they compatible?

Policy makers should be asking, "If there is no universal solution to failing schools, what is the best course of action for protecting the interests of the children left behind?"

INEVITABLE COMPLEXITY

Another lesson learned after 15 years of school improvement initiatives is that complexity invariably results from greater government involvement. In a provocative book entitled *The Utopia of Rules*, David Graeber (2015, p. 9) proposes the "iron law of liberalism": "any government initiative intended to reduce red tape and promote market forces will have the ultimate effect of increasing the total number of regulations, the total amount of paperwork, and the total number of bureaucrats the government employs."

Although No Child Left Behind is not regarded *primarily* as an initiative designed to promote market forces, it certainly endorsed school choice and offered charter schools as a possible way to help the children left behind. The bigger point, however, concerns the expansion of government bureaucracy at both the federal and state levels. From special school turnaround offices to pages of rules and regulations pertaining to the lowest-performing schools, America's efforts to improve failing schools expanded red tape and the educational bureaucracy at all levels. The insistence on data-driven decision making and complicated school improvement plans added to the workloads of already taxed school administrators and teachers. District offices regrouped in order to monitor school performance and oversee compliance with new rules and regulations.

Then came Race to the Top and waivers to No Child Left Behind. Complexity once again increased. In order to receive waivers, states had to meet additional federal requirements, including implementing performance-based evaluation systems for teachers and school administrators and promoting college and career readiness. Writing about what federal waivers did and did not accomplish, Hyslop (2013, p. 41) observed: "Halfway through the 2013–2014 school year, the year NCLB envisioned universal student proficiency, school accountability is more tenuous than ever. These systems have never been more complicated, and they have never been more dramatically different from one state to another."

One cannot help but wonder what gains in performance might have been accomplished if the money and manpower invested in managing accountability had been employed directly in the education of the children left behind.

THE ADVANTAGE OF LOCAL SOLUTIONS

In reflecting on the examples of school improvements discussed in this book, locally generated initiatives frequently have been the most successful. Evansville, for instance, developed the internal lead partner model eventually endorsed by the state of Indiana. Cincinnati's Elementary Initiative demonstrated what stable, enlightened district leadership and broad-based community support can accomplish. Denver's efforts to promote school choice and back it up with an innovative transportation system provide yet another example of the power and potential of local action.

It is not surprising, of course, that many of the most highly touted efforts to help the children left behind have resulted from local initiatives. Context, as already has been noted, is critical to the improvement process. National and statewide initiatives often fail to take into account the idiosyncrasies of particular localities. These idiosyncrasies, of course, may hinder as well as help improvement efforts, as the Buffalo case sadly illustrates. But it stands to reason that local policy makers, educators, and community members have more of a vested interest in improving failing schools than state and federal officials.

In his informative book *School Reform from the Inside Out* (2007, p. 227), Richard Elmore reminds us that "improvement is a developmental process, not an act of compliance with policy." He goes on to observe that schools get better "by engaging collectively in the acquisition of new knowledge and skills, not by figuring out what policymakers want and doing it."

Policy makers can foster the sense of urgency for change that provides an impetus for action and they can frame the long-term goals that need to be achieved, but they are not in a good position to assess the local capacity for change or the opposition to change that educators are likely to face. Hill, Campbell, and Harvey point out in *It Takes a City* (2000, p. 106) that for an improvement effort to succeed, "its leaders must build as broad a [local] coalition as is consistent with a focused initiative and either channel opposition in productive ways or meet it with countervailing ideas, organization, and political pressure."

Actions by states to address failing schools only should be taken as a last resort when localities are unable to mobilize the resources and political will needed to protect the interests of the children left behind. Such dire circumstances compelled Louisiana to create the Recovery School District and Massachusetts to launch the receiver takeover model.

THE POTENTIAL OF SOLUTIONS TO BECOME PROBLEMS

Another lesson derived from 15 years of efforts to help the lowest-performing schools is that any solution can become a problem if it is not well thought out, poorly designed, or improperly implemented. Mention already has been made of the unintended impact of federal regulations associated with No Child Left Behind and Race to the Top. Besides burdening school and district educators with compliance requirements, these measures have occasioned an unproductive increase in complexity and bureaucracy.

We also have seen that closing low-performing schools solves nothing if the only realistic options for students are other low-performing schools. Downsizing large schools, under certain circumstances, can provide students with smaller, more productive learning environments, but New York City's experience also suggests that small schools can increase racial and ethnic segregation. The same outcome can result from choice programs and charter schools. Innovation may lead to school improvement in some cases, but it also can lead to foolish ventures that waste time and scarce resources. Efforts in Chicago to ensure parents had a major role in school governance backfired in many schools and led to poor selections of principals and dysfunctional school councils. The heavy emphasis on test performance and the requirement of sanctions when test targets are not met have led some failing schools and districts to engage in cheating in order to avoid punishment.

Once again, the message is clear. There are no panaceas when it comes to low-performing schools. Every strategy, no matter how well intentioned, has the potential to derail improvement efforts. This is especially important to bear in mind because of the tendency for isomorphism to characterize improvement efforts across schools, districts, and even states. These entities, in other words, track what others are doing and copy or adopt similar strategies without necessarily determining if the fit is a good one. Witness what happened in Michigan when the state tried to adapt Louisiana's Recovery School District model. Prudence would dictate, at the very least, pilot testing a strategy from elsewhere before committing to widespread adoption.

MISSING BENCHMARKS MAY NOT MEAN FAILURE

If we judge hospitals by their morphology rate, the rate at which admitted patients die while in the hospital, it would be in the hospital's best interests to admit only patients who were unlikely to die. But what is the point of a hospital? It is to serve the needs of sick patients, no matter how ill they may be.

The analogy between hospitals and schools is appropriate. Under current accountability provisions, it is not in a school's best interests to enroll students who are unlikely to pass state tests. Public schools, however, do not have this option, unless they are allowed to have entrance requirements, as was the case with some Buffalo schools. Public school educators, in fact, complain that they are judged by the performance of virtually all of their students, even those who have just transferred to their school and students who are chronically absent. Buffalo teachers argued that it is unfair to include the performance of these students in determining whether a school is failing. Their point is a valid one. Schools in poor neighborhoods may have mobility rates in excess of 40%, and 15% or more of the student body may be absent on any given day.

It is quite possible that some failing schools would not be judged to be failing if recent transfers and chronic absentees were excluded from performance ratings. Principals and teachers, after all, have no control over student mobility and absenteeism.

Many students in Priority and Focus Schools are making consistent improvement. It's just that they were so far behind to begin with that they are not hitting predetermined state benchmarks. Other students in these so-called failing schools actually are meeting benchmarks. Subjecting the schools serving these students to threats of sanctions and eventual closure is analogous to punishing hospitals because some patients fail to recover from serious illness.

No Child Left Behind set a high bar for public schools: 100% of stu-dents achieving proficiency on state tests in reading and mathematics by 2014. Waivers granted during the Obama administration pushed back the date for attaining this lofty goal, but the goal did not change. Has any other sector of society been held accountable for a 100% success rate? Medicine? The military? Business? Government? Social services? There is nothing wrong with aiming high, but punishing people and institutions for missing the mark is another matter altogether.

FUTURE CONSIDERATIONS

A discussion of recommendations for what to do about our lowest-per-forming schools might begin by asking if there are any measures that have not been tried. Policy makers, for instance, have refrained from calling for the development of publicly supported boarding schools for the children left behind. A case could be made that the best chance for these children's academic success lies with their removal from homes and neighborhoods where poverty, poor parenting, and peers conspire to undermine school success. The cost of such a drastic measure, however, would be enormous, and some parents are unlikely to support having their children live elsewhere. Besides, there is no guarantee that boarding schools would have a better track record than district-run schools or charter schools.

With the exception of several states, there has been no significant effort to combine urban school districts and neighboring suburban school districts as a way to promote greater educational equity. James Ryan (2010) has shown how the Nixon administration laid the groundwork for removing such mergers from the bargaining table. The Nixon administra-tion agreed to pour millions of dollars into urban school systems in re-turn for their tacit agreement not to press for urban–suburban integra-tion. The time may have come to reopen discussion of this option, though great resistance from suburban residents can be anticipated. A less con-troversial option adopted by some states permits city students to use vouchers to attend public schools in nearby suburbs.

Another measure that has yet to be tried on any significant scale is a law, modeled after Public Law 94-142 for disabled students, that offers students in low-performing schools the same protection and assurances as special education students. Given the red tape, regulations, and costs associated with such action, however, school districts are likely to mount vigorous opposition.

If we take another tack and ask about the current approaches to help-ing the children left behind that appear to have a reasonable amount of support, it is clear that the public favors educational accountability but not necessarily the heavy emphasis on state standardized tests as the sole basis for holding educators accountable. Expanding access to educational choices, both district-sponsored options as well as charter schools, also has garnered increasing public support. Choice programs enable parents with limited means to select schools that they believe are most likely to provide the right learning environment for their children. It is hard to argue against increased options for poor parents when well-to-do parents are free to make choices for their children.

Parents directly affected by the sanctions associated with current accountability programs in general oppose closing the schools their children attend. It is unclear whether significant numbers of parents also oppose replacing large percentages of teachers at their children's schools, as required for the turnaround and restart options under Race to the Top.

After examining America's efforts to improve its lowest-performing schools and after noting some signs of progress, the conclusion must be drawn that impediments still stand between the children left behind and a high-quality education. Among these obstacles are the following:

- continued politicization of school improvement initiatives
- new mandates that deflect attention from turning around the lowest-performing schools
- inflexible rules and regulations that stifle local customization of improvement efforts
- intervention strategies that focus on individual schools rather than feeder systems
- insufficient numbers of competent and committed principals and teachers willing to work in low-performing schools

Political paralysis. At the national level, Congress failed to reauthorize No Child Left Behind for years, largely because Republicans and Democrats could not agree on the best course of action for raising student achievement. At the state level in places like Indiana and Michigan, governors undercut state superintendents, while in New York the governor battles the mayor of New York City over what to do about low-performing schools. Locally, mayors seek control over schools by limiting the authority of school boards and superintendents. In far too many state houses and city halls, the willingness to compromise and pull together in a common direction is in short supply.

Is there a solution to political paralysis? The simplest solution would be for American voters to elect representatives who are not ideologues and who believe in seeking common ground. That too few such individuals get elected probably reflects divisions in the electorate, though perhaps not divisions on educational issues per se. The Idealist reminds us, however, that bipartisan support for improving the lowest-performing schools is possible. Witness the progress made in Massachusetts, Louisiana, Cincinnati, and Denver.

No end to new mandates. It is hard enough to turn around persistently low-performing schools, but when the federal government and state governments continue to issue new requirements, the task becomes virtually impossible. No sooner do teachers develop lessons and pacing guides based on one set of state standards and state tests than states adopt new standards and tests. States apply for federal waivers, but in return they must implement complicated new teacher and principal evaluations. Educators in low-performing schools feel as if they are being asked to tackle a never-ending agenda for change.

Is it possible to give educators involved in improving the lowest-performing schools some breathing room? One possibility would be to declare a moratorium on new mandates for schools and districts engaged in the turnaround process. Allow teachers to close achievement gaps and meet existing curriculum requirements before raising the requirements.

The crush of compliance. Even without new mandates, existing rules and regulations regarding the lowest-performing schools lead educators to focus on compliance at the expense of educating children. We know that principals can have an impact on student achievement if they are free to function as instructional leaders. Too often, though, they are expected to be compliance officers, monitoring arcane regulations, compiling reports, and meeting with state officials.

No one is in a better position to lead the school turnaround process than principals. District and state authorities should be asking what they can do to free principals of bureaucratic responsibilities so they can spend time working with teachers, observing in classrooms, and analyzing student performance data. One answer might be to assign a compliance officer to each low-performing school in order to relieve principals of their reporting and red-tape responsibilities. Alternatively, rules and regulations could be drastically reduced.

Focus on feeder systems. There are far more examples of successful elementary and middle school turnarounds than high school turnarounds. One reason for this is that high schools are more complex organizations, larger in size and subject to a greater variety of rules and regulations. Another reason concerns the fact that high schools inherit the accumulated learning deficits of students whose elementary and middle school programs have been subpar.

In order to address the challenge of improving failing high schools, it may prove more productive to conduct turnarounds with an entire feeder system—high school, feeder middle school or schools, and feeder elementary school or schools. Instead of working with content specialists in isolation, consultants and district experts then could engage content teachers from all three levels, thereby increasing the likelihood of coordinated and articulated instruction. Exchanges between teachers from different levels could ensure that students moving from elementary to middle school or from middle school to high school would receive the special attention that they might require. Addressing the feeder system as an integrated unit also would promote collective accountability.

A pipeline for failing schools. The greatest impediment to improving the lowest-performing schools involves staffing. There simply are not enough highly qualified principals and teachers willing to tackle the challenge of improving failing schools. This is especially true for African American and Latino educators. When capable educators are assigned to the lowest-performing schools, they frequently leave after a few years. The high turnover rate ensures that low-performing schools are invariably staffed by high percentages of novices.

Is there any solution to the staffing dilemma? Higher salaries could help, but they are no guarantee. Creating principal pipelines that place talented leaders in low-performing schools could make a difference, since high-quality teachers are more likely to stay in schools that are well led. But perhaps the most crucial move when it comes to staffing is the removal of current disincentives for working in a low-performing school.

Under current regulations, principals and teachers who accept positions in the lowest-performing schools place themselves at great risk. If the schools do not meet state benchmarks within a specified period of time, these educators could lose their jobs. What's more, being assigned to teach struggling students can have an impact on one's earnings, since teacher evaluations now are tied to student outcomes. If pay-for-performance remains, the base (assured) salary for teachers in the lowest-performing schools should far exceed the base salary of their counterparts in high-performing schools.

BACK TO BUFFALO

Nowhere has America's struggle to improve its lowest-performing schools been more apparent than Buffalo, New York. When we left the discussion of Buffalo in chapter 2, it was early spring in 2015, the city was searching again for a superintendent, and Governor Cuomo was searching for a state strategy for dealing with low-performing districts like Buffalo. By this time, Buffalo had five schools classified as "persistently struggling" and 20 schools considered "struggling" (Buckley, 2015).

On April 20, 2015, New York legislators passed a bill that placed all persistently struggling and struggling schools in receivership of their districts' superintendents. This move reflected the state takeover model in Massachusetts that so impressed Cuomo. The fact that Buffalo only had an interim superintendent at the time the new law was passed had to strike many observers as predictable.

The new law gave superintendents one year to improve the persistently struggling schools and two years for the struggling schools. In the event they were unsuccessful, the state education commissioner would appoint an independent receiver to take over. Independent receivers had two years to show "demonstrable improvement." Receivers were permitted to utilize a number of options, including extending the school day and school year, renegotiating collective bargaining agreements, and converting schools to charters or community schools offering wraparound services.

School board members in Buffalo, not surprisingly, were divided in their reactions to the new law (Thompson, 2015). Some complained that the time allowed for turnaround was too brief. Others welcomed the opportunity to renegotiate teacher contracts. Interim superintendent Darren Brown wondered what the state considered "demonstrable improvement."

Buffalo's search for a district leader continued through the summer, with some potential contenders withdrawing their names after meeting with the school board. Meanwhile the clock continued to tick on the deadline for developing 25 school turnaround plans for the district's struggling schools. Whoever accepted the superintendency would be faced with an enormous task and precious little time in which to accomplish it. The one positive factor was that, under the new law, the superintendent's authority as receiver for the 25 struggling schools exceeded that of the school board. For a year, the new superintendent could proceed relatively unfettered by a divided school board.

In August, with schools set to open in a few weeks, the school board selected Dr. Kriner Cash to be the new superintendent. The vote was seven to zero. By September 30, he was expected to submit intervention plans for all 25 schools. One of his first actions involved convening groups of parents to learn of their ideas for turning around the schools.

What will happen to the children left behind in Buffalo and across the United States remains to be determined. Fifteen years of intense effort may have reduced their numbers in some places, but elsewhere their numbers have increased as the percentage of public school students from low-income families continues to climb. Although the ambitious expectations of No Child Left Behind and Race to the Top have not been realized, the struggle to improve our lowest-performing schools must not abate. We may not yet be able to guarantee that every child will thrive academically, but we must assure them that we will not give up the cause.

REFERENCES

Buckley, E. 2015, July 22. School leaders head to Albany to learn about "Receivership." Retrieved from http://news.wbfo.org/post/school-leaders-head-albany-learn-about-receivership.

Elmore, R. F. 2007. *School reform from the inside out.* Cambridge, MA: Harvard Education Press.

Graeber, D. 2015. *The utopia of rules.* Brooklyn, NY: Melville House.

Hill, P. T., Campbell, C., & Harvey, J. 2000. *It takes a city*. Washington, DC: Brookings Institution Press.

Hyslop, A. 2013. *It's all relative: How NCLB waivers did—and did not—transform school accountability*. Washington, D.C.: New America Education Policy Program.

Layton, L. October 25, 2015. Study: Testing overwhelming schools. *Washington Post*, A-3.

Ravitch, D. 2010. *The death and life of the great American school system*. New York: Basic Books.

Ryan, J. E. 2010. *Five miles away, a world apart*. New York: Oxford University Press.

Schorr, L. B. (1989). *Within our reach: Breaking the cycle of disadvantage*. New York: Anchor Books.

Thompson, C. July 21, 2015. Buffalo education leaders, with 25 schools to turn around, seek details on receivership model. *Daily Journal* (Indiana). Retrieved from http://www.dailyjournal.net/view/story/9a42e5ea4b4840189bf06094f6bd55ba/NY--Buffalo...

Epilogue

On December 9, 2015, the U.S. Senate, by an 85-to-12 vote, passed the Every Student Succeeds Act (ESSA), thereby bringing an end to an era in education policy. As was the case with ESSA's predecessor, the No Child Left Behind Act, the bill received bipartisan support. However, instead of Republicans and Democrats joining ranks to expand the federal role in public education, as they had done in 2001, the two parties agreed to diminish Washington's role.

The ESSA still requires states to test students in reading and mathematics in grades 3 through 8 and once in high school, and to publicly report the results according to race, income, ethnicity, disability, and whether students are English-language learners. Decisions regarding what to do with the lowest-performing schools, however, will be left to the states. States also will determine how to judge school quality and how to evaluate teachers. Supporters of the bill promised that the ESSA would produce a wave of innovation and boost student achievement.

As an era of unprecedented federal focus on the lowest-performing schools draws to a close, there are many questions that remain to be answered. Will those states that resorted to takeovers of struggling schools continue to do so? Will pressure to close failing schools subside? Freed from the threat of federal sanctions, will education leaders curtail initiatives aimed at helping the children left behind?

Fifteen years of concerted effort by federal, state, and local leaders produced a heightened sense of urgency regarding the plight of the lowest-performing schools, unprecedented funding for school improvement, legions of external providers offering technical assistance, new strategies for raising student achievement, an expanded range of choices for many of the children left behind, and a modest number of sustained school turnarounds.

Are we better off as a result? If states use the reauthorization of No Child Left Behind to back off their commitment to improve the lowest-performing schools, the answer will be "no." If, however, the momentum for addressing the needs of struggling schools continues and policy makers consider the lessons learned during the past decade and a half, perhaps a more positive assessment will be warranted.

Index

About the Author

Daniel L. Duke, internationally known specialist on school improvement, has written extensively on how to turn around low-performing schools. Besides conducting numerous studies of the turnaround process, Duke has designed training programs for turnaround specialists, conducted trainings, and consulted with states and school systems on ways to improve struggling schools.